THE CLASSICS
OF **WESTERN**
SPIRITUALITY

D1616106

THE CLASSICS OF WESTERN SPIRITUALITY
A Library of the Great Spiritual Masters

President and Publisher
Mark-David Janus, CSP

EDITORIAL BOARD

Editor-in-Chief
Bernard McGinn—Naomi Shenstone Donnelly Professor of Historical Theology and the History of Christianity, Divinity School, University of Chicago, Chicago, IL

Editorial Consultant
John E. Booty—Professor of Anglican Studies, School of Theology, University of the South, Sewanee, TN

Joseph Dan—Professor of Kabbalah, Department of Jewish Thought, Hebrew University, Jerusalem, Israel

Louis Dupré—T. L. Riggs Professor of Philosophy of Religion, Yale University, New Haven, CT

Rozanne Elder—Executive Vice-President, Cistercian Publications, Kalamazoo, MI

Michael Fishbane—Nathan Cummings Professor, Divinity School, University of Chicago, Chicago, IL

Karlfried Froehlich—Professor of the History of the Early and Medieval Church, Princeton Theological Seminary, Princeton, NJ

Arthur Green—Professor of Jewish Thought, Brandeis University, Waltham, MA

Stanley S. Harakas—Archbishop Iakovos Professor of Orthodox Theology, Holy Cross Greek Orthodox Seminary, Brookline, MA

Moshe Idel—Professor of Jewish Thought, Department of Jewish Thought, Hebrew University, Jerusalem, Israel

Bishop Kallistos of Diokleia—Fellow of Pembroke College, Oxford, Spalding Lecturer in Eastern Orthodox Studies, Oxford University, England

Azim Nanji—Director, The Institute of Ismaili Studies, London, England

Seyyed Hossein Nasr—Professor of Islamic Studies, George Washington University, Washington, DC

Sandra M. Schneiders—Professor of New Testament Studies and Spirituality, Jesuit School of Theology, Berkeley, CA

Michael A. Sells—Emily Judson Baugh and John Marshall Gest Professor of Comparative Religions, Haverford College, Haverford, PA

Huston Smith—Thomas J. Watson Professor of Religion Emeritus, Syracuse University, Syracuse, NY

John R. Sommerfeldt—Professor of History, University of Dallas, Irving, TX

David Steindl-Rast—Spiritual Author, Benedictine Grange, West Redding, CT

David Tracy—Greeley Professor of Roman Catholic Studies, Divinity School, University of Chicago, Chicago, IL

The Most Rev. and Rt. Hon. Rowan D. Williams—Archbishop of Canterbury

Hasidic Spirituality for a New Era
The Religious Writings of Hillel Zeitlin

SELECTED, EDITED, AND TRANSLATED BY
ARTHUR GREEN

PRAYERS INTRODUCED AND TRANSLATED BY
JOEL ROSENBERG

FOREWORD BY
RABBI ZALMAN M. SCHACHTER-SHALOMI

PAULIST PRESS
NEW YORK • MAHWAH

Cover art: Photograph of Hillel Zeitlin, courtesy of Dr. Arthur Green.

Cover and caseside design by Cynthia Dunne, www.bluefarmdesign.com
Book design by Lynn Else

Copyright © 2012 by Arthur Green

All rights reserved. No part of this book may be reproduced or transmitted in any form or by any means, electronic or mechanical, including photocopying, recording, or by any information storage and retrieval system without permission in writing from the Publisher.

Library of Congress Cataloging-in-Publication Data

Hasidic spirituality for a new era : the religious writings of Hillel Zeitlin / selected, edited, and translated by Arthur Green ; prayers introduced and translated by Joel Rosenberg ; foreword by Zalman M. Schachter-Shalomi.
    p. cm. — (The classics of Western spirituality)
    Includes bibliographical references and index.
    ISBN 978-0-8091-4771-7 (alk. paper) — ISBN 978-0-8091-0603-5 (alk. paper) — ISBN 978-1-61643-143-3 1. Zeitlin, Hillel, 1871–1942—Teachings. 2. Hasidism. I. Green, Arthur. II. Rosenberg, Joel.
    BM755.Z38H37 2012
    296.7—dc23

2012007191

Published by Paulist Press
997 Macarthur Boulevard
Mahwah, New Jersey 07430

www.paulistpress.com

Printed and bound in the
United States of America

CONTENTS

Contributors to This Volume

ARTHUR GREEN, who edited this volume and translated the selections in *Hasidism Then and Now* and *Judaism and Universal Religion,* is rector of the Rabbinical School and Irving Brudnick Professor of Jewish Philosophy and Religion at Hebrew College in Newton, Massachusetts. Recognized as one of the world's preeminent authorities on Jewish mysticism and spirituality, he is the author of more than a dozen books. These include *Radical Judaism* (Yale University Press), *A Guide to the Zohar* (Stanford), and *Menahem Nahum of Chernobyl* in the Classics of Western Spirituality series (Paulist Press). He is former president of the Reconstructionist Rabbinical College and Philip W. Lown Professor at Brandeis University.

JOEL ROSENBERG, who translated and introduced *Prayers: Songs to the Eternal,* holds the Lee S. McCollester Chair in Biblical Literature at Tufts University, where he is co-director of the Program in Judaic Studies, member of the core faculty in the Program in International Letters and Visual Studies, and co-founder of both programs. Author of *King and Kin: Political Allegory in the Hebrew Bible,* he was also translator of *Kol Haneshamah,* the Reconstructionist prayer-book series for Sabbaths, Festivals, and High Holidays.

ZALMAN M. SCHACHTER-SHALOMI, author of the Foreword, is widely recognized as perhaps the most important Jewish spiritual teacher of our time. Reb Zalman's teachings incorporate wide-ranging knowledge of the spiritual technology developed by peoples all over the planet. He is committed to a post-triumphalist, ecumenical, and Gaian approach. His many published works include *From Age-ing to Sage-ing, All Breathing Life,* and *A Hidden Light.*

Dedicated to the original dreamers of Yavneh:
Zeitlin's faithful readers in Poland and throughout Europe
whose names are lost among six million others

PREFACE AND ACKNOWLEDGMENTS

I was twenty years old when I first read Hillel Zeitlin's essay *Yesodot ha-Hasidut* ("Fundaments of Hasidism"). I no longer remember whether it was my late teacher Professor Alexander Altmann, or my longtime mentor and friend Rabbi Zalman Schachter-Shalomi, who first sent me to Zeitlin. I had already begun my lifelong love affair with Jewish mystical texts, and I had certainly read both Scholem and Buber. But Zeitlin's essay reached my heart more than any other modern writing on the subject, and I promised then and there that I would one day translate it into English.

A full half century later I am grateful to fulfill that promise in the context of this larger volume. I am happily surprised that no one has beaten me to the task over the course of this long delay. Nothing more than one or two poems of Zeitlin has appeared in English, and I feel he is unjustly overlooked as a key figure in the history of twentieth-century Jewish religious thought because of it. Now the English reader will have the opportunity to encounter some of Zeitlin's major writings, and I hope this will gain his place, especially in the history of neo-Hasidism.

A few words need to be said about that enterprise. The notion that the legacy of Hasidism has something to offer Jews and others whose way of life is far from that of the traditional Hasidic community began to take root in the first decade of the twentieth century. That period was a low ebb in the history of Hasidism itself, a time when it felt as if the once vigorous movement was in sharp decline. Only as the struggle of emerging Jewish modernity against Hasidism abated was it possible for this reexamination to take place. The leading figures of neo-Hasidism as an intellectual movement were Martin Buber (1878–1965), writing in German for a Western audience, both Jewish and Christian, and Zeitlin (1871–1942), writing in Hebrew and Yiddish. Both of these figures were philosophers and publicists; neither was a movement builder. The neo-Hasidic community of which both dreamed never came to be. Buber transferred his version of it to the kibbutz movement, founded indeed by many a scion of Hasidic families and bearing something of its legacy in highly secularized form. Zeitlin's dreams of community died with him in the ashes of the Holocaust.

Neo-Hasidism reemerged as a phenomenon in North America, beginning in the 1960s. It was largely the creation of two men, Rabbi Zalman Schachter-Shalomi, whose personal Foreword I am delighted to include here, and his friend the late Rabbi Shlomo Carlebach. Both were educated as Lubavitch *hasidim* (though neither was born into that community) and began as emissaries of the Lubavitch drive to transform American Jewry. Schachter and Carlebach both broke with their *rebbe* to go in very different directions. Schachter was indeed something of a movement builder, and the Jewish Renewal movement may be considered an embodiment of neo-Hasidic Judaism. But the influence of neo-Hasidism extends much farther, reaching throughout the Jewish community. Literature (think of Agnon, Singer, and Wiesel) and music have been important vehicles for conveying the Hasidic spirit, alongside the translation of Hasidic sources and the theological writing and teaching that have engaged this writer and others over the past several decades. I take special pride in several of my students who will carry this work forward. Now there will be a chance for Zeitlin to gain the attention of later generations of seekers.

I am grateful to my old *haver* Joel Rosenberg for his fine poetic translation of Zeitlin's prayers, a great enrichment to this volume. My research assistant for this project, Ariel Mayse, has done much of the footwork in finding sources but has also been a thoughtful first reader of the translations themselves. I greatly appreciate his efforts.

I am delighted that this book is appearing in the Classics of Western Spirituality series, with which I have been associated since its inception. It is to be hoped that it will reach thoughtful Christian as well as Jewish readers, as it surely should. The fact that it will appear in this series exactly seventy years after Zeitlin's martyrdom in the Warsaw ghetto is itself an important statement of transformed attitudes and relationships. All of us students and readers of Jewish religious literature are most grateful to the Paulist Press for its broad-based conception of this series and the many volumes of Judaica included within it.

—Arthur Green

FOREWORD

Zalman M. Schachter-Shalomi

The name of Zeitlin always had a certain early fascination for me, connected to Rabbi Shneur Zalman of Liadi. I was studying at the Lubavitcher yeshiva in Brooklyn, New York. Among the things I heard at farbrengens (sessions that *hasidim* have for celebration, inspiration, and guidance) was a tale that the founder of Habad Hasidism had to visit three outstanding scholars who were opposed to Hasidism; one of them was Reb Joshua Zeitlin, apparently an ancestor of Hillel. This was part of Hasidic lore. In passing I had heard of Hillel Zeitlin but had not paid much attention to him until 1959, when I visited Jerusalem. I was fortunate to meet Professor Hugo Bergman, who shared with me Zeitlin's vision of a new Hasidic community, to be called Yavneh. Let me state why I was so inspired on reading his *Yavneh*.

Our family fled Vienna and illegally crossed several borders to get to Antwerp in Belgium. There I met some people who would have made good members for Zeitlin's Yavneh community. They had all studied in *yeshivot* and were now working as diamond cutters in a workers' co-op where they combined work with prayer and study. Reading Zeitlin's call for Yavneh took me back to my association with these wonderful people, followers of the late Reb Mosheh Tchechoval, himself a student of Rabbi Abraham Schneerson (who was the father-in-law of my *rebbe*, Reb Yosef Yitzchak Schneerson) and Rabbi Yehudah Leib Zirelson of Kishinev. That group was steeped in Habad-style study and prayer. But its members were also avid readers of modern writers on the inner life, including the Danish Anker Larsen and Romain Rolland. Their parallel to the mood of Yavneh and the other works of Zeitlin stands out quite clearly to me.

In that group my emerging ideals found the soil in which to take root. With its support I was able to transcend the merely robot-like fulfillment of my religious obligations and to allow the longing of my soul to find expression. Singing, studying, and working together with the group was the beginning of my spiritual formation. Therefore Hillel Zeitlin's writings, when I discovered them, had great resonance for me. I had a deep longing to live again in intentional community. Alas, many of my colleagues from Antwerp had not survived the Holocaust. (Thank God, one of the leaders who took hold of my soul, the late Baruch Merzel, did survive, and I had the opportunity of meeting him in Israel later.)

There was another stream of awareness touching me at about the same time: the discovery of the Dead Sea Scrolls. My imagination was stirred when I tried to picture what the Qumran people were like. Here was an intentional community dedicated to serving God and to sharing all spiritual lights in common. The *Manual of Discipline* lit a fire in my imagination. The Cold War we were engaged in at that time gave an extra sense of reality to the Battle of the Sons of Light against the Sons of Darkness. We were just at that point becoming more aware of the devastation that Hitler had caused to the bearers and embodiers of our Jewish spiritual know-how. The lack of spiritual guides who knew more than what is to be found in books was very obvious. Would that we might have had a Noah's ark that could have collected and saved those people to whom discourse with God was second nature, who knew the varieties of spiritual disciplines practiced by Polish Jewry as well as the liturgical rites and all the variegated forms and melodies that now were lost.

We could not even hope to find survivors in Israel who would be the tradition keepers who could pass them on. The beginning of the state of Israel created a melting pot, dissolving much of the uniqueness of the various liturgical modes, ranging geographically and culturally from the Rhineland Ashkenazi to those used by the Jewish communities who had lived in diverse Islamic lands.

Inspired by my experience in Antwerp, by Zeitlin's model, and by my waking dreams of what it must have been like in the Qumran communities (as well as by Ray Bradbury's *Fahrenheit 451*, describing an intentional community of people who in their memory preserved the great classics after a time of terrible destruction), I dreamt of an urban monastic kibbutz that I described as Qumran USA or Bnai Or. We would seek out the different traditions of liturgy, praxis, and inward devotion within Judaism, and each of our members would learn to embody a different spiritual know-how, preserving the particular ritual of a lost community. I feared that otherwise these treasures would be lost in this era of devastation, movement of survivors, and resettlement in both Israel and America.

Now I take a backward look to the time between the two World Wars. By this time Hasidism had drastically changed. People whose ancestors had lived in small towns for many generations now, due to the burgeoning Industrial Revolution, moved to the large cities. After the First World War, the Ruzhin *rebbes* moved to Vienna, the Boyaner to Leipzig, and the Radomsker to Berlin. No longer was the *rebbe* the center of the *shtetl.*

Whereas previously one would have had to travel by foot or horse-drawn carriage for days on pilgrimage to visit the *rebbe,* it was now a matter of a railroad journey of a few hours. (In Warsaw Reb Shlomo the Kozhinitzer *rebbe* used to take his *hasidim* for small trips on the local trolley, symbolically re-creating a bit of the old spirit.) Much of the spirit and the ethos that fueled the Hasidism of the early generations collapsed as a result of the dynastic descent of *rebbes* who had to prove that they hewed to the ancestral ways, even when they no longer made the same sense.

For many who had been studying in the various yeshivas, the lure of *haskalah,* or modern "Enlightenment," was quite great. The city of Warsaw between the two World Wars was in ferment. Socialism and communism found many adherents in a culture that was permeated by demands for equity and social justice. Cultural Yiddishism and Zionism, both religious and secular, also flourished in this new atmosphere. The horizons of science and the humanities were expanding; all this penetrated deeply into the *bet Midrash.* Instead of debates over Talmud, periodicals and newspapers featured in feuilletons and columns fierce debates over fine points of ideological distinction. The bright minds of many former Talmudic scholars were now engaged by these. The opponents of these radical debaters were the now bourgeois and comfortable *hasidim,* often more interested in the easy solidarity of ethnic belonging than in finding a master who would teach them how to serve God.

It was not only a matter of intellectual discourse. Belletristic writings were coming into their own in salons and literary clubs organized around the works of people like Chayim Nachman Bialik. His Hebrew example, alongside that of Isaac Leib Peretz in Yiddish, encouraged young writers to express themselves in poetry, short stories, and novels. A Jewish secular literature emerged, giving an immense range of freedom to the people who had grown up with the poets and philosophers of the golden age of Spain, some seven hundred years earlier. Hebrew vied with Yiddish to be the medium of this emerging creativity.

In spite of the growing rigidity of the Hasidic world, that period also produced some brilliant leaders. Most impressive among the last generation of Polish *rebbes* was the then-young Reb Kalonymos Kalmish of Piasecna, who in his way succeeded in building a cadre of students and followers that lasted until the Holocaust, when he and they were martyred. An inspirer and brilliant educator, he read the hearts of his students and guided them. I do not know whether he and Zeitlin met or interacted before the ghetto years.[1] They would have had much to share, even though one was a forward-thinking scion of a real Hasidic dynasty and the other a would-be creator of a "new" Hasidism. Another bridge figure was Dr. Fishel Schneerson, a pioneer of humanistic psychology, but also a gifted novelist who described the spiritual world of his own ancestors around the vicissitudes of a fictional hero's inner life in his novel *Chaim Gravitzer*. The young Abraham Joshua Heschel grew up in this milieu, trying to bridge the identities of Hasidic scholar and Yiddish poet.

Hillel Zeitlin was raised among people who were of the contemplative elite of Hasidism. The lofty concepts of Habad he absorbed, together with his studies in Talmud and the codes, were joined by a curiosity that led him also to study the classical medieval Jewish philosophers. These provided him with a springboard to the worldly philosophers of his day whom he quotes, at times in agreement and at times in argument. The milieu in which he grew up greatly encouraged contemplation, with its accompanying introspective awareness. This also brought him to the kind of psychology that we now would call transpersonal. The dream of a society that would live by the values and ideals that pressed on him from the inside demanded to be expressed. He did this intellectually by writing and socially by seeking to organize a group that would embody those ideals.

Those who wish to live a committed and purposeful life in the presence of the living God have always known that they need a societal "container" in which inner ideals can be freely expressed and shared. Such groups use a language that is rich in connotations of the spirit, that shares a sacred aesthetic, and in which one does not need to apologize for one's longing to live the life of one's ideals. It was such a dream that made Zeitlin design Yavneh.

How might we open such opportunities for the contemporary Jew? The conditions in the United States are not like those in Warsaw. Jews raised here are not permeated by that city's unique and now lost blend of Yiddish, Hebrew, Hasidism, and socialism. Knowing how important it is to open Zeitlin to our current readers, we must be aware that it is not easy to render one who wrote for a world where a large field of connotations gave rich meaning to his words. Someone not steeped in a field that spans from Schopenhauer and Nietzsche to the Zohar, Habad, and Reb Nahman could not have done justice to rendering Zeitlin for the current reader. Arthur Green, who has not only brought to us his own very relevant teachings, but also has presented us with Reb Nahman of Bratzlav, Reb Nahum of Chernobyl, and the Gerer *Sefat Emet*, has now set about resuscitating Zeitlin for our generation. May our reading of this saintly and martyred teacher help us to become more available to renew our Judaism and to participate in *Tikkun Ha-'Olam*, the healing of the planet.

Although Qumran USA never came to be, Arthur Green gathered another kind of Yavneh in Cambridge and founded the matrix, the first of the many *havurot*, Havurat Shalom. It too was another fractal, a gestalting of Zeitlin's Yavneh. I was fortunate to be able to participate in that amazing first year. The study of the effects of that foundational time still awaits its chronicler. The influence of that year permeated all of American Judaism and even spilled over to Israel and Europe. The emergence of Jewish Renewal since that time is deeply connected to what happened there, as it is to Zeitlin's dreams of Yavneh.

Since Zeitlin's time we have experienced great changes. Auschwitz, Hiroshima, and Nagasaki, the moon walk, the Internet, advances in cosmology, quantum theory, string theory, and understandings that deal with the Zero Point Field have all shifted our cosmological paradigm. A new organismic view of life on this planet under the Gaian hypothesis, with its warning about global warming and the pollution of earth, water, and air, has come into view. We now have to deal with the good and the bad of globalization against the background of our earth crying out to be healed. At this time it is vitally important for Jewish theology to open itself to the Jewish mystic dream; to be refreshed and re-enchanted by the soul, the mind, and the heart of Zeitlin.

HILLEL ZEITLIN:
A BIOGRAPHICAL INTRODUCTION[1]

In 1928 Hillel Zeitlin published the following brief but highly revealing autobiographical memoir.[2] Because this document stands as the primary source for all further biography of Zeitlin, the reader should encounter it in the author's own words.

MY LIFE IN BRIEF[3]

I was born in the town of Korma, in Mogilev Province on the Dniepr in 1871 (not 1872, as it says in the Russian Jewish encyclopedia). My father, Reb Aaron Eliezer, was a highly learned man, a person of wondrously clear thought, a good heart, a believer in people, tending toward modernity (*haskalah*). My mother was entirely dream and song, devoted to Hasidism. My ancestry on my father's side was through the Zeitlin family, one of brilliant rabbis, including Rabbi Joshua Zeitlin (more properly Zeitlis), who was called the "Lord of Ustye."[4] Descent on my mother's side was from fiery devotees of Hasidism, especially my mother's grandfather, Reb Joseph "the old *hazzan*," a disciple of Rabbi Shneur Zalman of Liadi. He was a man of wonders, one who served God with complete self-negation, and a fierce fighter for ḤaBaD.

  When I was eleven years old, I became known as a prodigy in my town and the surrounding area. I stood out in powers of memory, as a quick learner, and as a lad of deep understanding. I studied Talmud and legal texts, forgetting almost nothing that I had learned. I did not study in *yeshivot*. I learned a straightforward way of under-

1

standing Talmud from my father. I spent more intense study time on books of Hasidism, ethics, homiletics, philosophy, and Kabbalah than I did on Talmud and the legal codes. Such books could readily be found in the large Lubavitch House of Study in my town. I heard ḤaBaD preaching in my town from one Reb Zalman, a deep religious thinker and a key disciple of that mystical genius Rabbi Yizhak Eisik Epstein (author of "Treatise on the Exodus," "Four Cups," "An Essay on Humility and Joy," "Ariel Camped," and more), a religious philosopher unique to his generation.[5] For more than a year I listened to ḤaBaD sermons, often from the Rebbe of Retsitsa[6] (brother of the Rebbe of Kapust, grandson of the *Tsemah Tsedek*,[7] and grandfather of young scholar Professor F. Schneersohn);[8] at the time these did not yet seem to be very convincing to me. But a while after I departed from Retsitsa I found myself consumed by divine fire. For more than half a year, when I was about thirteen, I was totally given over to Infinity (*eyn sof*). No one knew what was happening to me, since I was by nature a shy loner. Yet even today I recall with secret joy that time when I was almost able to see the "power of the Maker within the made" and to penetrate beyond the "physical, corporeal nature of things," constantly seeing "the divine power flowing through them in each moment, without which they are naught."

I found myself in a state of ecstasy that I had not known previously and have never yet attained again. Usually people are in such states for minutes or hours in the course of a day. But I remained in that ecstatic state all day and night. My thought was attached to God with hardly a moment's interruption.

To my great sorrow, this state did not last for long. As winter passed, the material world and its demands came upon me. Youthful lusts and various inner stirrings, including that of *haskalah*, overwhelmed me. The books of Mapu, Y. L. Gordon, Smolenskin, Shulman, and A. D. M. Cohen came into my hands.[9] Mapu was an especially great influence. The accusations of Gordon and Smolenskin against the Hasidic rabbis I did not believe; nevertheless "one had to consider them." I began to look at everything around me with a suspicious eye. My natural religiosity did not allow me to fall, but a great battle had broken out in my soul.

My youth was spent amid this internal struggle. Meanwhile, I was forced to leave my town. My father's financial situation had declined steeply, and I needed to go seek out my own livelihood. I wandered from town to town, village to village, having my fill of anger, hard labor, and trouble. My wanderings continued for about seven years, during which I learned all about how low and coarse people can be. But during that time I also learned languages and various sciences, my mind becoming especially attuned to philosophy.

I studied intensely the writings of Abraham Ibn Ezra, Maimonides, Rabbi Joseph Albo,[10] and also such moderns as Mendelsohn, Salomon Maimon,[11] Krochmal,[12] and others. I devoted even closer attention to the works of Spinoza, Kant, Fichte, Hegel, Schelling, and above all to the positivists: August Comte, Spencer, Darwin, Bokal,[13] Draper,[14] and several others. On top of all these were the works of those destructive critics Pisarev,[15] Chernishevsky,[16] Dobrolyubov,[17] Mikhailovsky,[18] and others.

My spirit became deeply broken when I encountered the conclusions of "Biblical criticism." I felt helpless to stand up against them. My soul sought only faith, but critical and positivist thought pushed me toward denial—or at least toward radical doubt—in matters of faith.

Bouncing back and forth amid sufferings of both body and spirit, I entered into a special spiritual bond with a young man in Homel named Shalom Sender Baum (he is "Uriel Davidovsky" in Y. H. Brenner's[19] stories). He was at once a man of total denial and despair and one filled with poetic holiness. It was then that I plumbed the depths of Schopenhauer, Hartmann, and Friedrich Nietzsche. It was these, the seemingly most absolute heretics, who drew me bit by bit closer to my own inner self.

This began with "Good and Evil," published in segments in *Ha-Shiloah*.[20] Its middle was "Barukh Spinoza" (by *Tushia*),[21] "Friedrich Nietzsche" (in the monthly *Ha-Zeman*, and one of its later chapters, "The Critique of Man," in *Masuʾot*),[22] "Thoughts,"[23] "Writings of a Youth" (in *Ha-Dor*), and lots more. It ended up with "The *Shekhinah*,"[24] "Sublime Beauty,"[25] and "The Thirst."[26]

Looking deeply into Hartmann and Schopenhauer, I was able to distinguish between their outward European, atheistic shell and their inward Indian and mysterious core. Beyond the outward extreme heresy of Friedrich Nietzsche I was able to discern one who sought God in the world, even to the point of madness. For this recognition I am grateful to the most original Jew I have seen in my lifetime: Lev Shestov.[27] From him and from his books I have learned all that I had previously felt in a subtle way, that out of the midst of colossal tragedy of soul one may come to true knowledge of God. I again sank myself deeply into the study of Kabbalah and Hasidism and came to a synthesis of profound pessimism and profound faith.

The many awful troubles that have fallen upon my brothers' heads, their economic decline and their inward ruin, pushed me into the public arena, making me "a man of conflict and dispute throughout the land (Jer. 15:10)." I will not say much about this, because my activities in this realm, which I came into by necessity, are so well known. Well known also are my struggles with everyone and against everyone. Whether I was right or wrong, the Merciful One will judge. One thing I will be able to say before God's throne of judgment, along with a hero of Shakespeare: "I am a man more sinn'd against than sinning."[28]

Since 1907 I and my household[29] have lived in Warsaw, where I earn my living as a journalist. Various waves have passed over me here, some of which sought to swallow me alive. I have acquired many enemies among the intelligentsia and the quasi-intelligentsia, but I have also gained many beloved and faithful friends among the masses of Polish Jewry, the youth, and individuals who see into the heart.

From the day I settled in Warsaw, I began to order and renew my Torah studies. I use all my spare time to study the two Talmuds, Midrashic works, books of ethics and philosophy, but most particularly books of Kabbalah and Hasidism. The more I study, the more I see how few there are among us who truly comprehend these sources. The slightest bit of what I have found in my studies in this realm I put into my articles "The Antiquity of Jewish Mysticism" and my book *An Index to the Book Zohar*. But my essential attainments in the study of Kabbalah and Hasidism are kept within me. Who knows whether I shall still find in my lifetime someone to whom to pass these on. "I have many coins, but no money-changer to whom to give them...."

I keep recalling, with a heart-breaking sigh, the words of the *Idra*:[30] "The days are few, the lender presses to be repaid, a message calls forth each day, the workers in the field are few, and those at the edge of the vineyard pay no attention and do not know...."

The picture of my inner life (and that is most of my life) would not be complete or accurate if I did not mention, at least briefly, the growth in my life of faith since the day the war broke out. In it and all that has happened since I see the "messiah's footstep," meant not metaphorically, and not simply referring to our national rebirth, but truly the footsteps of Messiah ben David.

In the years 1914 and 1915 I was enveloped in almost the same state of ecstasy that I had found within myself when I first encountered ḤaBaD. I became nearly a "visionary." The smallest bit of what I envisioned and felt is recorded in my book *Between Two Worlds*, a small part of which was published in *Ha-Tekufah*; the rest remains with me in manuscript.

All of my spiritual life in these years is the fruit of that wonderful ecstasy: my efforts to learn Torah for its own sake, to fulfill all the practical commandments in a whole and faithful manner, my attempt to found little brother-hoods of individuals called *Yavneh* and elite groups within them called *Beney Hekhala*, and two books that remain in manuscript. These are *A Word to the Nations*, one chapter of which was published in *Ketuvim*, and *A Book for Individuals*, a chapter of which, written in the style of the Zohar, I am now submitting to *Ketuvim*, along with various other works.

The Hebrew translation of the Zohar that I started with the 'Ayanot Publishing Company I have set aside for now, for various reasons that I will keep to myself.

My Hebrew and Yiddish writings are scattered not just over seven seas, but over seventy-seven. They have found no redeemer. Perhaps they, along with my Hebrew trans-lation and commentary to the Zohar, will be redeemed, if God grants that I spend the remaining years of my life in the Holy Land.[31]

The earliest writings of Hillel Zeitlin, including "Good and Evil" (1899), *Baruch Spinoza* (1900), and *Friedrich Nietzsche* (1905), hardly predict that within two decades their author would become a key figure of Jewish mystical piety, symbolizing in his person the possibility of a thoughtful modern's return to the life pattern and religious language of Hasidic Judaism. Zeitlin lived in an age when all the human "traffic," as it were, was moving in the opposite direc-tion; he was one of thousands of Jews who had fled *shtetl* life, includ-ing the influence of Hasidism, in favor of the "new Jew" whose emergence they were helping to fashion. One major group within this multi-pronged movement away from tradition was that of secu-lar, mostly Hebraist, Zionist intellectuals. It was to this circle that Zeitlin belonged in his early years in Gomel, Vilna, and Warsaw.

In fact, Zeitlin is to be counted among the followers of the most radical of Jewish spiritual revolutionaries, Micha Josef Berdyczewski (1865–1921). Influenced by the writings of Nietzsche, Schopenhauer, and others, Berdyczewski called for a total "transvaluation" of the Jewish cultural heritage and literary canon, primarily in the Nietzschean spirit. This implied great emphasis on human creativity (manifest primarily in literature, art, and thought) as the endless font of rebirth and renewal. The group called *Tse'irim* (Youth) in the Belorussian city of Gomel (Homel) saw itself as cultural shock troops ready to respond to Berdyczewski's call. (This is not to say that within this circle of young intellectual hotheads there weren't constant arguments with Berdyczewski, some of them reaching very high-decibel levels of controversy.)

A central figure of the group was Sender Baum, mentioned in Zeitlin's memoir, a charismatic and ascetic figure who seemed to embody the pessimistic philosophy that so enchanted young seekers in that age. Baum intellectually charmed a group of young men who formed a tight circle around him. These included, along with Zeitlin, the Hebrew writers Yosef Hayyim Brenner (1881–1921) and Uri Nissan Gnessin (1881–1913). Zeitlin lived in Gomel between 1896 and 1901, or from age twenty-five to thirty. It would appear that this was a second key formative era in his life, standing alongside the period of adolescent piety that he described above.

Writing some twenty years later, Brenner (by then a rising star of Hebrew literature and a culture hero to many in Palestine since 1909) had some not entirely kind memories of Zeitlin from their Gomel days. While naming Zeitlin as his first literary mentor, he recalls him as follows:

> His worldview then was fiercely pessimistic, which was also his usual mood. But there were other things alongside worldview and mood...chief among them: life itself, meaning relations with others, the need to seek a livelihood, the difficulties of domestic life, national concerns, helping relatives....
>
> He was a madman, one who suffered from his madness. But he also enjoyed it and took pride in it. In general—I hope my words about him are not too harsh—he was a person of great pride who thought highly of himself. This despite the fact that in truth, on the basis of his literary nature, I think he was merely a second-rate figure....
>
> This was his tragedy: he was less great than he thought he was. He had moments of sublime elevation, he loved humanity and his people Israel, and he was compassion-

ate. Together with these there was an inner chaos, a certain anarchy....He sought liberation from it by exhortation, by engaging in worthwhile literary activity.[32]

This somewhat harsh evaluation was written in response to a rumor of Zeitlin's death that had reached Brenner. Ironically, Brenner himself died in one of the earliest Jewish-Arab violent encounters only a year after these words were penned. In mourning him, Zeitlin was significantly kinder.[33]

Most interesting in Brenner's memoir is his capturing of the mood of Zeitlin and that group. They apparently had turned pessimism into something of an ideal, almost a new religious value. Pessimism meant a realistic confrontation with a godless world as well as with the beastliness of human nature. Unlike the Marxists, these pessimists did not believe that the destructive urges within the human self were the remediable effects of socioeconomic forces. They were deep-seated realities. To point them out and portray them in artistic media might have some spirit-soothing value, but ultimately they could not be changed. To advocate such pessimism as a worldview demanded cultivation of an appropriately serious downward glance. These pessimists made light of do-good attempts to relieve suffering, setting them somewhat at odds not only with the traditional religious world from which all these people had come, but also with both Zionism and socialism, the positively oriented trends that so captivated much of Jewish youth in early twentieth-century Europe.

Zeitlin went through a mighty struggle with this pessimism in the years between 1896 and 1906 or 1907. The fact that Sender Baum committed suicide shortly after the turn of the century undoubtedly had a great impact upon him. So too surely did the advent of a new century, as it had upon so many in that era. His meeting with Lev Shestov ("the most original Jew I have ever encountered") in 1904, a figure as morally impressive as Baum, but one drawn away from Nietzschean pessimism by a new attraction to religion, was formative in Zeitlin's quest. The young seeker's growing body of published writings, going from "Good and Evil" (1899) to "The Thirst," "Intentions and Unifications," and "The Longing for Beauty" (1907), bears often searing witness to this struggle.

Two issues came to engage Zeitlin in this formative period, the same two that would follow him throughout his life and to its tragic end. One was the crisis of faith, the search for an old/new religious language that might uplift him, as it had Shestov, from the abyss of despair. For Zeitlin, already so deeply rooted in the sources of Hasidism, this would have to be a Jewish language. Although Tolstoy and others were important models for him, he could not follow Shestov in his attraction to Orthodox Christianity, and there is no evidence that he was even tempted in that direction. Yet he was open, then as well as later, to learning from non-Jewish spiritual teachers. His collection of prayers includes adapted translations from Christian sources, a daring step for one writing in Hebrew and Yiddish in early twentieth-century Warsaw.

The other issue that plagued Zeitlin throughout his life was his deep awareness of Jewish suffering, especially that of the many poor among East European Jewry in the pre-Holocaust decades. The Jewish national awareness that had initially propelled Zeitlin toward Zionism arose out of his awareness of the plight of the impoverished, especially as he had encountered them in the *shtetlekh* of Belorussia during his years of wandering. In Warsaw he came to see and know the urban Jewish poor, identifying deeply with their situation as well. The Kishinev pogrom of 1903 and the increased persecution of Jews in the Czarist empire after the failed revolution of 1905 also contributed to his conclusion that the situation of Eastern European Jewry was simply untenable, politically and economically as well as spiritually, and that one had to work toward the most immediate form of relief on all of these fronts.

Attending the Fifth Zionist Congress in 1901, a representative of the Gomel delegation, Zeitlin came away with a feeling of disillusionment and dismay. While Theodor Herzl himself was most impressive to him, he felt that the princely central figure of political Zionism was too far removed from the Jewish masses to appreciate the urgency of their need. Yet he was also not drawn to the other leading faction within early Zionism, that which centered around Ahad Ha-'Am (Asher Ginzburg, 1856–1927), the "cultural" Zionists, with their strong commitment to building up Erez Israel as a "spiritual center" for a renewed Jewish people, a large portion of which would remain in the diaspora. The problem he saw so keenly was that this diaspora existence was insufferable in its current state, crying out for immediate relief. Zeitlin thus became a supporter of the Uganda Plan when it was proposed, seeing the idea of an East African Jewish colony as a more immediately available release valve for the Jewish masses than the slow pace predicted for acquisition and settlement in Erez Israel. When the Uganda alternative was roundly rejected by the Zionist leadership, Zeitlin joined Anglo-Jewish writer Israel Zangwill (1864–1926) and others in turning away from Zionism to create the Territorialist movement. The key principle here was that Jews should seek territories anywhere they might be offered (Polish Galicia and Argentina were very much under discussion in the early years), including but not limited to Erez Israel, where Jews could establish cultural as well as economic hegemony.

Zeitlin's status as a dissenter from Zionist circles (the truth is that he vacillated between Zionism and Territorialism, depending upon both the latest events and the context of the debate) made him the object of fierce polemical battles within the flourishing Hebrew and Yiddish press. So too did his critical stances toward Bundist socialism and, especially as he went along on his own spiritual journey, his denunciations of contemporary Orthodoxy and Hasidism. Zeitlin was truly a man who belonged to no party but lived at the very heart of journalistic and literary Warsaw, the center of the highly politicized world of early twentieth-century East European Jewry. Too religious for his fellow territorialists, too modern and universalist for the *hasidim*, critical of the emerging orthodoxies of both Zionism and socialism, refusing to choose sides between Yiddish and Hebrew, it is no wonder that Zeitlin devoted much of his literary career to an ongoing series of controversies, giving and taking the sharpest sorts of barbs, and being depicted by many as one who simply thrived on conflict.

But throughout the years in which Zeitlin was so involved in controversy, often played out on the pages of Warsaw's Yiddish dailies *Heynt* and *Der Moment* (both of which he had helped to found), he was continuing to produce a remarkable series of essays on the inner life of Judaism, chronicling his intellectual development and his quest for a religious language and viewpoint he could call his own.

These form the true heart of Zeitlin's literary and spiritual oeuvre, providing the essential contents of this volume.

The journey that led Zeitlin back from the precipice of total pessimism and toward religion can already be seen in his first published work, "Good and Evil," which appeared in Ahad Ha-'Am's *Ha-Shiloah* in 1899. It is clear that the young Hebrew writer was much under the influence of Russian thinkers, including those most inclined toward religious questions: Tolstoy, Dostoevsky, and Vladimir Solovyev. German philosophers Schopenhauer and Hartmann, the anti-heroes of pessimism, were also on his reading list, as was Nietzsche. But perhaps most interesting is the significant amount of space that Zeitlin devotes to Buddhism and its identification of suffering as the central religious problem of human life. He views this as an attitude from which the West had much to learn, although he manages to identify the biblical book Kohelet (Ecclesiastes) quite fully with Buddhist teaching. Zeitlin seems to have read a good deal about Buddhism, popular especially in the Tolstoyan circles, and about which several books had been published in late nineteenth-century Russia. "Good and Evil" is a wide-ranging historical survey, touching on the Hebrew Bible, Greek philosophy, early Christianity, the rabbinic tradition, and medieval philosophy, Islamic and Jewish. Finally its author turns toward the Jewish mystical tradition. He is interested in Isaac Luria as the Kabbalist who took evil most seriously, seeing human history as a long evolutionary process toward *tikkun,* or redemption. Sabbatianism is depicted as a reflection of impatience with this long process. Non-mystical Judaism, or the rabbinic view, is much less attractive to Zeitlin because it is essentially optimistic, and that means superficial. Modern Judaism tends to follow it and hence has become hollow.

From Tolstoy and Solovyev, Zeitlin takes the notion of overcoming suffering by a turn inward toward a world of inner truth, a deeper look at existence that nullifies external worldly suffering by the discovery of a more holistic view of reality. This turn is, of course, also shaped by all of their contact with Buddhism. Unlike conventional Western religion, there is no justification or apology for evil's existence in a world created by a God of good (*tsidduk ha-din*). Instead, there is a turn away from outer reality as illusion or as superficial perception of truth. Of course, the Positivists would call this the greatest illusion of all, but Zeitlin, who read Comte and other Positivists as well, decided to leave them behind.

A page before the end of the book, he summarizes: "Among those who see the awful gap [in the human condition] between the wholeness that is needed and the lowliness that actually exists, some despair entirely; these are the extreme pessimists. But there are others whose love overcomes all. Examples of these: in Israel, the prophets, the Ba'al Shem Tov, and Rabbi Nahman of Bratslav; among the nations, the early Christians, Tolstoy on the one hand and Nietzsche on the other." Here Zeitlin has already identified his key Hasidic heroes with the "love" or compassion that Buddhist teaching places front and center in its confrontation with the reality of suffering. The bridge between them is Tolstoy, who has constructed a Christianity fully identified with this principle. Paired with him, perhaps surprisingly, is Nietzsche, who has overcome pessimism by the force of creative will, soon to be identified by Zeitlin with the power of *hiddush*, or creative renewal, that he finds in Hasidism.

Zeitlin's next work (actually the first to appear in book form) was *Baruch Spinoza: His Life, Works, and Philosophical System.* The young author presents himself as a fully convinced Spinozist, willing to defend the sage of Amsterdam against all his critics, including those who found in Spinoza an unacceptable lack of divine and human free will, both pillars of classical Jewish theology. When it comes to discussing the bans on Spinoza, that of the rabbis as well as that of the Catholic Church, Zeitlin displays no sympathy at all for religious authority. The final chapter of the book, "Spinoza's System and Judaism," tends to minimize the Jewish influence on Spinoza and specifically dismisses any thought that Kabbalah might have played a role.

At the conclusion of that chapter Zeitlin turns explicitly to the question of Hasidism. Hasidism, he notes, referring especially to the sort of contemplative ḤaBaD tradition in which he had grown up, is known for the pantheistic tendencies in its thought. One might expect that Zeitlin was about to proclaim some common ground between the two as a way toward renewed Jewish appreciation of Spinoza. But such is not the case.

"Spinoza's strength," writes Zeitlin of 1900, "lies not only in his pantheism but in the freedom of his thought and his scientific point-of-view, as well as in the way he makes these consistent with the idea of God." This is hardly an attitude to be found among the *hasidim*, who "from beginning to end are very far from a scientific view of the world." He then goes on to discuss the alleged intellectual parallels between Spinoza and Hasidism:

> From this it appears that those who find complete equal-ity of views between Spinoza and the leaders of Hasidism, particularly ḤaBaD, are mistaken. Spinoza's primary assumption that nothing ever departs from the laws of nature in any way whatsoever is totally inconsistent with the teachings of Hasidism. Aside from this, they are divided by their views of God, even though the *hasidim* are also pantheists to a certain degree. According to Hasidic views, God "fills all the worlds" and "surrounds all the worlds." Spinoza would have God "fill all the worlds," or, in his words, be the internal cause of all things (*imma-nente*), but not "surround all the worlds," meaning that God is not their external cause (*transcendente*). In the Hasidic view, even though God already incorporates nature within Himself (since the Kabbalists had already noted that *elohim* [God] is numerically equivalent to *ha-teva'* [nature]), God also hovers above the bounds of nature. For Spinoza there is finally nothing beyond nature.
>
> If there is anything in Spinoza's system that accords with the teachings of Kabbalah and Hasidism, it is on the poetic side. God as the center of all ideas, the spiritual love of God, and the joy and devotion to Him remind us of enthusiastic statements in the writings of the Ba'al Shem Tov's disciples.[34]

To "all the worlds" Zeitlin appends a footnote:

> "All the worlds, according to this, are a reflection of His blessed self." Occasionally they do think like pantheists, but they generally stand within the bounds of theology and consider God to be a specific being in every sense. Even when they express things that tend toward panthe-

ism, it is mostly out of theological enthusiasm. If they knew where the things lead, they would be taken aback.

Zeitlin in his twenties is still enamored of the scientific worldview. His pantheon of greats includes Darwin and Spencer along with Spinoza, and it is the rational and scientific character of Spinoza's thought that makes him so significant. The unscientific character of Kabbalistic and Hasidic reflections (mostly taking the form of high-flying scriptural homilies, after all) leaves Zeitlin cold. A vague bit of poetic fancy is all he can offer to their credit. Perhaps most significant (and not entirely inaccurate) is his comment in the footnote that Hasidism is far from being a consistent pantheistic system, such as Spinoza's, but is rather a theism that leaves room for enthusiastic outcries that have a sort of pantheistic ring. Some more recent readers of Hasidism have seen it that way as well.

This evaluation and self-positioning changes dramatically over the course of the ensuing decade. By 1910, the next time he compares the two, Zeitlin is identifying with the Ba'al Shem Tov rather than with Spinoza. The subject matter is somewhat different here, but so is the tone with which Hasidism is treated:

> Had the BeSHT conceived of divinity as Spinoza did, he would have had to say together with Spinoza that all conceptions of good and evil, whether perfect or imperfect, are entirely human. Pure divinity has nothing to do with them. Because people have imperfect ideas, they think that one thing is good and another is evil. The universal Self—Nature—God is neither good nor bad. People love, rejoice, suffer, live, die. But this has nothing to do with God.
>
> But the BeSHT, even though he was a pantheistic thinker like Spinoza, even though he always saw God and world as one, conceived of it in an entirely different manner. God and world are one, but God is not bounded by the world, which is itself a sort of illusion or fantasy of God's. If He wants, it is already done with. On the one hand, the world is divinity itself. On the other hand it is a creation, a work of art, a masterpiece. As a creation it has

its goal. As time goes on, it comes closer to that goal, reaching higher and higher, purer and purer.

Spinoza's God is without life, a pure idea. The BeSHT's God is one that lives, strives, grows, blossoms, suffers and composes, thinks and creates that for which the heart is torn and the soul longs. The BeSHT's God is in man, even in his lacks and sufferings, his sin and smallness.[35]

Here the identification is clearly with Hasidism, and one can see quite dramatically the change that has taken place in Zeitlin over the course of a decade. Hasidism is personified by the Ba'al Shem Tov, a figure about whose teachings Zeitlin was about to compose a major essay.

What is the nature of this change? Over ten years Zeitlin has moved from commitment to a scientific worldview to one much more identified with poetry and spirituality. Within his own Jewish context he has repeated the move made by Shestov, embracing a religious language that saves him from the depths of pessimism. His pantheist position is not sacrificed (he had it, after all, first from Shneur Zalman of Liadi and only second from Spinoza), but the tone in which he articulates it is now very different. Zeitlin of 1910 is concerned not with philosophical consistency, but with the religious and emotional power of ideas. Hasidic pantheism is saved from the logical conclusions of Spinoza by its sense of the world's unreality. If this God-filled world is, from one point of view, mere illusion or fantasy, a "masterpiece" spun out of the divine imagination, God indeed remains transcendent to the world. While the sources to justify such a view are clearly found within Hasidism, one suspects that Zeitlin's readings in Indian religion and Buddhism also bolstered his ability to express them in this very direct manner.

Zeitlin's major religious writings of this highly creative period (1905–10) will be introduced individually below, so there is no need to discuss them further here. But their roots can be seen a bit earlier in an essay entitled *Kavvanot ve-Yihudim* ("Intentions and Unifications"), published in *Luah Ahiasaf* 10 in 1903. This work might be viewed as a modern update of the classical *Perek Shirah*, a hymn to the beauties of Creation and the way all of nature sings the praises of its Creator. In those days Zeitlin was living in Roslavl, close to the then-untamed Belorussian countryside. The piece reflects long periods alone in the woods, lost in meditations on nature that inevitably took the form of prayers.

> I pray and the trees pray with me.
> I bend and they bend with me;
> I bow and they bow with me.

Man and nature are joined in their devotions. Although Zeitlin has begun his journey back to the conventions of daily prayer, he here openly expresses his preference for the lone company of hills and trees, field and forest, over that of any human community of worshipers. The theme of mystical pantheism or oneness with God is also given expression here:

> We pray...and with "One" we mean simply that the blessed Holy One and His name are one, that all is one, that all changes and differences, separations and oppositions, reversals and contradictions, permutations and transformations, are mere illusion.
>
> We have but few specific intentions [in our prayer], but rather one grand one: that not only the Torah is composed entirely of the names of God, but the entire world as well.

Here Zeitlin has already arrived at the radically pantheistic/poetic worldview that will remain with him throughout his later years. One can still clearly see Berdyczewski's "transvaluation of values" in these passages, but with a greater emphasis on the mystical/religious side. These views will often manifest in Zeitlin's later writings as readings of Hasidic sources or as the teachings of the Ba'al Shem Tov. There is no more talk of "objectivity" or the value of science in Zeitlin, whose writings over the course of his lifetime may be seen as giving increasing rein to the imaginative, poetic, and ultimately even prophetic dimensions of his soul. While it is conventional to view this as a return from Spinozism to Hasidic Judaism, one may also say that the Nietzschean side of Zeitlin triumphs over the Spencerian (also Berdyczewski over Ahad Ha-'Am), or that the Russian mystic vanquishes the Western critic.

It was clear to Zeitlin by the beginning of the twentieth century's second decade that he sought to found a "new religious current," one that was to start with transformation of the inner life and build a sort of new Hasidism or religious revival within Judaism. Zeitlin did not use the term *neo-Hasidism* to describe his vision, a term that was being coined in that decade to characterize a literary rather than a truly religious phenomenon (for example, Y. L. Peretz' "Hasidic" stories, and so forth).[36] The impulse driving him was not nostalgia for the lost *shtetl*; Zeitlin shared the deep ambivalence of many in his generation toward the world they had all left behind. He did not repent of criticizing that world's narrowness of vision and disinterest in anything beyond its self-defined "four cubits." His call, though seemingly dressed in a longing for what might have looked like restored *shtetl* religion, was for a renewed spiritual life on a different plane. Yes, he dreamed that some of the spirit he sought had been there and been lost, while also knowing how much had been wrong with it.

> Zeitlin sought the personal experience of divine nearness, an inward and unmediated relationship with God. His was not an ordinary call to a religious life of fulfilling the *mitzvot*, a living out of religious obligation as detailed in the sources. His was neither a faithfulness to the ways of his ancestors nor an allegiance flowing from a defined theological position. All of these created a certain separation between the person and his Maker. Seen carefully, Zeitlin did not pull away from normative religious life, but he saw it as proceeding from the mystical experience of intimacy with God.[37]

Zeitlin's memoir tells us that the early years of World War I were a period of renewed mystical arousal for him, recalling that of his adolescence. It would seem that it was during this period that Zeitlin turned back to a full pattern of traditional Jewish observance, something with which he had been struggling for more than a decade. Unfortunately, we do not have documentation from those years. While Zeitlin refers the reader of his memoir to the passages published in *Ha-Tekufah*[38] under the title "On the Border between

Two Worlds," that publication in fact comprises a journal written later, in the spring and summer of 1917. In any case, it seems fair to say that the war years were critical in Zeitlin's religious and moral development. Like most of middle Europe's cosmopolitan intellectuals, Zeitlin saw the war only bringing about greater impoverishment and suffering. Influenced by Tolstoyan pacifism, he sided with no party to the conflict but only with its many victims.

The 1917 journal[39] is an important document, one that reveals Zeitlin as a real human being struggling with his own religious growth, with fears of sin and temptation (especially around questions of gossip and slander or "evil speech," surely key issues in the life of a controversial journalist), with hopes raised and dashed by news of peace initiatives and by the February Revolution in Russia, and with his deep disillusionment with the Hasidic leadership of Poland, with which he had begun to come into contact. These realistic motifs are woven together with fragments of a dream diary from the same months, including accounts of flying (without benefit of airplane) and various other visions of grandeur, appearance before kings, and so forth. It appears that Zeitlin placed great store in his own dreams and flights of fantasy. The journal is quite uncensored, revealing a person of rather boundless ego, one who sometimes seems to see himself in the role of cosmic *tsaddik,* or messianic figure, bearing the sufferings of Israel just as Israel as a whole bears the pains of humanity. In his fantasies he is a sort of counter-Herzl, bringing about a fuller redemption to the Jews, including both body and soul, leading toward a vision of universal redemption as well.

It is in this period that Zeitlin's searing concern for the fate of Jewry combines with his religious passion and his openness to the influence of inner experience to push him toward what can only be described as the self-proclaimed role of prophet, predicting the near-immediate advent of messiah. This self-perception was to grow in Zeitlin's consciousness over the course of the following two decades, reaching the point where some of those around him came to dismiss him as delusional, perhaps even mad. His later published Hebrew writings, especially *Davar la-'Amim* (Warsaw, 1928) and *Demamah ve-Kol* (Warsaw, 1936), speak in a tone that recalls both the biblical prophets and Nietzsche's *Zarathustra.* They place Zeitlin clearly within the parameters described by Eli Schweid[40] and others as belonging to a large group of Jewish religious writers in the twentieth century who long for a renewal of prophecy and flirt with claiming its mantle. These include Ahad Ha-'Am, Martin Buber, Abraham Isaac Kook, and Abraham Joshua Heschel. Zeitlin goes farther along this path than the others, actually writing in the prophetic style. Any claim that this is evidence of "madness," of course, has to deal with the fact that Zeitlin did indeed come closer than almost any other observer to foretelling what was to be the utterly unthinkable fate of European Jewry, including himself.

Because Zeitlin's writings from this later period are sometimes dismissed as pseudo-prophetic rantings, it is worth quoting his rather sensible introduction to *Davar la-'Amim*:

A DECLARATION

I am neither a prophet nor the son of a prophet, nor am I so misled by my fantasies as to think that what I declare to the nations in this book that I now place before the reader was sent to me from above. I know that these words are mine, the product of my thoughts and feelings, the voice of my innermost soul. In that sense this book is similar to my earlier works, including "*Shekhinah*," "Transcendent Beauty," and "The Thirst," works characterized by a distinctive blend of thought and poetry.

Yet the book I now place before the reader is entirely different from those other works. In "*Shekhinah*" and the like I gave less than full expression to what my soul told me of its longing for transcendence, for distant and sublime worlds. In this book *Davar la-'Amim* I am expressing that which my soul tells me in its total melding with the collective soul of Israel.

Were the prophets Amos, Isaiah, Jeremiah, and Ezekiel to rise today from their graves and see the great World War, the bloody conflict like none other since the very first murder, the millions who died on the battlefield, and the people Israel, offered up on the altars of each battlefield and in the pogroms and slaughter of Russia, Ukraine, and similar places...and to deliver their burden to Israel

19

and the nations, surely their words would rise higher than mine as heaven is above the earth. But the outer revealed content of their message, I believe, would be the same as my *Word to the Nations*.

He knows he is the poet-thinker, choosing to don the prophetic mantle. This introduction may be seen either as modest—an assurance that its author is not claiming prophecy—or as utterly audacious, an announcement that in content, if not in sublime source, he is the contemporary spokesman for the prophets of Israel. The voice that speaks within him is indeed the prophetic muse:

GO AND SPEAK INTO THE EARS OF THE
GENERATION: BE PREPARED!

Thus says the word that speaks within my heart:
　Go and speak into the ears of the generation, saying: Close, close is that day of which the prophets have ever spoken.
　Behold, it stands behind us, waiting to pounce upon us like a lion, or before us, like a leopard in our path.
　Prepare!
　Sinners, repent! Defiled ones, become pure! Oppressors, cease your evil! Victims, renew your strength!
　Flee from sin as you would flee a snake. Cast aside your filthy thoughts and deeds. Your God and King gazes into the clefts of your hearts.[41]

The call for repentance, both individual and collective, will become the central theme in Zeitlin's later writings. Jews are to repent of their over-attraction to a modernity that has betrayed them, of their quest after money and the comforts it buys, leading them into business and speculation in ways that inevitably oppress and take ill advantage of others. They are to return to the authentic spirit of Sinai, the passionate commitment to Judaism as Zeitlin portrays it. In doing so, they will become the exemplary heart of the great universal repentance that must take place before the messiah can arrive, an event that Zeitlin needs to see on the immediate horizon as the clouds over Europe continue to darken. The nations are to repent primarily of the ways they have misunderstood and mistreated Israel, who stands at the center of the great messianic drama that is about to unfold. *Davar la-'Amim* contains specific "prophecies" addressed to the Russians, the Poles, the English, the Arabs, and the Americans, all of them reflecting the events and the dangers felt in the mid 1920s, with particular focus on the treatment or the effects of policies upon Jews. The Arabs are called upon to welcome the Jews, who have brought such prosperity and renewal to their land. Zeitlin has seen the emergence of fierce Arab opposition to Zionism and Jewish immigration, but (naively, from the perspective of eighty years later) believes it to be misguided. Once the Arabs are made aware of the blessings—corporeal as well as spiritual—that the Jews bring with them to their to-be-shared homeland, they will clearly relent. The Americans are asked chiefly to reopen their borders to immigration, after the notorious restrictions of 1924. (In both of these cries we see the frustration that led Zeitlin to Territorialism, his sense of East European Jewish desperation, and the need to keep open opportunities for emigration and resettlement.) America is also called upon to see its newfound great wealth and seemingly endless blessing of resources as a test rather than as a divine bounty to be taken for granted.

The spearhead of this great movement toward repentance that Zeitlin seeks to bring about will be a cadre of Jewish youth, both in Poland and in the Holy Land, who will create a new and rarified Hasidism, one appropriate to the spiritual language and needs of twentieth-century Jewry and humanity. Again, the key documents of this effort will be presented in this volume, so not much summary is required here. The would-be movement had several names, including *Ahdut Yisra'el*, *Ha-Bonim*, *Yavneh*, and *Beney Hekhala* or Children of the Palace.[42] Sometimes one gets the impression that these were to exist as concentric circles, the innermost mystically enlightened elite to serve as leadership and inspiration for a mass movement. Alas, Zeitlin was better at writing and dreaming than he was at social organization. There is no evidence that these groups ever organized beyond perhaps a single small circle that met in Zeitlin's home.

The turn toward Jewish youth, especially the large portion of it now growing up caught between a questioning of tradition and an ideological secularism (Bundist or Communist), became central to Zeitlin's writings in the interwar period. He senses, probably correctly, that this large undefined center is in search of a cause, wavering between Zionism, including its moderate religious forms (Mizrahi, Po'el Mizrahi), Jewish culturalism, and a degree of assimilation. He bemoans the decline of Yiddish among young people, seeing it as a sign of their increased desire to get ahead in Polish society, which he continues to see as alien and unwelcoming.

It should be said that Zeitlin's writing did have a large popular following, primarily in Poland but also in Erez Israel and even America, among those who read the Yiddish and Hebrew press. His articles appeared with great frequency in both languages. While he opined and argued on nearly every subject current in Jewish public life, Zeitlin had the particular role of writing about aspects of Jewish traditional life in press organs that were addressed to a secular public. Many of the readers of those journals were themselves of religious background and had made personal journeys away from traditional observance or identification with Orthodoxy. Nevertheless, they enjoyed reading about their past from the pen of such a thoughtful observer as Zeitlin. He also had the frequent habit of comparing a Hasidic figure or idea he was describing to something in Western philosophy, Russian literature, or Eastern religion, signifying to the reader that this was no mere pious or nostalgic evocation. This latter habit must have annoyed the Hasidic public greatly.

Two books embody Zeitlin's attempt to reach out toward youth. The first, *Der Aleph-Beys fun Yidntum* (*The A-B-C's of Jewishness*), was published in 1922. Written in Yiddish, it is addressed to young intellectuals attracted to universalist ideals, Tolstoyan pacifism, and critical perspectives on the Bible and on Judaism. Was there a significant Yiddish-reading audience that shared and was troubled by these viewpoints, even among his many readers? Or was the real "Jewish youth" Zeitlin was addressing a series of inner protagonists in his own ongoing personal struggle? Although purporting to be a popular work, his arguments are sufficiently shot through with references to philosophers (Spinoza, Kant, Schopenauer), biblical critics

(Wellhausen, Delitzsch), Haskalah writers (Mendelsohn, S. D. Luzzatto, and especially Nahman Krochmal), and contemporary Jewish thinkers (Ahad Ha-'Am, Joseph Klausner, David Neumark) that the readership would have been quite limited, and there is good reason to suspect that inner-directed passion rather than a real sense of audience lies behind this volume, this despite the fact that the second portion of it is constructed of alleged letters to Zeitlin and his responses to them.

The largest portion of the volume is taken up by two collections of "Letters to Young Jews," in which Zeitlin strikes the conversational tone of an older mentor, trying to bring his readers along to his way of thinking. The very essence of Judaism, as he presents it, is a sense of Jewish difference, chosenness, and special obligation. Eleventh-century poet/philosopher Judah Halevi and Hasidic master Nahman of Bratslav stand together as Zeitlin's past mentors, each speaking in his own way about Israel as the heart of humanity and the world. Zeitlin's Judaism here might be called neo-prophetic more than neo-Hasidic; Israel's unique place in world history, and hence its special burden as bearer of God's word, is his essential truth. Zeitlin is surprisingly close to the nineteenth-century Reform version of Jewry as "a light to the nations," as ever-suffering bearers of the prophetic message. While he is attracted to the universalist pacifism of Tolstoy, the World War has forced him to realize that the human capacity for evil must not be underestimated. Jewish morality, with its insistence on deeds and on the values of realistic self-control, is the best tool in humanity's ongoing struggle to overcome the beast within. Ultimately he shares the universalists' dream of a world without the need for law or self-restraint, and he points proudly to such proclamations in the Jewish corpus with regard to the messianic future. But he sees us as far from ready to declare that era to have come.

The same is true with regard to private property and Judaism's view of the struggle between capitalism and socialism, very much a current topic within Polish Jewry of his time. In one of a series of chapters on the early history of humanity and religion, Zeitlin, ever the thoughtful autodidact, describes the emergence of private property (first tools, then the home, produce, and finally land). He is at pains to point out the ambivalent attitude of the Torah toward private ownership, especially of the land, which belongs to God. He hopes to show the reader that Judaism at its best shares the ideals of socialism, only seeking to bring them about over the long haul by education of the human heart and peaceful persuasion, rather than through violent revolution. The Torah is completely sympathetic with social progressives in their concern for uplifting the masses from poverty and obliterating distinctions of class, which have no place in the ideal world the Torah is seeking to bring about.

If all these lofty ideals are not to be seen in the reality of Jewish life, either past or present, it is because historical circumstance has hardly ever permitted Jews to create a society where Torah (as Zeitlin understands it, to be sure) could be fully enacted and thus put to the test. The prophets of the First Temple period bear constant witness that their message had not penetrated the people, who continued to worship idols. The leadership, both royal and priestly, was also less than ideal, as prophetic writings make very clear. The prophets were contrarians, rejected from all sides, much as Zeitlin sees himself to be. Judaism did thrive for some time in the early Second Temple period, perhaps its best era ever. But by Hasmonean times the conflict between parties became crippling to its ongoing development. Once the Romans took over the political power, Jewish practice began its long march toward being crammed into certain restricted areas of life, thus becoming petty and small minded. This was more true once the Temple was destroyed and the agricultural laws were suspended. Over the centuries Jews living as oppressed minorities under Christendom and Islam were so concerned with self-preservation that the highest—and potentially most universalist—teachings of Torah were suppressed.

The return to Judaism that Zeitlin seeks, he insists, is no call back to the ghetto or to an idealization of Jewish life as it had existed in the recent past. It has more to do with creativity and self-actualization than with conventional notions of repentance. Despite Zeitlin's piety and self-proclaimed distancing from some of his former mentors, it is easy to discern that they still reside within him:

> What is it that I seek? A Judaism that is a melding of people-hood and humanity, of humanity and that which transcends it, of good deeds and holy intentions, absolute justice in the public sphere and purity and holiness in the lives of individ-

uals. I seek the love of all creatures and the love of their Creator, the cool detachment of the scientist and the fiery passion of prophecy,[43] the great longing and the silent peace of the holy spirit ("Israel is symbolized by a dove…"), the truth of this world and that of higher, purely mystical realms.…(pp. 56f.)

…In the depths of the national soul, somewhere very deeply buried, beyond any awareness or conceptualization, there lies a secret creative energy that will at some point be revealed. It will break forth with a fierce power that will surprise both the world and the Jews themselves.…(p. 62)

…Returning to our ancient, eternal people bears something else with it. It is a return to ourselves. It is hearing that which your own deepest, eternal Jewish soul says to you. It means appropriating from others such gracious, beautiful, and profound teachings, or personal qualities and practices that befit the Jewish spirit or at least are not contrary to it. It also means liberating oneself from such teachings, qualities, and practices that are poisonous to your soul. It means hearing God's voice as it rings forth at all times, in every generation, placing yourself beyond all temporal gods, fashions, and ways of living. It is a return to the everlasting Source, to one's true Jewish nature, to divine creativity, to prophecy. (p. 67)

It is not hard to see in this description a pious version of the "new Jew" that various competitors with Zeitlin's ideology, including some who saw themselves as very far from him, also wanted to create.[44] Zeitlin's "new Jew" would have lived in Poland as well as Erez Israel, leaving the city behind for an idealized agrarian or craft-based livelihood, and devoting many hours to introspection, inward prayer, and a life of spiritual and artistic creativity. Such ideal communities might serve, in Zeitlin's broader fantasy, as hubs of larger radiating circles that would work for Jewish and universal human efforts toward redemption.

The second volume of Zeitin's call to youth is *Sifran shel Yehidim*, which appeared in 1928. The title of this slim (sixty-four pages) collection of essays, written in Hebrew (plus a few in Aramaic), has been translated above as *A Book for Individuals*. But it might also be read as *The Book of the Elite*, *yehidim*, as in *yehidey segulah*, the chosen few. The volume's subtitle makes its intent quite clear: *Deep Secret, Pure Thought, Proper Conduct and Deed for Those Lonely Souls Looking toward Eternal Redemption in These Years of "Messiah's Footsteps."* Writing now in the language of the educated, Zeitlin seeks to constitute his elite corps. On the verso of the title page appears the following notice:

> Now [I turn] not to the entire folk, but to certain individuals within it, those of strong faith and courageous and pure hearts.
>
> The Yavneh and Beney Hekhala groups that I suggest founding in this volume should not be confused with the Ahdut Yisra'el about which I have spoken extensively in the press. Ahdut Yisra'el is meant to include everyone, all of Israel, while Yavneh or Beney Hekhala (I call the elite within the elite by that name), should they be established, will be associations of single individuals for the purpose of inner uplift and seeking healing for the ills of the nation and the world.
>
> A small attempt was made in this regard in 1923–24. That attempt did not succeed. After my call in the press, a few pure and upright young people responded. But they were not sufficiently clear of sight or deep enough in their inner knowledge.
>
> Perhaps that which did not succeed then will now have its chance.
>
> In this book I turn toward those individuals who are not only upright and pure, but also filled with deep faith, feeling the great pain of the Jewish soul, strong of heart and powerful of spirit.
>
> Whoever wants to live in accord with what is found in this *Sifran shel Yehidim* should turn to me by letter (60 Szliska Street, Warsaw). I will not respond to idle queries,

objections, or arguments. But to whoever wants to walk the path I have outlined in this volume, but has doubts about one aspect or another, I indeed will respond.

Zeitlin's admission that this volume is already a second attempt, along with his dismissal of what had taken place four years earlier, probably gives us a glimpse of his failing in the role of community organizer. Our volume includes two letters in which he urges the founding of Yavneh groups in Erez Israel in the late 1920s, again showing no evidence that he had achieved any success in organizing them in Warsaw.

The other literary activity that occupied Zeitlin in the 1920s and 1930s was his ongoing study of the Zohar, the central text of medieval Jewish mysticism. Zeitlin's love affair with the Zohar is manifest in a series of essays around that work's history and meaning, published in the early 1920s, but especially in the long-term project of a Hebrew translation and commentary to the original Aramaic text. This aspect of Zeitlin's career has been documented thoroughly by Jonatan Meir, and I too have had occasion to write about it in another context.[45] In the end, only his translation and commentary to the Introduction to the Zohar were published, first in S. Rawidowicz's literary annual *Metsudah* in 1943 and then reprinted in the postwar volume *Be-Fardes ha-Hasidut veha-Kabbalah*, along with his Zohar-related essays. These materials had been in Rawidowicz's possession since the mid 1920s, when he and Zeitlin had hoped to publish them under the imprint of Ajanoth. Based on this surviving initial fragment we may surmise that the Zohar project was a huge and time-consuming occupation over much of two decades. Whether we can believe the report that he had completed this project, the results buried in the Warsaw ghetto ashes, we will never know. But it is fair to say that much of Zeitlin's energy in his later years was devoted to it.

The prophetic impulse in Zeitlin's later writings caused him to lash out against the Jews as well as against the nations of the world. As much as the nations were fully to be blamed for their wickedness and defilement, Israel's refusal to repent and return to the God of its ancestors was surely a key factor in delaying the redemption for which Zeitlin yearned in ever-increasing measure. In *Demamah ve-*

Kol (1936), the only significant book he published after Hitler's rise to power, he portrays himself as an isolated figure, one who has been predicting such a tragedy (he uses the word *sho'ah* for the current and coming situation of the Jewish people, probably the first to do so) for over a decade but has been ignored and betrayed. He traces the increasing desperation of East European Jewry, from the pogroms at the beginning of the century down to the present, repeatedly condemning the Jewish leadership for failure to see clearly or to act forcefully. The greatest sins of Israel seem to be those of partisan conflict and small-mindedness. These paralyze the people, keeping them from acting as a whole, even on the key questions of emigration and the saving of Jewish lives from both oppression and starvation. Zeitlin in 1936 still has concrete suggestions to offer. These include international appeals, the systematic organization of emigration (but to where? He has lunged back and forth on the Territorialist question but now seems open to any solution that will offer immediate relief), the establishment of a Jewish bank, a Jewish high court, and so forth. It seems clear, however, that he has left his readers behind. The frustration, anger, and sense of "I told you so but was betrayed" that overwhelms this volume cannot have made it popular reading in the late 1930s.

The very last significant publication of Zeitlin's lifetime was sent from Warsaw to a new Paris-based journal called *Oifn Sheydveg*. It was published in April 1939, just four months before the outbreak of war. The opening section of "Have We Fulfilled Our Mission?" is devoted to a slow retelling of the tale of the prophet Jonah and his attempt to flee from God. Zeitlin shifts the tale into our own day, imagining a pilot in a small seaplane flying overhead, looking down through his telescope at the people casting Jonah into the sea. He would assume, of course, that Jonah must be a terrible criminal and notes that the sea does calm down after he is thrown overboard.

Zeitlin's reading of Jonah as parable is surprising and off center. The nations of the world are about to cast Israel into the sea. The Jewish people has fled from its God-given mission, that of leading the world to know God. The great repentance, of which the world might be capable with proper Jewish leadership, has not come about.

The world blames the Jews for its woes and seeks to throw them overboard.

Zeitlin then goes on to quote at length from the biblical prophets' passages describing Israel's election and mission in the world. The verses are mostly taken from Deutero-Isaiah, but he turns also to the original charge of Exodus 19:6: "You shall be unto Me a kingdom of priests and a holy people." The flock of this collective priesthood is the whole of humanity, and the nature of the redemptive mission is clear:

> It is to bring on good deeds (*tsedakah*), right and justice (*mishpat*) in the world. It is to demand right and justice not only for ourselves, but for *all* peoples. We are to teach pure God-consciousness to all nations (as a "kingdom of priests"), to conduct a strictly holy way of living, and to provide an example to all ("a holy people"). We are to feed the hungry, clothe the naked, care for the homeless ("Are you not to spread forth your food to the hungry, take the miserably poor into your house, clothe the naked when you see them?"—Isaiah 58). You should not satisfy yourselves with philanthropic and humanitarian good intentions. You have to *battle* for right and justice. You must stand always on the side of the oppressed against their overlords. You need to free the enslaved and rescue the hurt (the same Isaiah passage).
>
> Have we *fulfilled* this mission of ours in the world?

Zeitlin then turns to the enemies of the Jews. Most anti-Semites, he tells his Yiddish readers in 1939, including the Nazis, who have made Jew-hatred a "science," are hopelessly and irredeemably set against us. Inborn wickedness, he calls it. But there is a second sort of anti-Semite, a distinct minority, that interests him more. These are in the position of his airborne observer: they see that Jews are hated and oppressed everywhere and believe that they must somehow deserve it. Some, he suggests, are even good people, but are carried away by the shallowness of vision that they have concerning the Jews, just as our airman's telescope cannot penetrate the depths of the sea.

29

The article then proceeds into a précis of Jewish history, showing how Jews have almost never gotten to fulfill the task to which they were called. Zeitlin implies, without daring to say it quite openly, that this is why the second group despises the Jews: they never lived up to their great promise. The best pre-modern attempts, he believes, took place in the Hellenistic era, when in Alexandria and elsewhere Jews were reinterpreting Torah in Greek cultural categories (Philo) and also seeking out converts. Persecution made this impossible to continue, and Jewry for hundreds of years was cast into a narrow need to concentrate on its own survival. Historical conditions simply did not allow Israel to pursue its mission in the world.

In modern times the situation is different. Persecution abated, and Jews might have taken on the task for which they had suffered so long. But modern Jews are divided in two. Eastern Europe's Jews are strongly rooted in their own uniqueness, staying close to the covenant of Jewish existence itself. Even the nonreligious among them reflect a commitment to the *berit-'am* (he is playing off Isaiah 42:6), the national covenant. But they fail to look beyond themselves toward the greater task. Western Europe's Jews have come to appreciate the "light unto the nations" mission, standing proudly at the center of many movements for human betterment. But their own Jewish roots have become too shallow and weakened by ignorance (American Jews, though many in number, were apparently not even worthy of consideration). The strengths of these two communities need to be recombined in order for the true mission of Israel to find expression, a task still unfulfilled. Finally, Zeitlin turns to contemporary Jewish nationalism, leading up to his concluding prophecy:

> Modern Jewish nationalism, whether in its general form or in the specific Zionist garb, generally strives to secularize Jewish life and render it profane, making the Jews a people like all others. Modern Jewish nationalism struggles mightily against assimilation without noticing that in the course of this secularization it in fact is striving for the very same thing as the assimilationists—"Let us be like all the nations." But the prophet Ezekiel thousands of years

ago foresaw that demand, reacting to it with the following harsh, but at the same time encouraging, words:

"That which has arisen in your minds will surely not come to pass, when you say 'Let us be like the nations, the families of the earth, worshiping sticks and stones.' By My life, says Adonay your God, with a strong hand and an outstretched arm, with rage poured forth I will rule over you" (Ezek. 20:32–33).

"Rage poured forth" is the precise meaning of the present fierce tempest that now seeks to sink the Jewish ship in many lands.

But the prophet does not speak only of "rage poured forth," but also of a "strong hand" that will lead the Jewish people, willingly or not, toward the divine kingdom, toward that great future light.

Can Zeitlin be accused of blaming the victim, of saying that the Jewish people, not having lived up to its mission, is in part responsible for its own fate? Can we bear the thought of his saying this so late in the decade, after the Nurnberg Laws, after the expulsions and the first concentration camps, after Kristallnacht? Seeming to know how harshly his readers will judge him if he says it outright, Zeitlin dances around the claim without ever quite making it explicit. But as history had it, this became his last testament to us, and its message is clear.

Zeitlin lived in the ever-worsening conditions of the Warsaw ghetto until September 1942. His younger son, Elchonon, a literary critic, poet, and essayist, died of illness (probably the typhus that was rampant in the ghetto); his is one of the last graves in the vast Warsaw Jewish cemetery. Zeitlin's elder son, the well-known poet Aaron, was away on a lecture tour in the United States when the war broke out, and he could not get back to Poland. He lived in the United States until 1973. His wife and child were killed at Maidanek. Hillel Zeitlin's wife, her son-in-law, and her grandchild (Rivka's child) died at Treblinka.

Hillel Seidman, a survivor of the ghetto, brought out with him the only eyewitness account of Zeitlin's martyrdom.[46] When his block was called forth to the notorious Umschlagplatz, the assembly point for the forced march to Treblinka, Zeitlin came out wearing *tallit* and *tefillin*, with a copy of the Zohar in his hand. He joined the march in this way but died along the road, thus saved the final indignities that would have met him there. It was the eve of Rosh Hashanah of the year 5703, perhaps the darkest in all of Jewish history.

Zeitlin loved the Zohar and studied it all his life; it is no surprise that he would carry it at this moment. But I also suspect that he had in mind a key line, originating in the Tikkuney Zohar but widely used in the literature of Bratslav Hasidism, which Zeitlin knew and loved so well: "With this book will Israel go forth from their exile."

May his memory be a source of blessing.

HASIDISM THEN AND NOW

1. The Call for a New Hasidism

Translator's Introduction

In the years following the First World War, Zeitlin sought to sow the seeds of what he hoped would become a new Hasidic movement, one built around principles he was beginning carefully to outline. He approached this project with great enthusiasm, though apparently it met with little or no organizational success.

The earliest version of this call by Zeitlin appeared in an article he published in Martin Buber's journal *Der Jude* in 1916. There he says:

> Polish Jewry has another very great and holy task. To say it more precisely: a holy and glorious endeavor, a great and vital responsibility. It was in Poland that Hasidism was born. There it flourished and branched forth, diversified and divided. There too it dissipated and declined in various ways. But Polish Jewry needs to preserve that treasure in a strict, serious, and artful way, a treasure granted to it by the gracious right hand of the Eternal....
>
> Hasidism in Poland has to return [or "repent"] if it does not want to die (and it must not die, for "thought that proceeds from sublime Wisdom is not to be destroyed"). It must return to the Ba'al Shem Tov and his disciples, those bearers of divine compassion. Hasidism needs to be restored to its source. Then it will nourish the spirit and soul of all humanity.

In one of the only writings Zeitlin ever published in a language that was read by non-Jews as well as Jews, he added:

> The holy Hasidic word needs to be carried far, far beyond the boundaries of Poland, even beyond the bounds of the entire Jewish people. The inner power of this word needs to call forth to all humanity, arousing them to true love, true justice, and the true "kingdom of heaven."[1]

The first two documents translated below originally appeared in Yiddish in a pamphlet called *Di Teyvoh*, published in Warsaw in the spring of 1924.[2] The title means "The Ark," but Zeitlin may also be playing off a well-known early Hasidic reading of "ark" as "word." The pamphlet claims to be written by Zeitlin but "published by the religious-ethical circle *Yavneh*, associated with the *Ahavat Re'im* Society." Both of these bodies, so it appears, existed chiefly in Zeitlin's wishful imagination.

The three Aramaic essays were added when the original *Di Teyvoh* documents were translated into Hebrew as part of *Sifran shel Yehidim* in 1928.

The first essay, in which journalist Zeitlin "interviews" himself, constitutes his neo-Hasidic manifesto. In its 1928 version it is entitled "The Hasidism of the Future." The new religious movement he seeks will differ utterly from the corrupt and discredited version of Hasidism that currently dominates the scene. But it will also (after an initial denial) differ from that of the Ba'al Shem Tov in three interesting ways. Regarding each of the three loves that the BeSHT said his soul came to earth to fulfill, Zeitlin wants to open wider vistas. He wants the love of God to "shine forth and burn even more brightly" than in former times, Israel serving as a beacon to lead the entire world toward passionate engagement with a God present in all things and all moments, the great truth that he finds in Hasidism. "Love of Israel," a key teaching of the BeSHT and all later Hasidic tradition, will be expanded into "a great worldwide love of humanity." Love of Torah will no longer be limited to traditional rabbinic and Talmudic studies, but will be sought out in "all the finest works of art, in all of worldly knowledge."

This is indeed a revolutionary program, one that would transform Hasidism beyond recognition to anyone living in the Warsaw of 1924. It may be said that Zeitlin the Berdyczevskian disciple still lurks beneath the Hasidic *kapote* that Zeitlin had by this time taken to wearing. As will become clear from the fifteen rules or "admonitions," Zeitlin is quite classically pious regarding several key traditional issues, but without compromising his expansiveness of vision.

The other new point in Zeitlin's approach to Hasidic piety is his consciousness of class and class conflict, something not yet articulated in the Ba'al Shem Tov's day. His sharp anti-capitalism comes out even more strongly in the admonitions. In an era when Jewish craftsmen and factory workers were still numerous, he urges members of Yavneh to earn their keep by physical or skilled labor. Anything else leads one down the path of oppressing others, or at least gaining benefit from their inadequate compensation and dehumanization. Business, especially that characterized as "speculation (meaning stocks, bonds, and investments in general)" is utterly corrupting. So too is the quest for creature-comforts and luxuries that characterized the rising Jewish bourgeoisie of post-industrial revolution Poland, encompassing not a few Hasidic and once-Hasidic households. At all this Zeitlin lashes out with the beginning of that prophetic wrath that will so characterize his later works.

The three brief Aramaic chapters show Zeitlin at his most poignant and vulnerable. He passionately seeks disciples who share his deep inward vision of divine light, the all-present radiance of *shekhinah* filling each moment of life. Even a *longing* for such a presence will suffice to make one a disciple, a member of the innermost circle that will become his new movement's leaders. His personal street address, posted at the end of the admonitions, as at the conclusion of several other such calls, makes the point clearly. If you are serious about living this life, come see me. Knock on my door. Let's talk.

From the letters to disciples in Erez Israel, as well as from negative evidence (lack of later mention of such groups in Poland), we have the impression that very few came. A small study circle met at his home in Warsaw, as the second letter indicates.

One reason for this may have been the growing edge of messianism that already makes itself present in these early post–World

War One documents, a tendency that was to grow as conditions for Poland's Jews worsened. As with most messianisms, it was accompanied by a terrifying vision of the nearing apocalypse. The growing darkness with which Zeitlin spoke was not likely to attract the sort of idealistic young followers he sought, who surely would have preferred a message of greater hope.

Religious and idealistic youth were finding that hope primarily in Zionism. The Religious Labor Zionism of Po'el Mizrahi and Po'aley Agudat Yisra'el offered the closest actualist platform to Zeitlin's Yavneh vision. The socialist Hasidism that he was proclaiming probably was, as his letters indicate, easier to live out in the back-to-the-soil atmosphere of 1920s Palestine than in the context of ever more urbanizing Poland, where the flight to the cities did little to improve growing economic deprivation and ultimately desperation. While a messianic message may have been tempting in such circumstances, the hard grind of daily life left little room for realizing the romantic communitarian dream that Zeitlin had to offer.

It should be said that Zeitlin's vision stands in the context of a long history of real and fantastic intentional communities strewn through the history of Judaism. While full monasticism (after Qumran) lies outside the boundaries of Jewish self-definition, mystics in every era have sought to create intense brotherhoods of shared spiritual quest, some of them leaning toward an idealized communitarian vision. The paradigm for all later such communities is that of Rabbi Simeon ben Yohai and his loving disciples as described in the pages of the Zohar, which Zeitlin so greatly revered. This band of wandering souls, now understood to be a literary creation of Kabbalists in thirteenth-century Spain, may indeed reflect the life and aspirations of a real community, though one living a millennium after the setting in which it is described. But groups of masters and disciples in such diverse places as Safed (late sixteenth century), Padua, Jerusalem, Frankfurt, Miedzybozh (eighteenth century), Bratslav, and Przysucha (early nineteenth century) all lived in the glow of that community and sought to re-create it. Zeitlin's Yavneh, while shaped by modern ideals as well, is in part another link in that ongoing chain.

His passion is still stored away in these essays, waiting to be unwrapped in another time and place, a very different era in which his call so very much seems to strike a tone that might yet find response.

Szliska 60 is no more, but Yavneh still waits to be created.

WHAT DOES YAVNEH WANT?

(A Dialogue)

What does Yavneh want?

Yavneh wants to bring the old Hasidism, that of the BeSHT,[3] back to life and establish it on foundations that are more acceptable in the present time of "Messiah's footsteps."

Of what does this old BeSHTian Hasidism consist?

Three loves: the love of God, the love of Israel, and the love of Torah.

How did the BeSHT understand the love of God?

Until the BeSHT, even the purest love of God (and we speak here only of the love of God in its purest form. Those who love God because He gives them health, length of days, glory, and wealth, are not being considered here at all) was conceived only like the love of a glorious king or a great sage. Maybe, in the best case, it was like the way one loves a father. But the BeSHT came and taught that one must love with a terrible thirst, a terrible burning, terrible suffering that fills the entire soul and body in such a way that no room for anything else remains.

Was the BeSHT the first to conceive of the love of God this way?

Long before the BeSHT there were those who saw the love of God as entailing suffering as long as the person remains in the body and does not have an actual "outpouring of the soul."

Who were they?

R. Eleazar Rokeach, R. Yehudah he-Hasid,[4] and in the time of the BeSHT, R. Hayyim Ibn Attar.[5]

And how did such enlightened Jews as R. Bahya Ibn Pakuda,[6] Maimonides, and many others understand the love of God?

They understood "love" as an act of the mind, of consciousness, of knowledge.

And did R. Eleazar Rokeach, R. Yehudah he-Hasid, R. Hayyim Ibn Attar, and the BeSHT think that "love" is not an act of mind, consciousness, or knowledge?

They respect these as well. But they demand that the love of the Most High take in the entire person. It is the highest form of passion, the desire of all desires. It embraces all particular wills, all of a person's senses, the totality of passion, all one's lust for life, all thoughts, all words, all deeds!

Did they come to this all-consuming love just out of their own souls, or were they somehow aided by the ancients?

They saw this love in the words of the poet: "As the hart pants after streams of water, so does my heart pant for You, O God"…"My soul thirsts for God, for the living God" (Ps 42:2–3)…."Who else do I have in heaven? I want none but You in the earth….My flesh and heart wear away, O rock of my heart; God is my portion forever" (Ps 73:25–26).

If Rokeach, Yehudah he-Hasid, the BeSHT, and Ibn Attar saw this in the words of the poet, what did they add to it?

Everyone knows these words of the poet. But they are taken as just that: poetry, meaning unique and special moments of divine inspiration. Along came the Rokeach, R. Yehudah, Ibn Attar, and the BeSHT, and they made it a requirement for every individual in every hour and moment, like the air we breathe.

And what did the BeSHT in particular add to this?

For the Rokeach, R. Yehudah, and Ibn Attar, this all-consuming love was a positive commandment, alongside all the others. But for the BeSHT it is the foundation of everything. He never stops talking about it in all his teachings, stories, and aphorisms.

And how did the BeSHT understand the love of Israel?

He once said to someone: "Believe me, I love the worst Jew in the world much more than you love your favorite child." This is what love of Israel meant to the BeSHT.

And what did the love of Torah mean to him?

If you understand "Torah" only as sharp-minded, expert, deep learning, you can find love of Torah among other great sages and righteous folk, perhaps even more than in the BeSHT. But the BeSHT's love of Torah touches especially upon the light of Torah, the hidden light, attachment to God through the letters of the Torah, the "worlds, souls, and divinity" that exist within every letter. Those letters combine to form words, and out of the joining of these words are formed awesome unifications, bringing near the coming of messiah.

And why do you call all this a "return to the original Hasidism" of the BeSHT? Why don't you simply say: "to Hasidism"?

Because today's Hasidism is very far from the pure Hasidism of the BeSHT.

In what way has today's official Hasidism turned away from the pure Hasidism of the BeSHT?

Simply in the fact that it no longer possesses that love of God, Israel, and Torah.

What do you mean?

Very simple. Today's *hasidim* still *talk* about all these things. But they mix all sorts of incidental things in with them—fanciful interpretations, homilies, intellectual games—until the real point is obscured. Second—and this is really the main thing—for some of today's *hasidim* their Hasidism has become a purely external matter. They study without a real taste for it; they pray in the same way. They pursue wealth and glory no less, and sometimes even more, than non-*hasidim*. They're always busy praising their own *rebbes* and castigating all the others, along with their disciples. They've set up *rebbes'* courts and dynasties and get all involved in the politics of these. They spend a good part of their lives fighting about rabbis, ritual slaughterers, and other religious officials. They consider only themselves to be proper Jews and everyone else to be nothing at all. They make Hasidism consist entirely of external manners, outer dress, and outward customs. They regularly mix fanaticism with piety. They chase away the young people over petty and foolish matters, sometimes pushing them far from Jewish religious life with their very hands....

Are you claiming that today's *hasidim* contain even less true and pure Judaism than the non-*hasidim*?

God forbid! First, I'm only speaking here about a portion of today's *hasidim*, not about all. Certainly there are other sorts of *hasidim* present today as well: those who bear a deep inwardness, a deep attachment, a passionate love of God. They have love for all Jews, a love of truth and a longing for peace, a strong, clear understanding of all that is happening around them. Second, even the other *hasidim*, those of outwardness and dress, still have lots of good qualities, things that belong to all Jews. Whatever failings a contemporary *hasid* may have, he still bears a certain sense of shame, a fear of God, a brokenness, something of modesty, humility, a leaning toward lovingkindness, goodness, and love. But all—the inward *hasidim*, those who concentrate on the externals, and just ordinary Jews—today need a new light that will shine into their souls, a Hasidism of the future, rays of messiah's light.

Does Yavneh want to be that "Hasidism of the future," that "ray of messiah's light"?

That Hasidism is not yet here. The rays of messiah's light show themselves hardly at all, only to those most pure of sight. But Yavneh wants to *prepare* for that future. Yavneh seeks, bit by bit, to qualify individuals for it. It wants to create vessels to contain that light, which must come sooner or later.

And in what way will the "Hasidism of the future" be differentiated, not only from today's external Hasidism, but from that which is inward, and even from the Hasidism of the BeSHT?

Differentiated from inward Hasidism and from that of the BeSHT? Not at all! On the contrary, it will be built entirely on the Hasidism of the BeSHT. But what then? It will go farther, broader, and deeper, appropriate to these messianic times.

What will that "going farther," in both breadth and depth, consist of?

In the time of the BeSHT it was enough for Israel to shine a light for itself. In these times, in a time when a world has been destroyed and a new one is being built,[7] Israel has to be a light for itself and for all peoples, as in the verse: "I the Lord call you in righteousness and hold fast to your hand, making you as a covenantal people, a light to the nations" (Isa 42:6). And scripture also says: "Is it easy for you to be My servant, to raise up the tribes of Jacob and restore the guarded ones of Israel? I have made you a light unto the nations, so that My salvation may reach the ends of the earth" (Isa 49:6). And it also says: "Then I will turn all the nations toward a clear tongue so that they all might call upon the name of the Lord, to serve Him together" (Zeph 3:9).

And in what else?

In the time of the BeSHT Jews sought the light of Torah only in the Torah itself. Sometimes they also sought it out in ordinary folk-tales, in which they discovered a hidden light. ("Declare His glory among the nations" [Ps 96:3], according to a profound remark of Rabbi Nahman, means that "the glory of God cries forth from all things, even from tales told by the non-Jews.") But in the times of this final great purification we need to seek out the Torah-light in all the finest works of art, in all forms of worldly knowledge. We need to approach these with a certain light in our hands, with a particular kind of foresight. "A candle of the Lord is the human soul, searching out all the belly's chambers" (Prov 20:27). It will have to separate, seek out, and nullify, casting aside heaps of lies in order to get at the kernel of truth....

And in what else?

In the time of the BeSHT the class conflicts among people were not yet so sharply defined. The demand for social justice had not yet been articulated with full seriousness and honesty. Today we are undergo-

ing horrible evils that are taking place in the world. But these are leading us to a more just and honorable relationship with those who work
with sweat on their brows. The "Hasidism of the future" will incorporate all that is healthy, pure, and honorable in Socialism. But it will
with great bitterness cast aside all in Socialism that is petty, egotistical,
merchant-like in its materialism, unjust, jealous, or vengeful. It will
reject the dark and wild tyranny of the masses and of those adventur-
ers who climb up on the backs of the masses.[8]

In the Hasidism of the future the love of God will shine forth and
burn even more brightly than it did in the days of the BeSHT. The
"Love of Israel" will be transformed into a great worldwide "Love of
Humanity." Nevertheless, Israel will always be recognized as the firstborn child of God, the one who has borne, continues to bear, and will
continue to bear the godly light. "Love of Torah" will spread forth
over all that breathes with sublime wisdom, after the inner light
teaches the Jews to distinguish between that within the worldly sciences which is of the divine mind and that which is just self-
proclaimed human conviction, error, and lies. "Justice, justice shall
you pursue" (Deut 16:20) will be spread through all social relationships. Justice will be demanded not only of the opposing class (as
both the capitalists and the proletariat do today), but people will
demand justice *of themselves*. Pursuit of justice will be not only a public matter (as it is today), but rather one of individual concern. Each
person will think not about how to avoid being exploited, but rather
about how to avoid exploiting the other.

**Perhaps you could outline for me, just briefly, how you see the
hasid of the future, that for which the Yavneh member is preparing.**

I'll try to do so. The *hasid* of the future will live only from his own
physical labor. He will exploit no one in the world, doing not even the
slightest harm to anyone. He will partake of God's own holiness, living
in uninterrupted communion with the Endless. He will walk through
divine fire while praying, will study Torah with an inner godly light,
will seek and find everywhere the light of Torah and messianic light.
In all his thoughts and deeds he will strive only for true peace and
unity. He will be filled with love and compassion for every Jew and
non-Jew, for every creature. He will long to raise up the form of the
shekhinah in the holy land and to spread her light through all the

world. He will be a great seer and a great knower. In his own eyes he will be as nothing at all, having not just an external veneer of modesty but a deep inner recognition, a full consciousness that he is "just a small creature, lowly, dark, standing with but a weak mind before the One who knows perfectly." In that moment he will be a true "chariot" for the divine, a true servant of God, a faithful messenger.

ADMONITIONS FOR EVERY TRUE MEMBER OF YAVNEH[9]

(Fifteen Principles)

1. Support yourself only from your own work! Try as hard as you can to support yourself from simple physical labor and not from trade. Trade is based primarily on the deception of customers, and this means lies. And lies completely oppose what the blessed Holy One, who is Absolute Truth, demands of us ("God, our Sovereign, is truth." And, "the signet of God is truth.").

    If you are, brother, a worker, try to become an expert in your craft. Don't look forward, as so many do today, to leaving this work so that you can support yourself more easily through business. If you are not yet a worker, make the effort to become one. If you have not yet been given the opportunity to join a labor union for religious or moral reasons, try to establish, together with a few of the members of *Yavneh*, cooperative workshops, and the like.

    If you cannot work as a physical worker because of old age or infirmity, try at least to choose for yourself a type of livelihood that succeeds with a minimum of commerce in it, and help your friends who work with their hands in every way you can.

2. Keep away from luxuries! Luxuries throttle the mind and the strength of a person. Luxuries bring on acts of constant deceit, leading from there to thievery and robbery. Striving for the true Jewish life, and at the same time for a life of luxuries, is like dipping in a purifying pool while holding a defiling abomination in your hand.

43

Therefore, choose a life of modesty, simplicity, keeping yourself far away from all external luxuries. Refrain as much as you can from various habits that cost you money, that do not benefit your body, and that harm your soul. My friend, turn your steps away from the theater and from parties. Guard yourself from smoking, from liquor, from expensive clothes, from adorning yourself with rings, and the like. Seek not to adorn your dwelling with costly decorations. It would be better if you would purify and adorn your soul, my dear friend.

3. Do not exploit anyone! If you support yourself solely by the work of your hands, the length of your days will be surrounded by modesty, calm, and humility, by abstention from indulgence, luxury, and pleasure seeking. It will simplify your task if you fulfill the great and holy commandment to every pure mortal: do not exploit anyone! Do not "use" people, seeking your own benefit without their agreement, or even with their agreement, if a full exchange of value is not received. Every person is a complete world. From the standpoint of morality and pure religion, every business abuse, in any form whatsoever, is robbery and murder.

    A factory boss or supervisor who takes advantage of workers by paying them the lowest wage acceptable on the market, and not the full and proper sum for value received, is exploiting those workers. The merchant who takes unfair advantage in buying or selling exploits the people that merchant is dealing with.

    Abuses are to be found today also among politicians, journalists, doctors, and the rest of the people involved in the free professions. Every pressing of advantage that is not the result of the complete, considered, free, and serious agreement of the person involved is a sin. Protect yourself from all this as you protect yourself from fire, my dear brother!

4. Purify your family life. The family has always been a stronghold for the Jew. In the face of work, persecution, and daily troubles, the Jew found rest and comfort in quiet, pleasant, and pure family life. The family has always been the Jew's sanctuary. Even Balaam saw this, and against his will declared: "How good are your dwelling places, O Jacob" (Num 24:5).

Today, to our disaster, the anarchy of the street has broken into the Jewish family. This bulwark, the pure and pleasant Jewish family of Poland, has started to disintegrate since the time of the German conquest [World War I]. Now, this fall is deepening more and more. Further, this decline is abetted by the general moral ruin of the street, the theater, the movies, the pulp journals, and obscene literature. And a good bit of the so-called better and more serious literature abets this. Knowingly and unknowingly, many of those who declare themselves artists contribute to this decline.

Protect your soul from this catastrophe, my dear brother! Strengthen yourself to protect the quiet, the peace, and the love in your family!

5. Sanctify your sex life altogether! The preservation and sanctification of the covenant, these are the exalted bases of both interior and exterior holiness. Concerning this, we are charged: "Be holy" and "One who sanctifies oneself a little here below, will be greatly sanctified from above." "The sexual organ is the fundament of the body, sign of the holy covenant." One who is pure in this matter is holy; one who is impure in this area is defiled. In this one must be guarded not only from actual sin but also from sinful thoughts. And the proven ways to this are—always to be occupied with work (at best, physical work), and also with the learning of *Torah* with concentration and depth. "There is no room for sin except in a heart that is void of wisdom," says the RaMBaM. "*Torah* is good when joined to work; the exertion of both cause sin to be forgotten." Actual work—on no account idleness. Idleness brings on all misfortune.

6. Guard yourself from forbidden foods! "You will be defiled by them" (Lev 11:43). Read this as, "You will be *blocked* by them." Forbidden foods defile the body and soul; forbidden foods create vile and impure blood in the human body. If some of today's Jewish youth have a tendency to go toward evil, this is mainly an outcome of not protecting themselves against forbidden foods. Be careful, my brother, of forbidden foods, and thus you will save yourself from impurity, evil, and quick temper.

7. Sanctify your *Shabbos!* The Sabbath is not just an ordinary commandment, but the basic foundation. One who weakens the Sabbath, Heaven forbid, desecrates the God of Israel. A person who doesn't sanctify the Sabbath is like one who worships idols. "Keep" and "remember," the single God uttered at once. Unite with the holiness of the Sabbath, and in this way, commune with the blessed Holy One. The Sabbath, however, must be kept not only on the outside, but also within. This means prayer, learning, a basic stocktaking of the soul, concentration of the mind on holy and pure matters. *Shabbat* upholds the entire Jewish people. The Community of Israel and *Shabbat* are truly a pair, and in them resides the Holy Ancient of Days.

8. Keep your home holy! Not only the synagogue, the house of learning, the prayer room, but also every Jewish house is a small-scale sanctuary. When can this be said? When the house abounds with words of *Torah*, prayers, blessings, *Kiddush*, and *Havdalah*, and when these are expressed seriously, truthfully, with profound and intent sincerity! When a mother and a father, a brother and a sister, live in calm and true peace (for in a peaceful place, there is the blessing of the Father of Peace); when the children are educated in the spirit of the serious and pure *Torah*; when all the children of the house speak the Jewish tongue and are full of love, honor, and recognition for every Jewish thing.

    But what is today the structure of a house of an average Jewish merchant? Mostly, it is a place of selling and buying, sometimes a feverish stock market, sometimes a club for a game of cards, and sometimes a hall for parties. The father goes out in search of "pleasures," and the mother seeks her own. In the house—a constant ill will, continual arguments behind the backs of others, or worse, to their face. The daughters no longer speak Yiddish; the sons are being prepared for empty careers. Even where *Shabbat* is kept in an exterior way, it is without joyous celebration, without soul, without life. They pray, and when they have the opportunity, they fulfill commandments and customs, but everything is mechanical.

In a place where there is no light and no fire, no love or devotion—there is no resting place for the almighty God.

Yavnehite! Don't allow your house to become secular and commercial. Let your house be suitable for a Jew—a small sanctuary of the Lord! See that the Jewish language is heard in your house, allow the voice of *Torah*, words of peace, heartfelt prayers, taking part in the immense and tragic mystery of Israel, and silent hopes for redemption.

9. Live always amid the whole Jewish people and for the whole Jewish people. Don't be concerned about yourself, but about all of Israel. The pain of all should be your pain; Israel's joy, your joy. Every single Jewish soul is a part of the *shekhinah,* called *kenesset yisra'el* because She is the totality of Jewish souls. The Community of Israel is the lower *shekhinah*, the kingdom of heaven on earth. The suffering of a Jewish soul is distress to the *shekhinah*, as it were. So how can you, Yavnehite, cause pain to any Jew? Whoever works honestly and wholeheartedly for the redemption of Israel—as he understands it—is working to redeem *shekhinah*. Blessings to anyone who does something good for the Jewish people—even if his views are far from our own! Blessings to any hand that is stretched out to bring help to Jewry!

    Yavnehite! In all your thoughts, all your longings, all your words and deeds, do not have yourself and only those close to you in mind, but rather the entire great holy Jewish people. Bring yourself and your loved ones into that whole. The salvation of the whole will be yours as well.

10. Remove yourself from party politics. Though you are bound to live as a part of the general society, and work especially for the community, do not join any particular party, be it ever so close to your heart. As long as the party is occupied with politics, it is bound for the furtherance of those politics to transgress the limits of justice and communion of all of *Yisra'el*. If you are a member of a party, and you find it difficult to leave it, especially if the main purpose of the party is the building up of the nation—set your heart to scrutinize every act and deed of the party. Your humanity, your Judaism, your hidden

treasure, is a thousandfold more important than even the best and loftiest party.

Whether you are a member of a party or not, you can and ought to participate in the work of any party, to the extent that it directs deeds to the building of the whole nation, and to the unification of the nation, and you are bound to remove yourself from it, when it divides Jews, or when, to achieve its purpose, it uses means that are contrary to the Jewish spirit, which is that of love, justice, and holiness.

11. Remember and never forget the three loves! The Yavnehite is bound to seek religious perfection, meaning avoidance of sin and the fulfillment of commandments in actual deeds. But we are especially bound to awareness of the three loves—the love of God, the love of *Yisra'el*, and the love of Torah.

12. Subdue pride! Pride is the most profound and strongest idol. Pride is the "strange god" within one's own body. Pride has deeply rooted itself in us, and in order to uproot it, concerted effort over decades is necessary. We must combat it all the days of our life. As long as it rests in us, it hides God, it hides others, and it hides the world outside ourselves. We cannot reach the light of truth as long as pride rests in us. "Pay attention to this cursed one—and bury it!"

13. Sanctify speech! Speech is the expression of the soul. Guard the covenant of the tongue; the holiness of the tongue. Not one word of evil speech! Not one round of gossip! No idle words at all; and it goes without saying, not to defile your tongue with filth. Do not think that there is no damage from speech. What difference does it make? A vulgar joke? Whom does it hurt? No, dear brother! A word has the power to build and destroy worlds. It is your duty, Yavnehite, to be a builder, a creator, repairing lives that have been destroyed. Therefore, let your words be holy.

14. Sanctify your inner life! Let not a day in life pass without taking stock of your soul. Learn or hear *mussar* [moral teachings] every day. Books like *The Duties of the Hearts, The Path of the Upright, The Way of the Righteous, Tanya, Select Counsels,*[10] should always be your companions.

Even if you are busy and cannot afford more time, separate yourself for five to ten minutes every day, in your chosen corner, for a short and precise tally of your soul. And at this same time, let there be a short silent prayer in your heart:

"Sovereign of the world, set me on the right path, on the path of light."

NOTE: Any reader who has firmly decided to start living in accord with the fourteen principles outlined above, even if gradually, in steps, may turn in this regard either orally or in writing to Hillel Zeitlin, Szliska 60, Warsaw.

15.[11] Broaden and deepen the activity of "B'nai Yavneh." Wherever you encounter a person who is prepared to accept the views offered in this book and to seek to live by them, hold fast to him. Teach him, enlighten him, guide him. When you find a few people in your city ready to live in accord with everything said in this book, cleave to them. Enlighten and guide them; proceed together up the pathway that leads toward God. If the way is too far for you and you find it hard to fulfill everything said here, do not turn back. Fulfill first what is *possible* for you. Afterward try to go further. The God of heaven and earth will be there to help you.

Let one small gathering extend its hand to a second, the second to a third, until there is firmly established a whole assemblage of Jews returning to God in truth and wholeness, "doing His word in order to hear the voice of His word" (Ps 103:20).

THREE ARAMAIC CHAPTERS FROM
SIFRAN SHEL YEHIDIM

Into a Single Chamber![12]

To you, O children of the holy, sublime light! You know all the suffering and pain of *shekhinah*, all She has endured from the day of Adam's sin until now! You have known all the awful affliction, the loud outcries from amid the atrocities of the last years, surely the birthpangs of messiah.

I invite you all to join together in a single assembly. I call it Yavneh; it is an act of building, as in "the form and the building (Ezek 41:13)." It is also *binah*, the Supreme Mother, the World of Freedom, the World to Come.[13] It is repentance, but not like the old repenting amid cries and fasting, not even that of prayer and dancing. It is repentance like that of the people of Nineveh, about whom we are told, "They repented, each of his wicked way and the violence that was in their hands" (Jonah 3:8). On this the rabbis said: "Even if he had stolen a beam and built it into a tower, he knocked down the whole tower to restore the beam to its owner."[14]

The "*whole* tower" refers to all that people build for themselves by means of lies and cheating, that which is now called *speculation*, along with the whole misconceived building called *politics*.

Return to the place of Supernal Mother, She who calls out: "I am *binah* and *gevurah* (power) is Mine" (Prov 8:14). This is a power not based on the force and lies of this world, but rather the power of BeNaYaHu son of Yehoyada, who is called "son of a living man of great deeds, from Kabtse'el" (2 Sam 23:2). The holy Zohar tells us that "son of a living man" refers to "*Tsaddik*, Life of all the Worlds," and that "great deeds" means that He is master of all deeds and forces above. "*Kabtse'el*" refers to that precious and mighty Tree, greater than all. From what place does it derive? From *Kabtse'el* [literally "divine gathering"], the sublime, hidden realm that no eye has seen....[15]

But I come to you not with wordplays and hints, but rather with the powerful word of the God of heaven by Haggai His prophet (1:4): "Is this the time for you to sit hidden in your houses, while this House lies in ruins?" Now the "House" refers not to the Temple, but to the entire world, the House of God, that lies in ruins. The glorious light of *Tif'eret Israel* no longer shines in human souls! Sun is not joined to moon! The children of the Assembly of Israel go "each in his own wicked way" (Isa 56:11).

Even the small elite are like fishes washed up on dry land, each turning his own way and weeping. Earth is destroyed; no light shines upon it. Great sorrow and poverty fill the land. The sick and ailing cry out, but no one responds to them. The blessed Holy One calls out to people: "Why have I come and found no one, called out and received no reply?" (Isa 50:2). Come and see! The sublime light shines into human souls when they are joined together as one. But

50

when they separate from one another and no longer know each other, the divine light also separates from them, rising higher and higher, not shining upon humans at all. Then all dwell in darkness; the River of Light that flows and sustains life turns parched and dry.

Now I say to you: You who know this truth, join together in one assembly of love and prayer! Have great love for all the Holy One has created. Give light to all people amid holy and sublime love!

(Even though I said above that today's repentance is not that of outcry and fasting, or even that of prayer and dancing, but rather a repentance like that of Nineveh—the foundation of the final redemption—still it will need to be accompanied by constant prayer and supplication by us broken vessels, hard as stone and yet broken in the presence of God. The wise will understand.)

Come together in this single gathering, this Yavneh of which I have spoken, a single chamber, a great and powerful bond of faith! May the God of Adam, David, and Messiah be your help, pouring upon you many blessings, the very dew with which He will one day revive the dead. God grant you the inheritance of your father Jacob, an inheritance without end. Amen!

A Single Unity, That of the Ancient One

I now reveal to you, members of this holy assembly, a unification of God's name.[16] It is as old as that wine preserved with its grapes from the six days of Creation, yet as fresh as this morning's dawn. It is as bright as the sun shining through your window, like water drawn this very day, like the flight of birds just going by above my head. Yet you could also say that it is the most primal of all antiquities, the first thought of all, the primal will, the beginning point of all. So too is it the final act, the end of days, conclusion and fulfillment of all. It is the most hidden of all hidden things, secret of secrets, depth of depths, sealed up with a thousand seals. It is locked away in a cave as obscure as the very depths, a huge boulder set at its mouth, surrounded by a great snake. And yet it is the simplest of all simple things, the most revealed of revelations, known to all who study Torah, pronounced each day in blessings and readings, in prayers and supplications.

This unification, even though it is both ancient and known to all, has never been so clearly and distinctly revealed as it is now, in these days when messiah's footsteps can be heard.

Receive it from me, O holy assembly! When any one of you is aroused to study, to pray, to give alms, to recite a blessing, when putting on your fringed garment or your *tefillin,* or fulfilling any other commandment, intend with all the desire of your heart: "For the sake of uniting the blessed Holy One *and Israel.*"

For those who are used to reciting the formula "For the sake of uniting the blessed Holy One and His *shekhinah*...," the most mysterious unification passed down to us by those holy angels, the teachers of yore, you must now add to it this formula I have mentioned. This refers to the union and attachment of the blessed Holy One and Israel of the World of 'Asiyah, meaning Israel below, each and every Jew, those who work and strive and toil, suffering the yoke of exile. They utter sighs that could break any heart, yet their lives are so weighed down by heavy burdens that they lack the clarity of mind to set forth their prayers as they should. She [*shekhinah*] carries their inner cry upward, blasting through the air, breaking through all the heavens, smashing all the iron fences.

Come and see. Love for every single Jew is the beginning of everything. Anyone who does not have this love—all his good deeds remain within his own narrow space, bearing no fruit either above or below. Those good deeds have no vitality, no power to spread forth or bring about birth. But the one who does have love for every Jew in his heart—the good deeds he does do bear that holy life-force, the dedication and strength, the fiery flame from below that parallels the fire from above. (Of this it said that "even though fire comes down from the heavens, it is better to have it brought from a human source."[17]) All of such a person's good deeds become a spring out of which the Tree of Life is fed, seeds that will sprout forth in the grasses of Eden. Holy trees! Beautiful flowers! Birds whose wings will protect everyone in the world! Mighty high-flying eagles, carrying all of Israel on their wings as they journey from the darkness of Egypt to *shekhinah's* shining light!

Come and see! All the great ones among our nation attained the high rung they did only out of their abundant love for every Jew, even those who had sinned greatly against the blessed Holy One, including those who rebelled against Him. The Faithful Shepherd [Moses] handed himself over to death, saying, "You, if You would, bear their sin! But if not, wipe me out of Your book that You have written." Who were those for whom he was willing to risk death? Those who had sinned greatly, as he says: "Please! This people has committed a grave sin" (Exod 32:31–32)! Of King Messiah it also is written: "He bears the sins of many, defending the transgressors" (Isa 53:12).

All those who have prepared the way for King Messiah, such as the holy ARI [Rabbi Isaac Luria], the holy Rabbi Moshe Hayyim Luzzatto, the holy Ba'al Shem Tov, the holy brothers Reb Elimelech and Reb Zusia, the holy Rabbi Levi Yitshak, the holy Rabbi Nahman of Bratslav, and all who have labored in the field in every generation—all of these have attained what they did only because they preserved the flame of love for every Jew. Not only for every Jew, but for every human being![18] Indeed, for all that God created! This is not because all those faces are the same—surely their love for those who dwell in the holy King's own palace and for all of Israel, children of the King, differs from their love for those who stand outside that holy palace until messiah comes. Of that day scripture says: "Until Shiloh comes and the people assemble to Him" (Gen 49:10). This verse is translated to read: "Until the messiah's kingdom comes and all peoples will obey him." So too does it say: "Then I will change all nations to have clear speech, so that they all may call upon the name of God" (Zeph 3:9).

Yet their love was so strong that it poured forth like a mighty river flowing in every direction. They gave to all people and every nation to drink of their love, even the most distant of nations and creatures of God.

Come and see. "One who separates one of these ten *sefirot* from another is like one who brings about separation within You."[19] Whoever separates any one of the Children of Israel from the others is also like one who causes separation within the ten *sefirot*. There are "six hundred thousand letters in the Torah" and "six hundred thousand souls in Israel."[20] Anyone who says: "This one among the Children of Israel is pleasing to me, but that one is not" is like the "whisperer who separates familiar friends" (Prov 16:28).[21]

If the Children of Israel have sinned, let us bring them close to *shekhinah*. Let us pray and supplicate for them until they repent. Let us awaken the merit of the holy patriarchs, of the faithful shepherd, of all the generations. Let us seek compassion *for* them and *from* them, arousing the love hidden within their hearts. Let us blow on the holy spark within their souls until it bursts forth into a mighty flame. But let us not say to any Israelite, even to a sinner, "You have no place in the God of Israel." Surely we should not say to the many who have strayed from the path: "You have no place in the God of Israel."

[We are taught that] "all Israel have a place in the World to Come."[22] If so, they surely have a place in the God of Israel. Even those of whom that text says: "These have no place in the World to Come" can be purified and uplifted. Thus taught the great and holy priest Rabbi Tsadok[23] about those who "seek out the imprints," revealing the deeply hidden things and knowing that in the concealed heart of every Jew, even those who turn from the ways of faith and do every evil deed in the world, there remains a hidden point that is never separated from God. Because of that hidden point, such a person can return at the end of life, whether in this incarnation or another, to the Source of life. When King Messiah comes, he will reveal all those points of goodness within each Jew, uncovering that which is most hidden within their hearts. Then all the evil within them, even in those called "the sinners within Israel" (even though they will be punished, for how could judgment not be rendered?), will be shown to belong only to their outer selves, but not to that which lies within, and surely not to their innermost holy of holies.

For that reason, one who seeks to pray or do any good deed must join together with all the souls of Israel that have ever existed in the world, those that are present now, and those that are yet to be, linking all those souls to the one God. This is the secret meaning of "[The angel] Michael is the high priest who offers up the souls of Israel on the altar above."[24]

This is the revealed and secret meaning of *shema' yisra'el*.

"Listen"—*behold*.

"Israel"—*all the souls of Israel in every generation, all those that were present in the first man—whether in mind, heart, heel, or any other limb.*

"Y-H-W-H our God"—I and all the souls of Israel! I join myself to them with all the desire of my heart and the power of my love. Together we all take upon ourselves the yoke of heaven's kingdom. We cleave in complete union, with no hint of separation or blemish, to "Y-H-W-H is One!"

The Mystery of Thought

Thought is a person's inward palace; the innermost of thoughts is that person's holy of holies. That innermost point cleaves to the Endless with a love that never ceases. This is a "link that joins one to the blessed Holy One." But even if the person does not have the strength to rise to such a rung, but has only longings, passionate and painful desire—as in "Their heart cried out to God" (Lam 2:18)—that longing itself becomes God's dwelling, and this person too dwells within God. They are "One within one"—the Endless within the person; the person within the Endless.

If you, O child of the palace, do not yet have the strength to stand firmly on the rung of the "link that joins one" to God, be then on the rung of "his heart is troubled within him." Let your eyes fill with tears—like the "lower waters" that cried out, "We too want to be before the King!"[25]

At this time of messiah's approaching footsteps, especially in these final years when the imprint of those steps is revealed in the sands of "nations' desert" (Ezek 20:35),[26] overwhelming darkness surrounds us. Darkness perceives that its final hour has arrived; it rushes to send forth all its hosts and forces, both above and below. Seeing the kingdom of light drawing nearer, darkness trembles in terror and sets out to do battle with the light. It sends forth its shadow to swallow up all of light's forces, to consume all the world's goodness, to wreck, ruin, and demolish all that the "light sown for the righteous" (Ps 97:11) has planted.

Sometimes darkness sees that it cannot defeat a person, one who stands up like a firm pillar and does not allow evil desires or passions of the flesh to rule. Then the darkness appears in the form of a good angel, stealing its way into your heart and distancing you from God by way of sadness, a state of melancholy or small-mindedness that derives from the evil side.

Child of the palace, do not let that thief enter your heart! Keep your heart always both "broken" and "joyous." It was taught in Rabbi Simeon ben Yohai's name: "Have weeping firmly rooted in one side of your heart, while joy is in the other."[27] Sadness and brokenheartedness are not the same. The holy lion Rabbi Shneur Zalman taught that "sadness is having a heart as dull as stone with no life-energy within it, while a certain acidity and a broken heart, on the contrary, show there is enough life in that heart to turn it sour!"

When your heart is broken so that it has the energy to weep and plead before God, the "palace opened only by tears" will be revealed to you. Once the wellsprings of your heart are opened, a melody of attachment to God will burst forth on its own. Then a "palace opened only by melody" will become accessible to you. As your holy melody spreads through the upper worlds, a "palace attained only by joy" will open before you. As that palace opens, all forces of judgment and negativity will pass away, all accusing [or "guilt-producing"] forces will be hidden in the rocks, and the "shells" will be hidden in the cavity of the great deep. Then holy angels will come down among humans to hear words of Torah spoken by the faithful shepherd and all the other sages of that generation. They will rejoice and exult, dancing as at a festival of bride and groom. Forces of love will be revealed throughout the world, great blessings from above. Abundant love, desire, and grace will pour forth from before our Father in Heaven upon the holy people and upon all who live.

Remember, O child of the palace, what the pious of old have taught: "All the gates are sealed except those of tears."[28] "Tears *open* the gates—but joy *smashes* all the gates." You, child of the palace, must not forget even for a moment that "God is your shadow" (Ps 121:5)—the blessed Holy One is your shadow, being and acting toward you as you are toward Him. If you desire God, God will desire you. The whole world knows this, but people do not grasp it in an *inner* way. Even if they know it deeply, they do not *live* in accord with that knowing. Knowledge and life remain separate from one another. Even when their knowledge is enlightening, that light shines around them but not through them. For you, child of the palace, your awareness that "God is your shadow" must be your life, both within and without. It must be your inner light, your inner and even your innermost desire, your soul and the soul within your soul.

When this simple awareness becomes your inner light, an aura from above will descend and surround you. Your life of holiness and good deeds will allow you to absorb that light until it shines from within you. Then another light will descend, surrounding you again, and it too will be absorbed and united with your soul. And so onward, to the highest of rungs!

The most important rule: Let the blessed Holy One in every single moment be your *life*, the very *air* that gives you life. Let every breath you take be in God. There is no quick way to achieve this, but only that of lengthy service and ceaseless prayer, an inward prayer of the very simplest words, yet penetrating down into the very depths.

Pray like this:

My beloved Father, desire of my soul! You have sent me into this world. What have You sent me for? Surely to bear Your message! Teach me, beloved Father, what I am supposed to do this day and every day to fulfill Your will. What should I be saying to people—all of them my brothers and Your children? What should I be doing—right now and at all times—to make my life pure and holy, as You desire?

My Father, my Heart! Grant me all those sublime lights and all that contains them. May I have the brilliance of soul, bodily health, clarity of mind, and clear awareness— all the abilities and powers needed to do that with which You have entrusted me.

And you, holy souls of each generation! You who have fulfilled God's will throughout your lives, in holiness and purity, accompany me on my path! Help me in my actions! Pray with me and be with me in all the good I seek to do.

Light of lights! Soul of all souls! Send me all those holy souls who are close to my own soul-root! Let them hold fast to me, and I to them. Raise us all up and carry us on the wings of endless love.

This is the sort of inward prayer that a child of the palace should offer every day. It may be prayed with these words and phrases or others; the main thing is that it be *constant*.

It is the prayer of the poor and brokenhearted, yet at the same time the burning desire of a child to see his Father's smiling face.

WITH RABBI ISRAEL BA'AL SHEM TOV

(An Imaginary Conversation)

TRANSLATOR'S INTRODUCTION: This little fantasy first appeared in *Sifran shel Yehidim* in 1928. It offers an interesting glimpse into what Zeitlin saw as essential to the Ba'al Shem Tov's teaching as applied to his day. The historical context should be kept in mind. A decade after the great hopes raised by the Balfour Declaration, the Versailles Treaty, and the League of Nations, nothing had improved in the lot of Polish Jewry. Fascism and anti-Semitism were on the rise throughout Eastern and Central Europe. Jewry remained divided and its situation without hope.

What's happening with you, down there in the lower world?

It's bad, very bad, O master.

Don't say that, my son. Evil does not really exist. There are only multiple levels of the good. That which you, down in the lower world, call evil is really only a lower rung of goodness. When the broom hits the child, pain and distress come along with it. But there is a need for that broom. When Pharaoh tormented the Children of Israel, they cried out to God from the midst of their labors. In the order of things, there had to be room for Pharaoh and his decrees. Didn't you learn, my son, on "Pharaoh drew near" (Exod 14:10), that he "drew near the hearts of Israel to their Father in Heaven"?

Is it easy for you, master, to say things like that, because you are now in those hidden places above? But what shall we who live in this world say about sufferings unto death? About the pogroms?

What is that word *pogroms*? What does it mean? I never heard a word like that while I dwelt on earth.

Pogroms, master, refers to those murderous acts that the Haidemaks and Cossacks did in your day, the murders and rapes. The difference is that when such catastrophes happened in your day, there was an expectation that "catastrophes come to an end." But now they are constant. They poison and contaminate every moment of our lives. They don't leave us for an instant. When slaughter ceases in one country, it raises its head, like some deadly grass, in another. In your day those who slaughtered Jews were empty-headed bums. Today, they include professors and students. Today, actual governments are involved in these acts of murder.

How can that be? Governments? What do the upper princes [the angels who rule each nation] have to say about that?

You must know that better than I, master.

I have nothing to do with them now. When I was down there in a body, I was able to move such angels about on each new moon of Nissan [whenever I needed]. But now I am stripped of all that. Your world, all its creatures, and all that takes place in it do not concern me at all.

And Israel? Didn't you once say that you came into the world to teach three things—love of God, love of Torah, and love of Israel? Don't you now feel Israel's great pain?

I can't explain this matter to you as long as you are still in the body. We in the upper world see and feel things in an entirely different way.... I can only tell you one thing. I am with you now as I was with you when I wore the bodily form.

How? Our whole world is worth nothing to you, and yet still you are with us in our suffering?

I do not partake in your bodily nature, but I dwell in the pain of the divine spark that exists within every single one of you.

Even in the sinners?

Even in the sinners, my son. Did I not teach you that the word *sin* [Hebrew *het'* contains a silent aleph] has the cosmic Aleph hidden within it? Within every sin lies the deeply hidden divine spark

that gives it life. "Her feet descend unto death" (Prov 5:5) means that the lower extremities of the *shekhinah* [*malkhut*] reach down into the realm of the demonic forces, giving them life. A divine spark lies buried and hidden within every darkness; that is the *shekhinah*'s exile. From there, from the depths of darkness, she cries out in weeping and supplication: "Get me out of here! Redeem me! Liberate me! Purify me! Cleanse me! Raise me up to my sublime Source!" The *tsaddik* does that uplifting, as in "He reaches into Sheol and raises up" (1 Sam 2:6). But every Jew does the same in every act of studying Torah, in the performance of each *mitsvah*, in inner intention —you know this as well. The sin of an Israelite is not like those of other nations. Back when I was still wearing the bodily garb, I once heard the archangel Michael, the great defender of Israel, offering this in their favor: "Even when a Jew does some forbidden thing, he's doing it to raise the money for his child's school tuition."

But all that, master, might be true when it comes to individuals who stumble into sin. Afterward they come to regret it in the depths of their hearts. This might apply to the *tsaddik* who awakens that "hidden love" within his heart, the divine point that had been asleep, as in "He awoke as God was asleep" (Ps 78:65). But surely it can't apply to whole multitudes who turn away from the path of righteousness.

This time too, my son, you've forgotten what I have said. Remember what I said when the Frankists departed from the House of Israel. These were my words then: "The *shekhinah* mourns, proclaiming that so long as the sickly limb remains attached to the body, so afflicted as it may be, there is still hope. That hope is lost once it is cut off."

I see you, master, still burning with that love of Israel that you had while in the body, living in this world. You don't want to push away any Jew, no matter who. But do you know that today entire vast sections of our people have turned away from the path of Torah? There is no hope for their return, because they think of themselves, and even especially themselves, as true Jews. They do their sinful deeds and consider them good. Have you ever seen a person repent of the good deeds he has done?

The Frankists were not able to remain hanging between apostasy and Judaism. They had to turn one way or the other, either Jew or Gentile. But those who turn away from Torah today are different. They have figured out various ways to deny the obvious consequences of their deeds. They live without awareness, without Torah, without Judaism, and yet at the same time consider themselves true Jews, even "committed" or "ethnic" Jews. How will they repent of these?

Teach me, my son, something of the ways of these various camps. Maybe there is still hope for them. "He thinks of ways that the lost one not be lost from Him" (2 Sam 14:14).

We have, master, four sorts of parties. First are parties who concern themselves only with the Master of the Universe. Second are those concerned with both the Master of the Universe and the Jewish people. Third are those concerned only with a certain sector of Jewry: craftsmen, working-people, and the like.[29]

Then it seems that all of them are striving for the good. Why shouldn't they form a single union, doing what is good in God's sight and building up the House of Israel?

This is the crux of the matter, master. They only *say* that they seek God or are concerned with the welfare of Jews, or with that of one sector or another. In their hearts there is only hatred and spite, whether they stand on the right or on the left. Not only spite and hatred, but disbelief and destructiveness.

If that is the case—disbelief, destructiveness, and baseless hatred, it is indeed hard to heal their pain, especially as long as that demon of baseless hatred is dancing about in their midst. But what do your leaders think? Don't they know that "the Second Temple was destroyed because of the sin of baseless hatred"? And that healing has to happen in precisely that point where the affliction lay?

Our leaders do know that. Sometimes they even like to talk about peace and unity. But even as they are doing so, the great pit of hatred is widening and deepening beneath them.

Why?

Because when our leaders call for peace or unity, they really mean, "Listen only to me and my party! Whoever doesn't do so might just as well not exist."

It really is hard to find healing for a distortion as great as this. You must remember what I told you when I was still in the body. "You have cast truth to the ground" (Dan 8:12). How is it that this precious pearl, truth, the seal of God, rolls about in the dust? Why does no one pick it up? The answer is that no one is willing to bend down. But you can't lift the pearl out of the dust unless you are willing to bend your body first! This means self-negation; "Go and make yourself smaller," as God once said to the moon. It is all about the self, your *self*ish nature. It is taught: "Sell everything you have and buy shoes for your feet." But the phrase "shoes for your feet [*min'alim le-raglav*]" can also be read to mean "a lock on your habits." In order to recognize truth, you have to negate and suppress all sorts of habits. To come to awareness, you have to let go of your private awareness altogether, as a higher divine mind begins to shine upon you....One who seeks to approach truth at least has to put aside all other motives, all pride, all lust for glory. Your leaders, I see, are not ready for all this self-negation. Even when they distance themselves from improper motives, from seeking glory or fulfilling their own desires, they are not ready for total and absolute sacrifice of self.

And the leaders who existed in your day, master?

Even in my day they were not free of conflict. You know, my son, how great a controversy raged around me, and how fierce a conflagration broke out upon my disciples after my death. This fiery conflict raged in Israel until it destroyed communities and towns, until sons rose up against their fathers and fathers against sons. Brothers from the womb became enemies without compassion. Precious young men, the truly pious, were forced to divorce their wives, flee from their homes, and go into exile. Wherever they went, they were followed by persecutions and bans, blows and torments.

But there were also other leaders in my time. There were those who had true fear of God, awesome and holy, before the great truth. Some attained absolute self-sacrifice, including the Rabbi of Polonnoye [R. Jacob Joseph], the admonisher R. Aryeh Leib, the author of *Me'ir Netivim* [R. Meir Margulies], the preacher of Zlochow [R. Yehiel Mikhl], the preacher of Rowno [R. Dov Baer], and others.

But what shall we do now, master? The lamb stands between two wolves. The shepherds are busy arguing with one another, cursing each other. Between one outcry and another, the sheep are attacked. There are some shepherds who take care only of themselves, eating of their own flock, shearing their wool, but fleeing for their lives when a wolf comes down from the plain to attack their sheep. Or even worse, helping the wolves.

I hear the cry of distress, the cry that of the soul in agony. But is there no ray of light breaking over you?

There have been such rays of light coming from the west, from [Western] Europe. We have also received rays of light from the east, from Asia, from the cradle of our youth, the land of our birth, our Holy Land. But now these rays of light have disappeared, and we walk about in even thicker darkness.

You are wrong, my son. Light that appears from above never disappears completely. It appears to do so only to the eyes of the flesh, but it remains forever, hidden in a stronghold above, ready to appear again when the time is right. The sun sets in the west not in order to remain there, but in order to rise again from the east. The light that has appeared to you, whether from east or west, did not lead you astray. It is a radiance of radiance, a faint glow of the great light of redemption.

What does "radiance of radiance" mean?

When the light of redemption is revealed in its full strength, there will be no more place for hiding. Then "all flesh together will see" (Isa 40:5). "The crooked will be turned straight, the hillocks into a valley" (40:4). "Then I will transform all nations toward a clear tongue, all of them calling upon the name of God" (Zeph 3:9). But

that redeeming light has shone upon you in the force of radiance of radiance. It shone into souls and then disappeared, for a shorter or longer time, from your view.

But why did that light of truth remove itself from our sight?

Because when the light came down to you it did not find vessels prepared to receive it. "Why have I come and there is no one there, called and received no answer?" (Isa 50:2).

And when will the souls be ready to serve as vessels for that light which is breaking above them?

Read deeply in the epistle I wrote to my brother Rabbi Gershov of Kitov [Kuty] concerning my ascent of soul in the year 1746. Then you will understand.

I have indeed done so, my teacher and master. But how can your epistle of revelation comfort me, since you said in it that messiah will only come when everyone will be able to perform acts of unification as you did? When will such a wondrous end arrive? When will everyone in the world, or even every Jew, know how to bring about unification like Rabbi Israel Ba'al Shem Tov?

You did indeed write in your epistle that you had been given three holy names and three prescriptions that would be very easy to learn. But what are these? How will these names and prescriptions help us, since you were not given permission to reveal them, not even to a chosen few, not even to your holy brother-in-law from Kitov?

It is indeed told of one saint (the rabbi of Neshchiz) that he would study your epistle regularly, and within that document itself, he claimed, one could find hints to those hidden things you were allowed to reveal to no one. But what good is even that opinion to us, since we do not know where or how these things are hidden?

From your epistle we know only one thing: that within each letter [of the Hebrew alphabet] there are worlds, souls, and divinity. These are joined together with one another; only afterward do the letters join together to form a word. Thus a true unification takes place within God. When this happens, all the worlds are filled with endless happiness and joy.

You even offered a metaphor for understanding this: "When you understand the joy of bride and groom on this small worldly scale, you will see how much more it is the case [when unification takes place] above."

We know this too from your epistle, that we need to bind ourselves to the letters and become one with them. That is, binding ourselves to the *lights* within the letters, whenever we study or pray. As we think holy thoughts or do good deeds, our soul rises up and is included within those "worlds, soul, and divinity" and partakes of their joy. But who are we that we should perform such acts of unification and partake of such sublime and holy joy? What do we know of all these things now? Lots of us still pray, study, and perform *mitsvot* by dint of "the learned commandments of men" (Isa 29:13) [that is, by rote]. An ever larger part of us has abandoned regular service of God because they became repelled by it. How can such as we rise up, reaching toward such "unifications"? Isn't this just a mocking tease?

You are wrong, my son, about two things. First, you do not yet understand the matter of unifications in a fully clear way. Second, you have forgotten the scripture that teaches: "Do not say that former days are better than these" (Eccles 7:10).

You are wrong about the unifications in thinking, as many do, that they depend on [esoteric] concentrations or permutations of lights, pointed to by the letters. That is really not the case. Of course one has to have such concentration and to effect permutations when bringing about such unity. But these have to be preceded by great [compassion] and bravery, by the bright holiness of the *human* soul of that one who undertakes all this. Don't you know, my son, that when they opened amulets I made for people, all they found in them were the words "Israel, Master of the Good Name"?...In that case know, my son, that new great lights will not come down because of people who study Kabbalah and imitate the deeds of the great Kabbalists. They will come because of those who light up their souls by the noble flow of divinity, who gird themselves with strength from above. These will become one in holiness and purity, bringing to everyone in the world the light of

wisdom, understanding, and awareness. These will come together with love, awe, and all the divine qualities, which will be awakened above as they are aroused below. As the forces of holiness become arrayed in a mutual way below, the same forces become arrayed above. Then new lights are born, such as "no eye has seen," and a tremendous bounty of life and compassion will pour forth from above.

But how can such a great wonder come to pass? It's easy to say: "By the binding together of souls." But particularly for those high souls, such binding is very difficult. They are separated by both heart and mind. This is especially true in our generation; the great souls are most deeply divided. "The holier one is, the more sharp his sword."[30] The vessels are indeed broken.

In this too you are wrong, my son. You think that in my day it was easy to bring people together? It was just as hard then as it is now. I too had a hard time taking those first steps. For a long time I searched for people like myself and did not find them. Amid a vast Jewish area, I walked as though in a desert. For many years I wandered from one mountain to another, from valley to valley, field to field, forest to forest. Even after I was "revealed," I had a hard time enlightening souls, purifying them, raising up and revealing all the holy sparks that lay within them. It was like splitting the Red Sea! Especially difficult was joining the souls of those who thought of themselves as righteous. I once read the Mishnah's statement, "Where is the place of sacrificial slaughter? The holy of holies…" to mean "Where does the biggest slaughter of the evil urge have to take place? Among those who consider themselves the holy of holies."

But "I was not turned back" (Isa 50:5)—I walked my path of service without turning away to right or left, not even a hairsbreadth. With unceasing effort, I sought out those souls that were near to me. I purified and polished them, bound them together into a single community, and brought forth lights for them and through them.

And you folks, what are you doing? It's pretty easy for you to wander off course. You are afraid of persecution, of wickedness, and of mockery. You are afraid that you'll be left alone, that people

will make fun of you. You believe too much in what "the world" says and put too little faith in what your own soul reveals to you in times of meditation. You worry too much about public opinion, even in the very hour when in your hearts you dismiss the whole world as being filled with stuff and nonsense. It is not that you of the present generation lack understanding or insight. Even depth is not missing from within you. What is it that you most lack? *Inner strength and inner freedom!* You don't have the toughness and courage to leave behind the chaotic world in which you find yourselves to go forward and follow the divine voice that calls to you from within your souls.

You are currently filled with despair. Your current lot really is a bitter one by human standards. You are being torn to pieces and smashed to bits; salvation seems far from you. But didn't all these things happen to us in former generations? All those woes, persecutions, and oppressions? But we always remembered, "When I dwell in darkness, God is my light" (Mic 7:8) as well as "Joy in Y-H-W-H is your strength" (Neh 8:10). Our joy would have been sevenfold as great had we merited to have seen what you have in your day.

What have we merited to see?

Just this would suffice: that you have seen the sun rise over the hills of Judea. Anyone in our day who wanted to journey to the Land of Israel had to pass through all the seven chambers of hell, and even then rarely reached the goal. It happened to me—how much I wanted to reach the Holy Land! I risked my life to do it, but in the end I had to turn around at Istanbul. You surely know about all the adventures of my great-grandson Nahman in the course of traveling to the Holy Land. And now you have a hundred and fifty thousand Jews living there. A hundred and fifty thousand Jews living in the Holy Land! A hundred and fifty thousand worlds.... Great lights are coming down into the world. Despite all the slaughters, all the destructions, they are coming!

In my day the workingman was like a beast of burden. Now *the humanity within him is recognized*. He fights for his rights and his honor. This is a long and hard struggle. There is still a long way to go until justice and honor, the recognition of each person's value, is achieved. But that light will surely come.

For Israel the way is two thousandfold more difficult, since they are between the anvil and the hammer. Both the ruling classes and the liberated strike at them, both servants and masters, capitalists and workers. But that is how new things are born. "The womb is not opened without blood."

The world is sinking today in defilement and cynicism. That is the greatest trial of your times. But "this too shall pass." *The world will finally look at its own image, shocked and trembling at its own darkness. Then it will stretch forth its hands in prayer and supplication, with a purified and refined heart, filled with faith.*

Those among you of high souls and strong hearts must gather together to bring that day more quickly. Join yourselves wholly to the Root of roots.

TWO LETTERS: ON ESTABLISHING YAVNEH IN JERUSALEM

I

To his student Yitzhak Landsberg.[31] Written in 1924.

To my dear student Yitzhak Landberg!

After you parted from me for the last time in Jerusalem, I hardly slept all night. I couldn't stop thinking about you and your fate. I had always known that you were created for greatness. But the path you now walk—and it is indeed a *holy* path—is filled with stumbling blocks that endanger both body and soul.

If only I, sitting now in Warsaw, could occasionally learn with you the Kuzari or the Tanya! Or even simply the Book of Isaiah (not the way they study it now in the Land of Israel, using biblical criticism, etc., a useless and distorting approach, but simply in the way our ancestors studied it)! Every now and then I would reveal to you some of the divine wisdom in the holy Zohar.

But what can I do for you now? I am here "amid the exile" and you dwell in the holy city of Jerusalem, thinking that just by hewing stones and work of that sort you are accomplishing all that needs to be done now. Hewing stones and building houses in the Land of Israel is indeed an awesome and wondrous thing. But there is also a need to hew stones for an entirely different sort of building, that of the upper Temple within the soul. It needs to be refined and cultivated. The ruined house of Judaism needs to be rebuilt by a joining together of companions who understand the great spiritual danger that currently confronts us and how to be saved from it. The ways are long, so long—as long as the exile!

I rely upon your intuition, trusting that you will take in my words deeply and comprehend my thoughts. I am sending to our friends Heisherik and Steinsaltz, from Warsaw, a few copies of my latest publications (in Yiddish). Take three of those from them and read them carefully. If you find that they speak to your soul as well, try to gather a few people together under the banner of "Yavneh." Let those friends engage in some occasional conversation with you about these matters.

I now have hope that a group like this will get together in the Land of Israel and will turn toward building an Israelite religious community in the spirit of the prophets and the saintly ones. The matter is well known.

Write me a few words, in any language you choose. The above-mentioned companions will give you my writings.

With true kisses,
Hillel Zeitlin

II

24 Sivan, Tuesday of the Torah reading "Send men...," 1925

Dear Aminah,[32]

You will surely recall the day we spent together in Jerusalem and the many things we discussed with one another. These included the isolation of the truly religious laborer in the Land of Israel, the difficulty of this holy matter [of uniting religion and socialism], with much opposition from both right and left.

69

You will do me a great favor if you keep me informed of the current situation in the Land of Israel, especially regarding your conflicts with both the right and the left.

Now I want something of you. I think that a small Yavneh group should be established in Jerusalem. This will be an association of working people who agree to live in accord with the fourteen principles I set out in my Yiddish pamphlet "The Ark." A group like this exists here in Warsaw, but I think that Jerusalem (or perhaps the Land of Israel altogether) is its true place. Members of "Yavneh" may belong to any political party; they only have to recognize the holiness of Israel and the exalted level of true Israelite religious life. They would come together to realize the fourteen points that I laid out in "The Ark." For people like you, *who live by the work of your hands and are filled with religious feeling and holy fire*, it will be easy to live by these rules. You will join together to defend these principles and to disseminate them among *all the laborers and people who toil on the Holy Land.*

I am sending you a bundle of thirteen copies (symbolically numbering "one") of "The Ark," ten copies of the seventh issue of "My Word" (it includes a letter to the members of "Yavneh," emphasizing its spiritual side), and various other recent publications of mine. Among these are "Hasidism" (in Yiddish), "Hillel Zeitlin's Pages" (I have no copy of the first issue), and "The Burning Bush." What do I ask of you? Please distribute "The Ark" and "My Word" among your friends and try to found a "Yavneh" group...that would meet weekly (no less) for shared study and discussion of true religion (here we study primarily the "Tanya" by the Rabbi of Liadi, the Kuzari, the works of the MaHaRaL of Prague, and similar materials) and life in the spirit of "Yavneh."

I have already written about this to two young people from Warsaw. They are Mr. H (inquire about him from M. of Kerem in Jerusalem) and Mr. S. (ask about him at the Jerusalem quarry).[33] To them too I have sent copies of "The Ark" and "My Word" for distribution. I also wrote them concerning the founding of a "Yavneh" group in Jerusalem. I ask you to meet with them and together to carry forth this great and holy matter. I hope for great things in the future, if only this society will be established in Jerusalem and elsewhere in the Holy Land.

I ask you to inform me soon in connection with that which I have asked of you. Reach me at the address of "Moment"—Nawelki 38, to my attention.

With great love and affection,
Hillel Zeitlin

70

2. The Fundaments of Hasidism

Translator's Introduction

This essay, entitled "Book One," is all that appeared of a planned longer work called *Ha-Hasidut le-Shittoteha u-Zerameha* (*Hasidism: Its Systems and Streams*). It was published in Warsaw in 1910 and later reprinted under the title *Yesodot ha-Hasidut* in the posthumous volume of Zeitlin's collected works called *Be-Fardes ha-Hasidut veha-Kabbalah* (Tel Aviv: Yavneh, 1960).

The work is preceded by a short note in which Zeitlin tells the reader that the materials used for this study all belong to Hasidism's earliest stratum, the teachings of the Ba'al Shem Tov (1700–1760) and his immediate disciples. Later works, those of the third generation of Hasidism, are only quoted sparsely, when required. The unique schools of Bratslav and HaBaD are not treated here at all, since they are to be the subjects of special chapters to come.[34]

This essay, then, is Zeitlin's attempt to re-create the teachings of the Ba'al Shem Tov and his successor Dov Baer of Miedzyrzec (1704?–72), the founding figures of the Hasidic movement. He does so in a powerful and highly evocative way, weaving together selected quotations from early Hasidic writings and brief bridges of interpretation and comment.

Zeitlin plunges directly into the mystical heart of Hasidism, beginning with "Being and Nothingness." It is clear that he is reading the Hasidic sources as a philosopher. Unlike his younger contemporary Martin Buber (1878–1965), who had begun publishing a few years earlier, Zeitlin has no interest in telling Hasidic tales or in highlighting personalities. His Hasidic literature is not the late chapbooks of stories so uplifted by Buber, but rather those works published early and most treasured by the *hasidim* themselves, the teachings and Torah commentaries, focused on the mystical path of devotion, *'avodat ha-shem*.

His opening chapters on "Being and Nothingness" and "*Tsimtsum*" are based on Hasidic usages of key Kabbalistic terms and symbols. He will go back to present these systematically in the last section, but first he wants to show them in the powerful way they are used in the Hasidic writings. His choices of text are, of course, selective; he is trying to present Hasidism in its most radical and uncompromising mystical form; he thus leaves aside many sources that are more hesitant or apologetic in discussing these same ideas.

As Zeitlin makes clear in his preface, the purpose of this essay is both historical and programmatic. He wants the reader to understand the Ba'al Shem Tov's worldview in the most unencumbered way possible, but he is also looking toward the emerging "new Hasidism" that has begun to appear in his day, offering this rich reading of the sources as a critique of the romantic and sometimes trivializing re-creations of literature that were gaining hold on many readers' imaginations. Hasidism teaches firmly held religious truths, and Zeitlin wants to make sure these will stand at the center of this emerging new movement.

At the same time, it is clear that Zeitlin comes to Hasidism as one who has tasted of the fruits of Western philosophy. The influence of Nietzsche is particularly strong in this essay. Zeitlin reads Hasidism as one who has absorbed much of both *The Will to Power* and *Beyond Good and Evil*. His sources are reliably quoted, but the selections and juxtapositions are very much his own.

* * *

In Place of a Preface

Many in our midst have written, and are still writing, about Hasidism—its nature, its history, the life of the *hasidim*, its stories, various visions and thoughts, the *soul* of Hasidism. But no one writes about Hasidism *itself*. I mean that no one has paid attention to Hasidism as an entire system, including its principles, its various branches, its ways of seeing and contemplation, and the diverse opinions within it. These include the distinctive approach of each *tsaddik* to the ways of serving God. They also comprise its first shining forth, its bright sun, the setting of that sun, and its decline....

This too: no one has yet offered us a *critique* of Hasidism. Some writers curse and vilify Hasidism. Others raise it higher than the stars. But denigration and praise do not yet constitute *criticism*....

The first one to try to present Hasidism as a complete system was Eliezer Zvi Zweifel.[35] Those who have come after him do not even reach up to his ankles. Zweifel had a fiery spirit and poetic soul; he combined the enthusiasm of a *hasid* and the suspiciousness of a scientist. Yet for all his articulate explanations and unique style, despite his thorough knowledge and sharp critique, he did not give us what he sought. His book *Shalom 'al Yisra'el*, with all its great qualities, is essentially an apology for Hasidism. When you are trying to seek out the good, it becomes difficult to remain critical….

Beyond that, Zweifel was concerned chiefly with the religious and poetic aspects of Hasidism. He did not go deeply into its metaphysics. He hardly touched at all upon the literature of Bratslav and ḤaBaD. And what *is* Hasidism without Bratslav's poetry and the philosophy of ḤaBaD…?

The presentation and order of Zweifel's work confuse the reader. All the various systems and opinions of Hasidism are jumbled together. The reader gets bits and crumbs from here and there, arguments back and forth, long discussions, irrelevant tales and parables. In the end there is no complete picture.

Decades have passed since the publication of Zweifel's works. Official Hasidism, then already in decline, has now reached its lowest rung. But just as its sun began to set, there rose that of an *artistic* Hasidism (the visions of Peretz, Berdyczewsky, Yehudah Steinberg, Sholem Asch, myself, and many others). This "new Hasidism" is still in need of comment, explanation, and *sharp critique*….

We need a new book that will cover all of Hasidism from beginning to end, reveal all its lights and shadows, criticize its principles and elements, and look deeply into it. What does Hasidism offer to *all* who seek God?

This book that I place before you, reader, is an attempt to fill that need.

Being and Nothingness

"The blessed Creator's life-energy is everywhere. Each thing that exists surely has some taste, smell, appearance, attractiveness, or some other qualities. But when we strip away the physical aspect of that thing and consider it only spiritually—considering, for example, the taste or smell without the physical object itself—we will understand that we are dealing with something that cannot be held in our hands or seen with the eyes of flesh. It is in fact grasped only by our life-force, our human soul. It therefore must indeed be something spiritual, the life-force of our blessed Creator, dwelling within that corporeal thing like the soul within the body."[36]

The meaning: Consider a fruit. Take delight and rejoice in it. What you have before you is a real physical object. But when you think about that fruit, raising it up in your memory, imagining it—that is a spiritual process. Concrete reality has been set aside; only the image remains. Of course that image too can be seen as a product of the senses. But now you analyze that image, keeping in mind its physical form, its species, appearance, size, quality, smell, and taste. When you consider any one of these specifics and go deeply into it, grasping at its very essence, there will be nothing concrete left before you, but only abstraction itself. This is something felt and fully grasped only by the soul, for this is the Nothing within each thing, the divine spark within it.

The Nothing is the spiritual essence of that which is conceived and the spiritual essence of the soul that conceives it.

"There are several rungs within Mind, namely consciousness, intellect, and speech, all of which receive from one another. Speech exists within time. So too does thought, for today you may have one thought and tomorrow another. But there is a quality that connects consciousness to mind, and that quality cannot be grasped.[37] It is the Nothing, the *hyle*, like the way an egg becomes a chicken. There is a moment when it is neither egg nor chick. No one can grab hold of that moment, for it is Nothing. So too when consciousness becomes intellect or when thought is formed into word, you can't grasp that which joins them."[38]

The Nothing is present in each person at that point where the rational intellect, that which is linked to the senses, ends, and higher mind, the divine within, begins. Thus it varies from person to person and from thought to thought.

"*Hokhmah* [Wisdom] is called Being, but the life-force within *hokhmah*, that which illumines it, is called Nothing (as scripture teaches, 'Wisdom derives from Nothing'—Job 28:12).[39] 'Nothing' is that which remains beyond the intellect and is not grasped. It sustains and enlightens the soul. All this is in accord with the person's intellect, whether greater or lesser. That which you grasp is considered 'being' to you, while that which remains beyond your intellect is called Infinity, that which gives life to the mind."[40]

Such is the measure of the Nothing in the soul of the one who grasps it and such is its measure within everything that is grasped. The Nothing is the innermost aspect of creation, the flowing Spring, that which exists beyond the border of what can be grasped by the senses or by ordinary mind. Intellect has a limit. The inward glance—or, more properly, the brilliant flash, the innermost exultation of the spirit, mysterious and hidden—is infinite.

The Nothing is the moment of wonder in creation, a moment that you cannot call by any name. Hence you call it Nothing. This wondrous moment, precisely because it is so wondrous, cannot be defined, regulated, or placed within bounds of space or time. Thus it constantly unifies opposites. Separations and oppositions have their place within Being, while the Nothing is always the One of equanimity.

"*Hokhmah* links things, making peace even between opposites like the elements. Were *hokhmah* not between them, fire and water could not dwell together. Yet we know that they exist in composite form. That is only because *hokhmah* links them, each of them perceiving the Nothing within it…."[41]

"Each thing in the world, when you take it to its root, can be transformed from what it previously was. Take, for example, the kernel of wheat. When you want to change it, bringing forth from it many more kernels, you need to take it to its root, which lies in the generative power in the soil. Therefore, it can grow in the ground, but nowhere else. But there too it will not grow unless rain falls and causes its original form to be disfigured [rotted] and lost. It is reduced to Nothing, to the *hyle*, which is the category of *hokhmah*. Thus scripture says: 'You made them all in wisdom' (Ps 104:24)."[42]

"Everything that exists passes from one nature into another. The linking of these natures is called Wonder. In the language of the Kabbalists it was known as *keter*, the power that links opposites and joins them in a wondrous unity."[43]

"Hylic matter is neither potential nor actual, but lies between the two. It is the starting point of all existent beings. Everything, from *keter 'elyon* downward, exists only because of it. Hyle does not pass away or go in and out of existence, since it is the beginning of existence itself."[44]

Because the Nothing is the essence of Creation and its innermost soul, it—the Nothing—is in fact the real Being, true existence, essential reality. That which we call Being—revealed existence, the sensory, visible to the eyes of flesh and grasped by the rational mind—is in fact naught but the blindness of the senses, illusory existence. It is a cosmic error that we must recognize and negate in order to be free of it.

All that we call existence, with all its charming and entrapping attractions: the blue heavens over our heads, the earth beneath our feet, endless stars, light and radiance, joy and pleasure, beautiful textures, plays of color, sorrow and tears, the roar of the sea and the whisper of springs, all that we pursue and seek out until flesh and spirit are wearied, all that we delight in attaining and all that we moan for when we lack—all of it is naught but illusion.

The more you reach the Nothing that lies within all being, the divine inwardness, the closer you are to truth, to the Godly, to the essence of creation. You reveal the mask and see before you the King in His glory, the endless light.

"There was a certain king who created an optical illusion consisting of walls, towers, and gates. He commanded that those who came in to him would have to pass through these gates and towers. Then he had the royal treasures scattered about at each gate. Some only came up to the first gate, gathered up some coins, and went back. Others—and so on. Along came the king's only son; he struggled hard to get to his father the king. Then he saw that there was no real separation between him and his father, that it was all illusion. The blessed Holy One hides behind various garments and partitions. Yet it is known that God fills all the world, that every movement and thought come from His blessed self. So all the angels and all the palaces are formed of God's own self, like the locust who spins his cocoon out of himself. In fact there is no partition that separates man from God."[45]

"God emanated the worlds and created Being out of Nothingness. The main purpose was so that the *tsaddik* could make Nothingness out of Being."[46]

"If you want to prepare to have God dwell upon you, the main thing is to understand deeply that you contain nothing but life-giving divinity. Without this you are truly nothing. That is the proper preparation for the indwelling of divinity. This 'dwelling' is as in 'Like an eagle rouses his nest, hovering over his chicks'—touching and not touching. If you grasp this (constantly and with all its power) you will be negated from 'reality.'"[47]

"Everything you see with your eyes, heaven and earth and all within them, are the outer garments of the King, the blessed Holy One. Through them you will come to take constant note of their inner selves, the life-force within them."[48]

Tsimtsum

The world was created *ex nihilo*, being out of nothingness. But just how did the Nothing become being? There is no place for this question when we understand the "Nothing" as the essence of being, when we see it as *keter 'eylon* [supreme crown, the highest of the divine emanations], the force of "Wonder" within all of Creation.

But there is still room for *this* question: Since all that exists is only illusion, being at its core the divine Nothing, how does Being come to be a separate entity? Why do we see the world as we ordinarily do, rather than always perceiving the divine power that courses through it?

In other words, the world is nothing but an optical illusion. But how did that illusion come about? The king's son breaks down all the partitions and comes to the king. But how did the partitions get there in the first place?

The Kabbalists' answer to this is *tsimtsum*. What do they mean by it?

In the school of Rabbi Isaac Luria we learned: "When it arose in the Emanator's will to create the worlds, there was no empty place in which they might stand. The Emanator's light flowed without limit. So He withdrew His own light, like that insect who spins his cocoon out of his own self.[49] He lifts the lights out of that space at the center and removes them to the sides. In this way a void is created in which the worlds can stand."

But this is still not enough. God is—all; "there is no place devoid of Him." Then it is still hard to understand how the lights were removed to the sides. How did that place become empty?

Furthermore, even if we accept that there came to be an "empty space," by what power did it exist? In the end it too relied on the power of God (since "there is no place devoid of Him!"). But in that case, everything is back where we started, and the question still stands: How did existence come to be imagined? How is it that we can think the world to be separate from God? How did that cosmic error come to be?

Hasidism thus explains *tsimtsum* in a different way. *Tsimtsum* is only from our point of view, that of the receivers, the created. *Tsimtsum* exists only in thought. The supreme Emanator sought to bring about diverse and separate entities, displaying His light before all creatures. Everything was thus created in a limited way, in accord with each recipient's power. Just like a father, when explaining some deep concept to his young child, reduces his own profound mind to the limits of that of the child, so does Mind—which is One[50]— descend from its high rung to a lower one.

Another explanation, by way of "king and servants":

"The Zohar says that when the King is in His castle, He is called the great King. But when He goes down among His servants, He is the little King. This was what they meant: The letters of Thought [the unspoken language of the mind] are large, since they transcend the letters of Speech. The King on His own has no need to speak. But for the sake of those who receive from Him, He has to reduce Himself from Thought to Sound and from Sound to Speech. Even though all is a simple unity and all is the King Himself, the vessels [i.e. the recipients of His light] are divided. 'When He is in His castle'—in Thought—[He is the great King]. 'But when He goes down'—into speech, so that His servants can grasp Him—He is called the little King."[51]

The act of cosmic illusion takes place in this way: the young child, as the great thought of the father flows into him, grasps the thought in his own small-minded way. When creatures see the world and its fullness, they grasp only its external nature, the outer garb of things, imagining that is all there is.

But all of these are only examples to offer the ear what it is capable of hearing, making analogy between the spiritual quality of humans and that of the cosmos. Thus we try to understand divine *tsimtsum* based on the reduction of the mind and its going down from expanded to ordinary consciousness, from thought to verbalization to speech. But we still do not know how the One became many. How did such varied and differentiated things come to be, each having its own existence and unique nature?

Tsimtsum is nothing other than the imaging forth of being, the act by which it became possible for being itself to appear as a distinct entity, separate from God. But that still does not give us the key to understand multiplicity, distinction, and the unique "personality" of each thing. We see not only a world, but also endless particular entities, each one (from the archangel Michael down to the smallest urchin in the sea) appearing as its very own world, a living reality all enclosed in its own microcosm. The question remains: How did the "All" split apart into all these tiny pieces?

The Hasidic answer to this is "the breaking of the vessels." This doctrine, taken from Kabbalah, has a distinct meaning in Hasidism. The best of the Kabbalists explained the breaking this way: the vessels were not able to withstand the intensity of the light that flowed ceaselessly into them, and they were broken. This is like a person unable to withstand a sudden burst of joy that overwhelms him. But the *hasidim* explain the breaking of the vessels in a more inward and deeper way. The essence of their idea will best be understood by comparison with more recent modes of thought.

What is the innermost, most natural, and most instinctive desire of each thing that is? The desire to exist. But what is the nature of that desire for existence? "Each thing tries as much as it can to continue forever in its own existence…since by that force of being it will continue to exist, so long as it is not destroyed by some external force,"[52] says Spinoza. The desire for existence is thus an inherent power, the force of eternity. Because the thing exists, because it is filled with the feeling of its own reality, it fears being lost.

Schopenhauer added that the desire to live is the absolute inner essence of all existence, realized in each in an individualized way. This cosmic desire, which creates the illusion of being as a whole, also creates the illusion of particular existence. The one who exists also thinks he can attain some understanding—and comes up with crumbs. The desire for life is no longer an inherent force, one that makes for eternity, but rather an active force, a power that spreads forth, flows, bears fruit, and fructifies.

Nietzsche came along and taught that the innermost nature of each thing is not the desire to live, but to rule. What is this "will to power"? It should not be understood in a popular and vulgar sense. Nietzsche's will to power is really the desire to reveal the "I," to manifest one's full inner powers, to have them rule and master the powers of others.

"The tree by my window—and this is its very nature—reveals its 'I,'" says Oscar Wilde.[53]

The desire to rule, that is the desire for self-manifestation, the feeling of being, is the heritage of everything that exists. This is the secret of personhood, of individuality.

Here we come to the true meaning of *malkhut* ["kingship" of God; the tenth *sefirah*], according to the *hasidim*. *Malkhut* is the manifestation of that which is, the spreading forth [of the self], the feeling of power, utterance, imperative, spiritual rule.

Now we come to the Hasidic understanding of the "breaking of the vessels." These vessels are what the modern philosophers and poets see as the beauty of creation, the individual identity of each creature. To the *hasidim* this is cosmic sin, the fall, the descent, the brokenness. *Malkhut* belongs only to the One who truly exists, the Creator. But since the creatures also rose up to seek rule, it was smashed into the tiniest fragments, each of them saying, "I will rule!"

"The brokenness comes about because each one says: 'I will rule.' The term *malkhut* (kingship) applies to each thing insofar as it is a thing in itself, with no need for anyone or anything else. But in truth this term properly applies only to God, because all others are needy, requiring nourishment from their divine Source. Each quality [or 'being'] has within it, from the moment it flows forth from that source, the inherent claim of 'I will rule,' which it had as part of its original Source. There in the Root the claim was appropriate; all of them were raised up there within that Root. In this way they came to have that natural sense about themselves even when it was no longer accurate, after they had been cut off from the Root and had their own force of life."[54]

The Power of the Maker within the Made

The *hasidim* do not understand *tsimtsum* in the ordinary way. Divinity did not really remove itself; it fills being with its light in accord with the abilities and mental capacity of each creature. Rather than a limiting of Divinity, what takes place is a special revelation of the Divine.

But while the *hasidim* take *tsimtsum* out of its original sense, they do interpret "the whole earth is filled with His glory" (Isa 6:3) quite literally. The Gaon of Vilna[55] followed others before him in understanding "His glory" as referring to providence. The *hasidim* said no, it is His glory *itself* that is truly present. Divinity is everywhere; it fills everything. Everything you see and hear, touch and feel, think and contemplate—all of it is God.

One of these depends upon the other. Because they do not take *tsimtsum* literally, they become literalists when it comes to "He fills all the worlds." Since the removal of divine light takes place only insofar as our eyes can see, but is not the absolute truth, divinity continues to dwell even in the very lowest of rungs, just as it does in the highest. From its point of view all is equal: heaven and earth, creation of the world, the time before and after creation, "I Y-H-W-H have not changed." "You are He before the world was created; You are He since the world was created."

"The blessed Creator's glory fills all the worlds. No place is devoid of Him. When you look at the world, you are looking at the Creator, bless His name. When you are talking to a person, you are addressing the soul within him."[56]

"This is a high rung: When a person considers himself to be near to God, God is surrounding him from all sides. He (the person) is at the center of the heavens and God is 'the place of the world.' God was there before the world was created and the world stands in the midst of God."[57]

"Whatever a person sees, he sees it only by power of the life-energy flowing forth from the blessed Creator. If you see people, for example, you notice their form, hear their voices and speech, learn from their wisdom—all this is the life-force flowing through them. This is true of everything you see or hear, for each thing has the structure and purpose befitting it, a particular appearance or smell.

81

All of this is the life-energy of the Creator within each thing, since all is from Him, just dressed up in diverse garments."[58]

The *shekhinah* is called "the total picture," since all depictions appear within the *shekhinah* like a polished mirror, as it were, reflecting back the form of that person who stands before it."[59]

God is called *El 'Olam*, "God of world," to teach you that "God" is world and world is "God."[60]

"'Forever, O Lord, Your word stands in the heavens' (Ps 119:89)—Your word that You spoke in saying 'Let there be a firmament' (Gen 1:7)—those very words and letters stand firmly within the skies forever. The words are 'garbed' within all the worlds, giving them life. Were those words to disappear even for an instant, returning to their Source, all of the heavens would be naught, as though they had never come to be. The same is true of all that is created in all worlds above and below, including inanimate objects in this very physical world. If the letters of the ten utterances through which the world was created in those six days were to disappear, they would return to absolute nonexistence."[61]

"Every creature and existing thing is considered truly nonexistent with regard to the power of the Maker and the spirit of His mouth within the made. It is this that constantly brings it into being and leads it forth from nonexistence. The fact that each creature and object appears to us as extant and real is because we, looking with eyes of flesh, cannot see the power of God and the spirit of His mouth within the creature. Were the eye permitted to see and grasp the life-energy and spirituality flowing through each creature, proceeding from God's mouth and its spirit, the physical, corporeal dimension of things would not appear before our eyes at all."[62]

The angels ask: "Where is the place of His glory?"[63] All the worlds are called "place," since each receives its revelation from the one above it and is nullified before it. All are called "place" [because each serves as a container or embodiment of that which comes from above]. But when the angels attain that rung where they realize that all is One and there is no category of "place" at all (for "I Y-H-W-H have not changed" [Mal 3:6], and before Him, blessed be He, all is equal, as He equalizes great and small), they *then* ask "Where is the 'place' of His glory?" for they understand that there is no category of "place" at all.[64]

Letters

Divinity has *hidden* itself in the world. But since the power of the Maker resides within the made, hints and signs are to be found within existing things and the revealed world that point to a more inward, elevated, holy, and pure reality.

The God who hides in the bastion of His strength sends His word to every person, calling them aloud, arousing their ears, speaking to their hearts, warning, reproving, teaching.

God from afar whispers to the person: "Seek Me, for I am close, within your own mouth and heart...."[65]

"'Each day a voice goes forth from Mount Horeb, calling out: Woe to people for disgracing Torah!'[66] Neither speech nor words exist above, in the Realm of Thought. The 'calls' that issue from the cosmic Ruler come by way of hints. We need to apprehend the message through our thoughts, through the glimmers of repentance that come every day."[67]

"When some fear is aroused in the world, know that you are being called to cleave to the Root of fear. When joy is aroused in the world, attach yourself to the joy of God's service."[68]

"'He looks through the windows; he peers from behind the lattice-work' (Cant 2:9). When an evil person sets out to commit a transgression in a closed room, he feels fear, as though some person were watching him. This is the sublime Fear that reduces itself to be within his heart at the moment, bringing him to fear the blessed Creator."[69]

"The person is clothed in physical or material garb. How can such a one be aroused to love the blessed Creator in a pure way, or to fear Him, or to any other proper quality? God's own attributes, as it were, reduced themselves into physical forms, descending rung after rung, spreading forth by means of cause and effect, until they reached into very lowly matters."[70]

Further, "Everything in the world, including all the qualities that exist within each physical or created thing, is but a metaphor through which to perceive the divinity that lies within them."[71]

Everything contains a pointer toward the most high God; it is there in every movement, feeling, desire, echo, in all that you feel, see, and hear. When you walk outside and hear people talking, go deeply into the meaning of their words. Join them together in a different accounting, purify them of their mundane afflictions, remove their coarse outer garments, raise them up to their essential cosmic spirituality—and you will see God within them.

"The blessed God's glory screams forth from all things—even from stories told by the Gentiles!"[72]

"The *Lieder* that the Gentiles sing—all of them are expressions of Love and Fear that have spread forth from above."[73]

"When I attach my thought to the blessed Creator, I allow my mouth to speak whatever it wants, because I bind those words to the Creator. Everything has its root above in the *sefirot*."[74]

Sometimes you just gaze at nature and its order and you are looking at its exalted Creator.

"'Look at the heavens and count the stars' (Gen 15:5)—You can best see the exaltedness of God by looking at the heavens and seeing the stars in their courses and their glowing light. From this you come to understand how exalted God is."[75]

"If indeed the suspension of nature [that is, the supernatural miracle] demonstrates Divinity to the eyes of all, showing how God listens to the voice of one who bears His spirit, it is in fact the very conduct of nature itself that truly attests to God's wonders! What power but God's could there be that never ceases behaving in such an ordered way, stretching from the six days of creation down to the end of the world!"[76]

So too when you see bad and lowly qualities, contemptible desires; contemplate their inner nature, the essential pleasure and power within them. Then you will see that they are naught but God in an alienated state, the exiled *shekhinah*.

"'A man who takes his sister...that is *hesed*' (Lev 20:17.)[77] The love that is cloaked in the forbidden sexual liaisons is the fallen fruit of sublime love, so that through it one might come to the love of God."[78]

"'God grabbed hold of Jeroboam by his garment and said: "Repent!"' The blessed Holy One, because He seeks love and not the death of the wicked, lessens Himself to reach each person where he is, on his own rung. This is called 'grabbing him by his garment'—whatever [moral] 'garb' he is wearing in that moment. That is

'Repent!' By means of whatever bad quality that is aroused in you this day, it is 'time to do for Y-H-W-H' and to return to Him.”⁷⁹

"Even in the lowest realm of hell it is possible to be close to God.”⁸⁰ There is a clothing of God even in the demonic realm, following "His kingdom rules over all" (Ps 103:19).

In the moment when you suddenly feel the flow of the most delicate, most spiritual, of thoughts, thoughts so pure that your heart cannot grasp them; when your inner eye so sharpens its glance as to embrace all generations, all that has ever taken place—it is your God calling to you.

You then feel with your whole being that there is an inner dimension to reality. All those things that you usually see as fleeting and low in value exist for a purpose—they have come to teach you about the most hidden level of being.

"There is not a single blade of grass, or even the tiniest of creatures, that does not point to the uppermost worlds!”⁸¹

"The *shekhinah*, when it is among birds of flight, is called 'eagle'; when among fowl, 'dove'; when among plants, 'lily.' As the world is divided into diverse categories, so too is there variation in the name of the *shekhinah*. But the person who is aware of his Maker will have the heart to understand that the *shekhinah* appears to him in varied ways, arousing his mind to seek God's blessed unity.”⁸²

Indeed, the hidden God reveals Himself to humans in these ways:

1. Through those thoughts of repentance that occur to a person every day. There you are, sunk in your desires, your worries, your problems. Suddenly you begin to think about your life ending in chaos, about how you have sinned to your own soul, about the vanity by which you are surrounded, about the God from whom you were taken and to whom you will return.
2. Through the sudden fear that comes upon a person. You sit in your hidden chamber, doing your ugly deeds, thinking your ugly thoughts. Suddenly you are taken aback, as though struck by a sword. What did you see? You saw the One who gazes and sees into the deepest depths of your heart.

3. Through the vision of nature's regularity and constancy. Wondrous order, cosmic wisdom, heavenly heights, endless expanses!

4. By the feeling of eternity in every great passion, through the devotion you feel to it…

5. In the grace that is spread forth over every creature, the glory of creation, the secret of *shekhinah*, lily among the plants, dove or eagle among the birds.

But the main revelation of God, according to Hasidism, is in Torah. The entire Torah, from beginning to end, is nothing other than God, garbed in earthly matters, human stories, human laws and statutes.

Torah is divine not only in a general sense, but every single letter within it is a special revelation of the Deity. The combinations of letters found in Torah are those same combinations by which heaven and earth were made.

When you immerse yourself in Torah, you not only fulfill the commandment of studying Torah, but you are enrobed in the divine Self. God surrounds you from all sides, is taken up and grasped by you, since "Torah and God are one."

The twenty-two letters of Torah are twenty-two ways in which divinity flows forth, twenty-two cosmic forces. In the links among those flows and forces you find the combination that lies behind everything in creation. Everything in the world, big and small, has some sort of voice, expression, revelation, and the twenty-two letters represent all of these in combination. The complex interlinking of these letters fills cosmic space. The wisdom of all these linkages is found in Torah, since "Torah emerges from sublime Wisdom."

"When it arose in the blessed One's desire to create the world, in order to do good to His creatures, He reduced Himself. Into what was He concentrated? Into the letters of Torah, through which He created the world."[83]

"Torah is the imprint of the world, and the world is the imprint of Torah. One who is aware of his Maker can find the letters of Torah in everything in the world. It all depends upon the strength of your awareness and your grasp of the multi-colored garb of Torah. The upbuilding of *shekhinah* depends on this."[84]

"A person's mind is his soul, and it is a part of the *shekhinah*, as it were. The 'Torah of light' is the blessed Holy One. Therefore a person who links his own mind and good consciousness to matters of Torah is bringing about the union of the blessed Holy God and His *shekhinah!*"[85]

"The uppermost chamber of God, the place where He dwells constantly, is Torah—there the person and God dwell together, the holy chamber of Torah surrounding both, as it were, from all sides, One just like the other, equally."[86]

"All consciousness, when it grasps a certain object, takes that object up and surrounds it. The consciousness itself becomes wrapped up in that object as it takes it into itself....When the subject is Torah, not only is the mind garbed in the wisdom of God, but that divine wisdom enters into it....This is a uniquely wondrous union. There is none like it anywhere in the corporeal realm, in which God and man are truly one, united in every single way."[87]

The main difference between any ordinary religious viewpoint and that of Hasidism with regard to the divine origin of Torah lies in this: others may view Torah as coming from heaven, derived from God. Hasidism sees Torah as "heaven" itself; Torah is not only divine in origin. In its most innermost sense it is God, divinity itself.

Just as, according to Hasidism, "God is world and world is God," referring to their deeply hidden roots, so too is Torah world, and world is Torah. Not only are "Israel and Torah one," but world and Torah are one as well.

Just as the entire world, in the Hasidic view, is naught but the outer garment of God, so too is Torah nothing other than God's outer garb. In both of them—world and Torah—you have to discover God, seeking out the secret hidden within them. To see this way is to gaze with the inner eye, with a love so pure and a joy so divine that it is tasted only by a few in each generation.

"The secret is a matter that no one can truly explain to another. Just as the taste of a food cannot be communicated to one who has never tasted it, the same is true with regard to the Creator's love. It is impossible to describe to anyone this quality of love within the heart. That is why it is called 'secret.' But those things that most people consider 'secret'—like the wisdom of Kabbalah—how are they secret? The books are open for anyone who wants to study!"[88]

Torah is eternal not only because God gave it for all eternity, but because it is eternity itself. And just as it is eternal, so too is it infinite, endless. For this reason: insofar as you grasp some bit of Torah, you are attached to God. "One who holds onto a single part of a unity in fact holds onto it all." On the other hand, with all your efforts and struggles, your reach and your grasp, your longing, devotion, attempts at union—you have still not touched anything of Torah. That which is endless, transcending both time and space, cannot enter or be grasped within any borders. You, O human, insofar as you live within this bodily existence, are subject to all those limitations.

Therefore "'The Torah of God is innocent' (Ps 19:8). She remains in her innocence—no one has yet touched her at all!"[89]

Raising Up Sparks

The vessels, not able to bear the intensity of the light, were broken. Some of them broke into pieces, others into tiny fragments. Some fell, others sank down, some sank into the deepest maw of subterranean chaos. They were all scattered in every direction, with no one to gather them up. These castaways, wherever they are, sigh in longing for the sublime beauty of their original home. Holy sparks are bound up in matter, in nature, in coarseness, in body and—worse than all these—in evil, impurity, ugliness, pettiness.

They call out to God with all their strength: Please save us from captivity, from heaviness, from sin, and from our scattered state! The vessels sinned when each proclaimed, "I will rule!" As those divine lights came to dwell below, their own inner godly essence, as it were, hid its face from them for a moment, so that every world and each creature came to see itself as a separate being, set off and able to stand on its own without the entire divine Self, that which dwells within all worlds and that which hides in a secret realm all its own.

Then, when everything scattered and fell apart, the sparks were beset by a powerful longing. They understood their sin and how it had alienated them from the light of God's face. They moan all their days, looking toward their salvation, seeking to be redeemed.

Wherein lies their redemption? In the human soul.

It is within our power to recognize God in each thing, the holiness and sublime beauty that lies everywhere. We can perceive the absolute oneness that lies within all this separation and scatteredness and understand the error of being. We can see through the cosmic optical illusion to perceive the God-of-world, breaking through all the partitions that separate us. When you know and see this, living within the Deity, you are able to uplift everything you see, hear, or encounter, restoring it to its root in the divine will. Everything you use or enjoy, the food you eat and the clothes you wear, every person or object with which you come into contact—all of them strip off their profane, weekday garments and are dressed in holy raiment. They come forth from the deepest depths and rise to the greatest heights. They shed all vulgarity and defilement, are purified to become their most noble selves.

You need to recognize this very clearly: you need to get to know not only the worlds and the God that fills and underlies them. You need to find the divine *shekhinah* in each single individual or detail of existence. You have to know the particular lights that abide within each and every creature, the combinations of these lights, how they descended into this one and how they can be raised back up. You must get to the particular inner meanings of each object, matter, and event. When you can direct each sight, hearing, and encounter in both thought and deed, then bit by bit you will begin to raise up the lowly, cleanse the defiled, and purify all that is thick and coarse in its bodily manifestation.

The opposite is also true: when you forget the source from which you come, get all wrapped up within yourself and consider yourself a separate being, you become a world destroyer instead of a redeemer. Not only do you fail to uplift those holy sparks that have already fallen into the depths; you actively bring down new bits of light from the shining heavens into realms of filth and ugliness, the "deepest shells." The human being, a creature of mind, consciousness, and choice, can both uplift all with which he comes in contact, joining it to oneness, or bring it down, defile it, separate it ever further from its root, sinking it into the depths.

The human, as a conscious being, has power not only over the lower world, but over that above as well. We are able to grasp not only the coarse and sensual; we have a sense of beauty, sublimity, purity, and abstraction. We hold fast to the highest heavens and the deepest depths, *binah*, the Mother above, and *malkhut*, the Mother below. We are attached to all treasures of the spirit, to everything most exalted. But through pride and bad choices, in those times when we say "I will rule!" or by lowly passions, by our natural attractions to the coarse and defiled, we separate all those glorious things from their place within cosmic unity as well as from one another. We make them small, reducing them down to nothing, or dress them in vulgarity until the holy spark disappears into the realm of defilement.

This is the secret of "the kings who died," the 288 sparks,[90] the exile of the *shekhinah*, the sin of the Tree of Knowledge, the generation of the flood and the Tower of Babel, the sin of Israel and its exile, all sin, twisting, and distortion.

What are the "kings who died"? The vessels became separated, they forgot for a moment their single divine root. Each of them got that feeling of power, not of the single collective divine cosmic Self, but individually. Immediately they fell from their exalted rung. "Whoever falls from his rung is considered like one who died."[91] And what are the "288 sparks"? The Emanator wanted everything to emerge from potential into actuality, to be created in a revealed, fully apparent way. To bring this about, He gave to everything both life and shadow, the shadow to complete and help show forth the light. Light is seen only in contrast to darkness. Cosmic light consists of holiness, purity, beauty, love, justice, and all the rest. Cosmic shadow: Defilement, ugliness, defensiveness, hatred, evil, and so forth. The former and the latter are intermingled in myriad ways, combined in endless variations, joined together into one glorious whole, a wondrous cosmic weave by the universal Artist.

Further, the One who brought it all forth wanted there to be someone to recognize His work, to know His mastery, and to stare into the cosmic eye. This is the human being. And what are we to do, here in this cosmic palace? The blessed Holy One created it all: good and evil, beautiful and ugly, with all their endless combinations, varieties, and oppositions. To humans God says: "Sort it out! Separate the wheat from the chaff, the pearls from the sand, the good and beautiful from evil and ugliness. Lift the sparks of holiness from among the shells. This is your task!"

The existence of those "shells" is necessary, down to the time of final clarification. But how do they exist? What is their hold on reality? Who gives them life and sustains them? If indeed "there is naught but Him" and "nothing exists without the divine light," how are these sustained? Their whole purpose is to serve as partitions that block out Divinity, to stand against it! That is why (according to Luria's Kabbalah) the 288 sparks went down into the depths at the moment of creation. They give life to the "shells," which without them would be nothing at all. Those light-sparks, burdened and oppressed as they dwell amid thick darkness, wait in longing for their human redeemer....

The exile of the *shekhinah?* "The glory of God rises ever higher," but He leaves His *shekhinah*, His indwelling presence, amid the lowly. And what does sinful-hearted man do? We take that sublime beauty and sink it in the mud! The human soul contains glory, a sense of the beautiful, and longing for beauty and holiness. But instead of raising that visible beauty up to its hidden analogue and source, tying together the upper and lower worlds, wedding *shekhinah* (visible divinity) with Her holy Spouse (the blessed Holy One, sublime mystery), in love, we separate them by force. We settle for only that which we can see and touch. But we go still lower: within the sensate universe, we go for fragmentation, sinking further, so much into sensation that we forget the source of all this beauty. We come to think there is nothing in the world but single occurrences, blind chance, conflicts, and pleasures of the flesh. We tear off the King's royal cloak and shred it, using it in a defiled manner.

The sins of the Tree of Knowledge, the generation of the Flood, the Tower of Babel—all sin, for that matter—has a single root. The essential nature of sin is this: "They said to God: 'Be removed from us!'" (Job 21:14). Adam sinned regarding the mind, the Flood generation about beauty (lust), the Tower builders around what is most high and exalted ("Let us build a tower whose top will reach heaven"; "let us make us a name" [Gen 11:4]). All sin comes from big-heartedness, from an exaggerated sense of self, the desire to spread oneself forth. In themselves, there is nothing wrong with these! On the contrary, they are the most precious and elevated of intentions, the secret heart of being. But you have to let the divine light into them, linking them to their root, the Source, the pure spring. You need to deal with them in a way that puts them into harmony with eternal truth and cosmic holiness.[92] Sinners cut these things off from their root, turning mind, beauty, and exaltation into idols, endless idols, until bit by bit they are distanced from their Source altogether. Once they become coarse and materialistic, they turn cosmic unity into separation, sublime beauty into pleasure of the moment and pain eternal, bravery into violence, the exalted into the brutal.

Then all of creation turns toward devastation and waste. Far from God its Father, it becomes hideous and ugly. The good and beautiful within it thirst for God, seek to be liberated and redeemed. "The lower waters cried out: 'We too seek to be close to the King!'"[93] With them weep all splendor and goodness; all stretch forth their hands, begging for redemption....

For this reason, the task of those select humans who identify with the pain of creation itself, seeing its fallen and lowly state, those who hear the outcry of the "captives" and know their prayerful longings to be saved—these redeemers take on a heavy but vital task in each generation. Not only do they have to set right that which has gone astray within creation: the broken vessels, the 288 sparks, the captured *shekhinah*. They also have to deal with the transgressions of all the generations that have come before them, lifting up everything they have degraded and defiled by their blindness and their brutal spirits.

The eternal God, "thinking of how the banished one may no longer be banished from before Him,"[94] brings before each human redeemer that which belongs to the root of his soul, those things that this particular person needs to redeem. Therefore every human redeemer lives in a world that is particular to him, sees what he needs to see, feels what he needs to feel. Each of us has our own level; try to hold onto someone else's rung, and you will wind up with broken shards in your hand.[95] But when you hold fast to your own rung, the whole external world around you, along with everything in it, belongs to you alone. It is as though it came into being just for you, approaching you to seek its redemption.

"Each person's food, clothing, dwelling place, and the items with which he does business"—say the BeSHT and those who come after him—"exist for the sake of raising up his own sparks. This is the secret meaning of 'Know Him in all your ways' (Prov 3:6)—to unify and uplift the sparks of his soul, which are sparks of the *shekhinah*. This uplifting stirs her waters, bringing about union above."[96]

92

"All that a person eats and drinks is really a part of his own sparks, that which he needs to redeem. All objects that serve a person are like his children."[97]

"'A man's steps are established by God who desires his way' (Ps 37:23)—all of a person's steps come from God, established for some reason, since God desires to direct him in that path. The person also comes to 'desire his ways,' for his own purposes. But it all fulfills the divine plan."[98]

"Every path a person walks is in order to gather up his sparks. The sparks long for that *tsaddik* who is of their root, so that they may be joined to him and rise upward."[99]

"The path itself desires greatly that the *tsaddik* walk on it to gather up his sparks that lie there in inanimate things, in the very soil."[100]

"'Better that the human not have been created'[101] —but why then was he created? The king lost a certain precious stone in the depths of the sea. He sent his three children to look for it. One thought that his father had cast him out, so he remained there. The second longed to return to his source, to his father, but did nothing about it. The third understood that he had come there for a purpose. He sought and found the precious stone, and brought it back to his father in great joy."

"Some people get lost in the vanities of this world, 'the depths of the sea.' For them it would indeed have been better if they had never been created. Others spend all their days longing to go back to their Source, their Father. They guard themselves from sin so that they will be able to return to the Father just as they came. But then there are those who struggle, seeking out and finding that precious stone, raising up sparks of holiness and bringing about great unifications above. It is for their sake that the world was created."[102]

"Man is a microcosm, containing all worlds and all creatures. All of them go up and down within him. When he rises up and cleaves to his Creator, all of them rise with him. The opposite is also true, as in 'the spirit of man rises upward, but the spirit of the beast falls to earth'"(Eccl 3:21).[103]

"There is nothing in this world that does not contain a divine spark, emanating from the blessed Holy One's word, which gives it life. This spark is the taste in something sweet to the palate. When a person eats it, the life-force ensconced within it, the holy spark, remains within the person. That spark unites with the person's own life-force; through it he gains nourishment and strength. When that person has complete and absolute faith that this is also spiritual sustenance, God's own self as garbed there, and is totally mindful of that inwardness, cleaving to the Root of all, the One from whom all life flows (and making use of the mental energy added to him by the power of that spark)—he then brings that holy spark, until now broken and exiled, back to God. God, blessed be He, rejoices greatly over this, since this is our essential task, to draw near all those sparks that had fallen into the shells or been broken, to restore them to their holy place."[104]

"Just as the bee turns all it consumes into honey, man can raise up every morsel from the realm of physical pleasure to that of shining *shekhinah*—light, spiritual joy.... In this way the person can make himself so holy that his own food becomes shining *shekhinah*-light, that which sustains the angels above."[105]

Raising Up Distracting Thoughts

Similar to the act of raising sparks is that of lifting up distracting thoughts. Their essential content is the same: to find the holy and pure within everything and to raise them up to the Endless. What is the difference between them? In the first matter, raising sparks, the human redeemer uplifts through his goodness everything with which he comes into contact. But when raising distracting or "alien" thoughts, you are uplifting the evil within yourself. The new idea here is that you should not be pushing evil aside or seeking to cast it away. Rather, you need to uplift it, to purify the fire of lust in the divine fire. When raising up sparks you are turning the profane into the holy. When dealing with alien thoughts, it is evil that you are making holy. You find the holy spark within the wicked thought (because "the life-force of holiness is present also amid the shells" and "*shekhinah* is also ensconced within the ten crowns of defilement, because 'His kingdom rules over all'"—Ps 103:19). When you hold fast to that spark, the rest evaporates of its own accord.

"An alien or not-good thought that comes to a person is a complete form, but damaged. If you push it away, you knock it off its rung and kill it. For that reason it is wrong to push it off; you need rather to redeem it. This is how to do it. First, when such a thought comes to you, draw upon yourself great fear and a sense of shame before God. Then grab hold of the thought. (Unless you do this, there is a danger that it might corrupt you, since you haven't pushed it aside. This is like Jacob's 'I dwelt with Laban'—[Gen 32:5].[106] That is why you first need to draw down fear, so the thought will not bear ill fruit in you.) Then examine the thought carefully, analyzing the good and evil within it. Separate out the evil and act upon or speak the good within that thought. You have then brought the thought forth into the World of Speech or the World of Action. The damage or stain within it has been cast aside, like a stain removed from a garment by applying heat. Now the garment is whole and the stain is gone."[107]

"I will teach you a great thing," says Rabbi Nahum of Chernobyl.[108] "If you ever feel that you have fallen into the hands of bad emotional qualities—especially forbidden love (God forbid!), know surely that these 'evil' thoughts want to raise you up, to take you to a higher rung by means of your own natural emotions, to open your heart to God's blessed love. This will bring you to encounter the giving of Torah from above. But before this uplifting comes a lowering. By falling into that place of forbidden love and seeing that God is there too, by standing in that bad place and using the very arousal energy of that forbidden love to defeat the evil urge, loving the Creator with the love aroused there, you are raising yourself to an exalted rung. Thus you can raise up all the fallen loves that have descended to that place back to the World of Love."

But how should a person raise up those bad qualities or that improper love, including base and coarse desire, to the Palace of Love? How can one merit, through purifying the senses, "the giving of Torah from above"?

This is explained by the author of *The Well of Living Waters*[109] through a subtle parable, derived from Plato: "A king commanded his workmen to build him a great palace compound, containing many chambers, one within another. Thus would it be built: palace within palace, building within building, chamber within chamber. Each palace, building, and chamber would be painted and decorated in a different color, none like any other. They would be linked together by the fact that all of them were to be exceptionally beautifully and gracefully done. Before the workers set about to create this magnificent compound, the king drew up plans on paper showing all the palaces, towers, and chambers, including every door and window, every entrance and exit.

The paper plans, showing this wonderful project, were very attractive. Even a person who had no real idea of how to read architectural plans found them impressive because of their own beauty. But for one who understood them, down to their last detail, these drawings truly brought about a great desire to contemplate the future palace. How much greater would the actual palace be than the mere drawings!"

The visible, revealed world represents the drawing of the sublime palace. Every line and dot in the world points to something in the upper worlds, the beauty of which is infinitely greater than that of the world before us. Two paths stand before us: We may cling to the beauties of this world alone, giving pleasure to our senses. In doing this we would be seeing only the paper plans, a series of lines and dots that is actually the lowest rung of beauty. Or we may allow those lines and dots to arouse in our hearts a powerful desire to see the majesty of divine emanation, the brilliantly shining worlds of the Ancient Holy One.

The one who uplifts his distracting thoughts is choosing the second option. More than others, he sees the radiance and beauty of the world. But he realizes that these are no more than the fallen fruit of the radiance above, the most sublime beauty. Seeing these fallen fruits arouses in him great longings for the holy "Tree" itself....

This is the path that leads from sensual pleasures to "the giving of Torah from above." One who has never tasted of this world's beauty is also incapable of encountering the higher beauty, having no way to approach it. The human redeemer has to experience worldly beauty, dwelling within it at certain times, but without getting stuck in it. From the beauty of the plan he has to be able to pass onward to that of the palaces themselves...

So it is with beauty, but so too with every quality or thought.

Generally human thought in all its detail breaks down into seven mental categories, deriving from the "seven days of the [sefirotic] structure." A person who wants to uplift a certain alien or superficial thought has to figure out from which quality it was drawn, from where it was that it fell into the broken state or the "shells." Now it longs to be uplifted and restored to its root.

You hear someone telling jokes, for example, and that makes you happy. Say in your heart: This belongs to the World of Love! See or taste something in which you take great pleasure, but say to yourself: This comes from the World of Joy! Be quite careful not to take that pleasure in its corporeal sense, but attribute it fully to the World of Joy above. In that case you will be sitting here but partaking of the World of Divine Joy! The same is true of glorification or pride. If someone glorifies you, or if a thought of self-glorification comes to you during prayer ("How intensely I am praying!"), hold fast to the true glorification of the World of Glory. If fear comes to you, hold fast to holy fear; triumph—to the triumph of God. The same with thanksgiving and binding. Be bound only to God![110]

Uplifting the *Middot*[111]

Hasidism, like Kabbalah, its mother, sees duality in everything: good and evil, purity and defilement, truth and falsehood, beauty and ugliness, the *sefirot* of holiness and those of the impure realm. Hasidic sources, like the Kabbalah from which they stem, frequently quote the verse: "God made this opposite that" (Eccles 7:14). Both try to show that everything found in the holy world exists also in that of the impure, and vice versa.

All this frequent talk of duality within Hasidism is, however, superficial rather than essential to it. I mean to say that all this came to Hasidism by inheritance from earlier Kabbalah and does not reflect its essential spirit. Hasidism believes in this duality in the same way it believes in all that it received in written transmission; it does not take it upon itself to contradict anything that had been set forth by the earlier Kabbalists. But this principle of duality does not proceed from the essence of Hasidism, from its hidden soul. Had Hasidism built its house on virgin ground, rather than on the foundations of Kabbalah, it surely would not have spoken at all of holiness and defilement or any other duality in oppositional terms. It would rather have portrayed them as a single unity, one that descends from the highest rungs down to the very lowest. From there it rises back up to its source, ever richer and ever clearer.

With regard to evil in general, the disciples of the BeSHT have reported in his name: Evil is just the lowest level of the good.[112] When it is redeemed, it is transformed into pure goodness. This means that good and evil are not opposites; they are a single reality. In its lowliest manifestations we call that reality evil; in its highest, we call it good. Thus when evil is transformed it becomes pure goodness.

Since the *hasidim* do not distinguish between natural and moral senses of good and evil, and since "the good is that which is close to God" and "evil is that which is far from God," it rationally must follow from the BeSHT's teaching that the whole issue of holiness versus the "other side," so much discussed by Hasidic and Kabbalistic sources, is really just an allegory.

This allegory, so widely accepted for thousands of years, teaches something very deep, not easily grasped by most human minds. Because a superficial reading of it points toward an absolute duality within existence, many people have gradually transformed that into a depiction of reality. They have come to think that this reflects the true nature of things.

That is why you find many passages even in the Hasidic writings that speak of the holy and the "other side" as two creations standing in absolute opposition to one another, both created by the single God, made to fight and struggle constantly with one another until the holy wins its final victory.

In seeking to present the essential teachings of Hasidism in consistent fashion, we have only the statement by the BeSHT and that which necessarily proceeds from it. On this basis we say that Hasidism recognizes no duality in creation, just as it knows none in the Creator. Hasidism sees only a single unified divine force, giving life in an absolutely equal way to all that is, both good and evil. Divinity, descending from "the Hidden of all Hiddens," is a force that proceeds from rung to rung, becoming ever coarser and more sensate. Only as it reaches the very end is it so hidden that it can barely be detected. When we contemplate those lower rungs, where no divine clarity can be perceived, we call them evil. The person who is attached only to them (their outer, not their inner qualities) we call an evildoer or a sinner. But when that very person abandons those lowly rungs and reaches higher, or when he begins to see divinity within those lowly rungs themselves, he is engaged in redeeming and uplifting evil. To say it differently: he is raising up God's own Self, hidden within the coarseness of material existence, restoring it to its Source.

When you raise up all corporeal and lowly things, you are uplifting sparks. When in this way you raise up your lowly and material thoughts, you are uplifting distracting thoughts. When you apply the same uplifting to your own *middot* [your emotions and your patterns of behavior], feelings, and desires, you are "breaking" all those *middot* and raising them all to God.

There is thus no essential difference between good and bad human traits. Every *quality* a person has, when it is stuck in coarseness and small-mindedness, may be called evil. When it is purified and elevated, we call it good.

"All that exists among the disciples of the wicked Balaam is also to be found in the disciples of Abraham our Father. Among them it exists in holiness; in Balaam's disciples, in defilement."[113]

The deeper meaning of this statement, as we understand it, is this: The essential quality of both groups is an elevated and expansive ego-self. For the disciples of Balaam, who have an eye only for themselves and their own pleasure, even that expansive ego is limited and reduced. It is stuck into a certain constriction, that of man's small world when he is cut off from Infinity, from all that depth, richness, and glory of infinite life, from the All. His constricted ego becomes an enclosed pond of water, turning ever more brackish and bitter. Abraham's disciples, because they link the expansiveness of their own ego-selves to the greatness of the Infinite, make their own being into a dwelling place for the *shekhinah*, their own little world a vessel for Divinity. The small channel flows into the cosmic sea. Of expansiveness like this scripture says: "His heart rose high in the ways of Y-H-W-H" (2 Chr 17:6).

The same is true of any matter or want, anything a person contemplates or desires greatly. It applies whether you are cruel or compassionate, angry or gracious, cursing or speaking softly. You may hate or love, feel pride or be lowly in your own eyes, you may isolate yourself or live among people, be a lonely ascetic or a family person, swear off the world or enjoy everything you see. All of it can be good, and all of it can be evil. When your spirit is pure, elevated, living within God, and everything is in harmony with the divine life—it is all good. If your spirit turns downward, sinking, forgetting the God who bore you, caring only for your own desire and private pleasure—it is all bad.

Therefore, the *hasidim* understand the moral good not as decreed from without, not as commandment or statute, but rather as a stream of inspiration flowing from the Source of the person's divine soul. In that stream we purify and refine all of our emotions, until they become heavenly. The emotional teachings of Hasidism are an alchemy of the soul. Just as the alchemists labored to transform base metals into gold, so do the *hasidim* labor to transform every human quality within their souls into a godly one....

The *hasidim* reveal to us all the methods by which this holy work is done. They know various and sundry ways to raise up each *middah*, not just a single one. All depends on the traits of the particular quality and its nature, varying also with the person's character, the conditions in which he finds himself, the social setting, and the time and place in which he lives.

The *hasidim* understand that a person's character today is not necessarily what it was yesterday. Your mood when stirred by all sorts of activities is not the same as that which you feel when you are all alone, living true to yourself, sunken into your most undisturbed inner places, without desires or distractions that cloud your consciousness. There you perform your own inner judgments, take account of your own self.

The *hasidim* know how the essential character of people varies, sometimes even in strange ways. They are also aware of the various odd circumstances that affect people, how different people's feelings are when they do either good or bad. Following the lines of these feelings, there is good that is evil and evil that is good.... They know the power of desire, all the charms of sin, the natural and compelling power of things considered evil. They understand all the difficulty and bitterness, even the near impossibility, of the "battle against one's inclination...."

They also know this: the more you struggle against your desires, the stronger those desires grow. When you struggle for victory over your urges, those urges bring forth their strongest weapons, sending poison into the heart of the God-fearing person in order to defeat him. This is like two people fighting in fierce anger. The more one is winning, the harder the other struggles to knock him out....

"A person should always be cunning in the fear of God." This statement of the Talmud[114] is parent to endless prescriptions found in Hasidic literature. The main point is not the *power* to make war, but the proper *strategy*. You have to know how to conquer the enemy within his own *stronghold*, how to steal his own sword and defeat him with it. The *hasid* battles with the evil urge not only by using the good urge, but by means of the evil urge's own powers.

You can only do battle with the evil urge by *looking* and *contemplation*.

Looking:

"The soul is the King's daughter, come down from the divine throne, blown into a physical body that has various desires. Drawn after the body, the soul has forgotten her heavenly Father. When you show her the heavens and the stars, the sun and the moon, and tell her that she was created from the same place as them, she is able to rise upward."[115]

"'Look toward heaven and count the stars' (Gen 15:5). God said to Abraham: Don't lower yourself by going down from your own rung toward worldly matters. 'Look toward heaven'—gaze at the greatness of God. You will be most able to see God's greatness when you look heavenward, seeing the stars keeping faithfully in their courses, shining their radiant light."[116]

["Rejoice in trembling" (Ps 2:11).] "'In the place of joy, there should be trembling.' When you see God's greatness in your mind, how all the worlds, angels, and sublime palaces declare His praise, all of them trembling in awe, you are filled with great joy to be serving the true God. But then you tremble as well, realizing before Whom you stand, speak, and sit. The words of your prayer come forth in awe and fear, with great shame."[117]

That is one sort of "looking." Here is another:

"You see the image of God in its perfection. You see a true *tsaddik*: his beauty, glory, splendor, his pleasant manner, his deeds, the way he acts. You see before you a symbol of perfection, lofty exaltation. This seeing affects your soul, making it better, higher.

"Every move of a person's limb when doing a *mitsvah* or a holy deed causes the soul to dwell in that limb. When the soul resides in a limb of the body, it moves by the soul's power. The difference in this movement can be seen from without, all according to the person's *deeds and movements*. That is why the movements of the *tsaddikim* appear so good and sweet to those who see them. They are moving by the power of the soul, which is 'a part of God above containing all goodness.'"[118]

It was said of a certain *tsaddik* that "Among all those who saw his holy dancing, there was not one who did not return to God. He would bring about crying and joy in the heart, all as one."[119]

A third way of looking:

A person sees the light of Torah, the light of a *mitsvah*, the light shining through the letters of Torah. He attaches himself to those letters and the holiness that hovers over them. As he sees the lights from above, awe before God falls over him.

"There is a hidden light, hidden in the holy Torah. Torah is dressed in garments so that each person, according to who he is, can behold the brilliant light through them."[120]

"A person is reading the Torah and sees the lights of the Torah's letters. Even if he does not understand the notations properly and mispronounces the words, God is not strict with him, because he is reading with great love and enthusiasm. This is like a young child, greatly loved by his father. When the child asks for something, even if he stammers and can't pronounce the word properly, the father takes great pleasure. So too when a person speaks words of Torah with love—God loves him very much and is not strict about the pronunciation."[121]

"The Torah contains musical notations, vowel points, ornamental crowns, and letters. But the light within it is the Nothing, beyond all of these. It is the source from which Torah flows, the Creator Himself. In this way God and Torah are one. Every person who studies Torah has to attach his own life-force to that light or 'Nothing.' It surely will then turn him to goodness, since he has been joined to the inner light. He will become a throne for God's own presence, which dwells and flows within Torah."[122]

"When (the *tsaddikim*) study the Talmud, they clothe themselves in fear and trembling before God's presence. Torah shines in their faces. When they mention an early sage or another bearer of tradition, they picture that teacher standing before them, alive with the root of his light in the upper chariot."[123]

A fourth, most elevated, form of looking:

Look at everything as though the *shekhinah* were standing before you. Sharpen your sight so greatly that you do not even see the outer forms of things. What I mean is this: Become so used to thinking about God that God is no longer an object of thought, an abstraction, or an emanation. God becomes something you *really see.*

"The Creator existed before the world was created. The world stands within the Creator. Therefore you need to be so attached to God that the main thing you see is God rather than the world, with God second to it. No! Your sight should be focused on the blessed Creator. When you see in this way, all the shells fall away, since they are only there to bring about darkness and separation between you and God. They keep the mind's eye closed from looking at the Creator."[124]

"When attaching yourself (to the Creator), go first into the World of Action. Then fly higher in your mind to the world of the angels. Then continue on to the World of Creation, until you feel you can fly to the greatest heights, the World of Emanation…. Take care not to fall down from those very lofty places in your thought. Use all your strength to stay up there with all your mind. Make something like a banister so that you do not fall."[125]

"*Devekut* [attachment to God] for the *tsaddikim* means that they imagine the light of *shekhinah* above them, wrapping them up in a cloak of awe. They tremble spontaneously and take great joy in that trembling."[126]

So much for looking. What about contemplation?

There are three sorts of contemplation in connection with the raising up of *middot*: (1) contemplation from the viewpoint of God and the world, (2) contemplation from the viewpoint of the soul, (3) contemplation from the viewpoint of the evil urge itself.

From the viewpoint of God and the world:

"Inner awe (before God) brings you to a sense of shame. That is the highest form of awe, a sense of contrition before the light of the Endless that is found garbed within Wisdom, within the most primal force, before which all else is naught. Through this self-negation, 'Wisdom gives life to those who possess it'" (Eccles 7:12).[127]

"A major principle in the service of God for ordinary people: It is essential to rule over the natural force in the left chamber [of your heart] by means of the light that shines into the divine soul within your mind. That light should rule over the heart as you contemplate the greatness of the Endless in your mind. Your understanding should give birth to a spirit of awareness and fear of God within your mind, leading you to turn from evil."[128]

"'Know Him in all your ways' (Prov 3:6)—With every act, every movement, any sight or hearing, any thought or speech that comes to you from any inner quality at all, bear in mind that this too is God, without Whom nothing could exist. Through that very quality attach yourself to God. Take this example: When some sort of love comes to you, rather than loving the material aspect (of that love object), understand that it is the inner life-force that makes this object attractive, causing it to be seen in this loving way. Therefore, attach your love to that inner life-force, to His blessed Self that gives life to all. When you become accustomed, in all your ways, your feelings, your actions, your encounters, to contemplate Him, blessed be He, in this way, it will be within your power to transcend nature and the created world. When you love a particular thing, your love-thought is concentrated within it and it comes to surround your entire mind. Then it becomes impossible to attach yourself to God, because you are separated from Him by the material barrier that surrounds your mind. But if you accustom yourself, including your emotions, not to be involved with corporeality at all, but to become attached to the life-force that inhabits the corporeal, which is God's own Self, then you are not garbed in the material world at all, but dwell outside it. Then 'the world is not your place,' but you [like God] 'are the place of the world,' since you cleave to the cosmic life-force, that which gives place and form to the world. In this way it is possible to rule over the world."[129]

How does one contemplate from the viewpoint of the soul?

"Great reductions [of intensity of divine presence] took place until the worlds were emanated and created. The purpose of all these reductions was the creation of the physical human body, in order to subdue the 'other side' and to produce a greater light coming forth from darkness.

"So too in reverse [lit. 'as the face in the water' (Prov 27:19)]. The blessed Holy One has abandoned or set aside His great, infinite light, hidden and concealed it behind various reductions, all for the sake of us lowly humans, to raise us up to God, for love presses the flesh, [seeking its transformation]. How much more should we be ready to leave behind all that we have, spirit and flesh, setting it all aside for the sake of attachment to God with longing and desire! Nothing should hold us back, nothing within or without, neither body nor soul, neither livelihood nor wife and children."[130]

"The breath that comes out in speech contains within it some bit of the life-force, an externalization of the living soul within the speaker. But that which comes out in the act of breathing itself is a more inward manifestation of that living soul within. In the same way, by analogy, there are endless degrees of distinction among heavenly beings, even between the angels, who were created from Nothing and live as externalizations of the life-force that proceeds from the Endless to give life to the worlds, and the human soul, which is drawn directly from the innermost life-force itself."[131]

Because of this, a person should have great compassion on his own divine soul, the soul that God Himself blew into the person from His own innermost Self. This soul has sunk down to the lowest of levels and is being used to sustain all sorts of base and defiled things. Pay attention to the poverty and suffering of this royal princess, who has so many coarse and servile labors heaped upon her!

If a person sins, his soul is with him in that sin. It is like capturing the King and sticking his head in the toilet!

If a person sins, let him have compassion for the divine spark within him, for the name of God, which dwells with him in his uncleanness, for the *shekhinah*, with him in exile, for God, whose greatness is unsearchable. "He fills all the worlds and surrounds all the worlds," filling and surrounding endless worlds and palaces, each of which is replete with angels beyond count who cry out, "Where is the place of His glory?" and answer "His glory fills all the earth!"—referring to humans. God has set aside all the upper and lower worlds, choosing only the human being, drawing him near in an intimate way, becoming attached to the soul until they are like two lovers kissing on the mouth and joined in spirit. This human being drags God down and makes Him wallow in forty-nine measures of defilement! Have mercy on the divine Glory and desist from sin![132]

That is contemplation from the point of view of soul.

And from the side of the evil urge itself?

Rabbi Israel BeSHT says: "Sin—the cosmic Aleph is hidden within it!"[133] He means that the letter *aleph* in the word *het'* (sin) is unpronounced but belongs to the word's root. It hints at the cosmic *Aleph*, the One, God who is the beginning, middle, and end of all. He also dwells within sin, within the evil urge itself, in its seductions and allures, its traps and its cunning, in every wicked deed that is done.

The evil urge does the will of its master, and man has to do that of *his* master. The evil urge does its master's will, fulfills its mission and task faithfully. It seduces man to sin and to rebel against God. Man has to do his master's will, not listening to the urge's enticements.

"'When you go to war against your enemy and take his captivity' (Deut 21:10). Through the claim of the evil urge itself you can conquer the evil urge.[134] If he, the evil one, is so skillful at his craft that he can seduce you into sin, while doing God's bidding, then you learn from him how to be that skillful at *not* following the evil urge."[135] To what may this be compared? Two men set up signals between them, unknown to anyone else, that if one says to the other to do a certain thing, he will understand that he is *not* to do it.[136]

Thus says the Lord to man from within the evil urge: Do not do what your urge seeks.

Sweetening Harsh Judgments in Their Root

Just like the raising up of sparks, of distracting thoughts, and of the *middot* is the task of "sweetening" harsh judgments.

The essence of these ascents and purifications takes place in thought. As you think holy and pure thoughts of the one God, all those sparks of holiness that had fallen into the "shells" are restored to their Source. Then the deed too [follows thought and] is uplifted and made holy. So do all the godly thoughts, those that were distanced from their Source through all the reductions and emanations, those that became alienated in the course of opposition and separation, even the impure and forbidden thoughts—all of them return to their Source. Indeed, every thought that is thinkable may be uplifted and made holy. The same is true of all the divine qualities that had fallen so far away from their Source. The inner man is raised up and sanctified; the "form" of divinity is built up and perfected. Then all suffering and harsh judgments, all terrible illnesses and frightening punishments, all wars, killing, and murder, all terrors and fears, all those deeds and sights that so disturb a person and embitter his life—all of these will be totally wiped away by the power of absolute good. The higher man, the free person within man, the absolute *tsaddik* within the person, in whose place dwell only strength and joy, will be raised up and proclaimed holy. "Wailing and anguish will be negated, set aside,"[137] as all the worlds rise higher and higher, as cosmic distress turns into the endless joy of being.

Thus "harsh judgments are sweetened only in their Source." Judgments are transformed only as *gevurah*-forces are taken up to their root in *binah*. In the language of the BeSHT: "When fear is joined to awesomeness 'all the workers of iniquity split apart'" (Ps 92:10).[138] Elsewhere it is taught: "All the suffering in the world derives from *malkhut* when she is not united with her Lover."[139]

This is the meaning of these things:[140]

"At the first engraving of the King,"[141] the primal divine will (*keter*, the "tip of the letter *yod*" of God's name), the hiddenmost of God's own qualities, also known as the inner divine "Nothing," desired to create the worlds. This was an arousal of *the joy of creativity*, hidden and wondrous, within the "Ancient of Days." Afterward, when that Nothing came to be revealed, or when the primal divine will began the movement outward from its innermost self, the "Ancient of Days" became the "Longsuffering Countenance."[142]

Then *keter* and *hokhmah* were drawn forth, meaning that the first thought—hidden, original, *all-embracing*—was conceived. The first "what" was made, since the consonants of the word *hokhmah* can also be read as *koah mah*, the "potential 'what.'" This was unformed existence, out of which any sort of vessel might still be shaped. Next *hokhmah* brought forth *binah*, which means that the all-embracing but hidden Wisdom was now broadened, interpreted, clarified, and rendered into endless specific beings. The Spring of Life became an ever-flowing River, an upper *shekhinah*, called Leah. This font of divine *hokhmah* bubbles forth unceasingly and the river flows like a mighty flood, ever broadening and spreading wider. The river could not exist without the spring that feeds it. *Hokhmah* and *binah* are therefore called "two companions who never separate."

But we are still dealing here with God as pure *subject*, divinity as it imagines all that is still to emerge within it. To say it differently, we are still concerned here with divinity as it knows its own self and only itself. As *binah* expands, deepens, and lends specificity to that which it receives from *hokhmah*, it also draws a picture of all that is to come. *Hokhmah* is a simple point, containing no picture. *Binah* brings forth an image of everything that will ever exist. We mean by this a sublime, godly image, "it imagines in potential all that will ever become actual." But there are not yet real *objects* within this divine cosmic picture. Divine thought is still devoted to its own inward glance.

On the next rung, divinity sees things as objects; it sees them as they will exist when they are external to it. It conceives firmly fixed, elemental, real beings. Its thought attaches itself to them and is joined to them. This is the *sefirah* called *da'at*.

"*Da'at* (Knowing) means being joined," say the *hasidim*. In our language *da'at* is consciousness, awareness, the state in which we have a fully developed image of the object and therefore can say that we *know* it. The *sefirah* of *da'at* within the Godhead refers to that stage when God sees all things throughout eternity as objects, having a full and clear picture of them. In other words, He sees all things *as they are about to be created*. …

Thus the will of the All-present, in both its inner hidden form (the "Ancient") and its outer form (the "Longsuffering"), as well as primal thought (in its three manifestations: hidden *hokhmah*, expanded as *binah*, clarified and defined as *da'at*) preceded everything. Only once *da'at*, the last of these, emerged, could creation itself begin: "the seven days of structure," the seven divine qualities.

First among all the qualities to be revealed was divine *hesed* ("the world is built by *hesed*"—Ps 89:3). God's very deepest desire, like that of any creator, is the joy of creativity. And what is this joy in its deepest essence? The desire to flow forth, to do good, to bestow life. Being created and drawing forth a form are one; when the Creator desires to flow forth, to influence, and there is not yet anyone into whom to flow, the Creator draws a form. The Creator creates a form and pours all his love into it. Contemplate this further.

The worlds were created, according to the Zohar, "so that they would make Him known." All the hidden, secret divine forces, locked up within themselves, unknown and unrevealed, were sunk in a deep trance. Now they were to emerge from that wondrous hiding, from Nothingness to real Being, so that all the worlds above and below would be created and recognize the divine powers, so that trance would give way to wakefulness, with all its clarity.

This idea of the Zohar is as profound as the very depths of existence. It grasps the very purpose of the cosmic artistry. It helps us know why the Endless brought everything forth from Nothingness. Yet we still stand and wonder: What would have been missing if it had all remained within the divine Nothing? Could it be that the Endless, called the Complete Perfection, lacked something without manifestation, acknowledgment, and recognition on the part of those created?

The *hasidim* explain these things with the help of words chosen from R. Isaac Luria and other great teachers who preceded them. All was created because of the Good's desire to do good. "The purpose of creation was to allow God to bestow goodness in accord with His desire.…The whole enterprise of existence and the way it operates, including all individual beings, is only one, as established by the One who brought them forth. His purpose is doing good unto perfection, in every imaginable way. The conditions that allow for this are those by which all exists."[143]

Thus says R. Moshe Hayyim Luzzatto, commenting on Luria. It is easy to understand how this ordering goes back to the quality of *hesed*. This is also the hidden joy within the divine will (the "Ancient One" in the realm of *sefirot*, but the "Primal Man" in the realm of worlds). The Creator sought not only to reveal His power and goodness, but that there be someone who could sense all this divine goodness. Thus began the process of emanation.[144]

Moreover, "the Endless wanted not only to do good in a perfect way, but wanted the recipients of that good to receive it without shame. He also conceived of a way to reveal His total unity, the fact that no obstacles or lack stand in His way. He thus set up a system, which He controls, in which evil can be transformed into good. He first allows a place for evil to act out, but then brings about the repair of all the damage wrought as evil returns to become truly good. In this way is unity revealed, the true joy of souls."[145]

This means that the Creator wants His creatures not only to feel goodness, love, and grace, but also to have a sense of freedom, of standing in their own domain. God gives us the eternal illusion that we, by our good deeds, actually create goodness. He wants us to view ourselves not as putty in the Creator's hand, but as fellow creators. The Source of Life wants each one who emerges and branches forth from Him to see himself as a source, a giver, not merely one who received everything as a gracious free-willed gift.

For the sake of this, a limit had to be placed on *hesed*, which was flowing forth without end.[146] Thus were created judgment, reward and punishment, and the possibility of evil. The divine light came to be locked away within itself. A hiding, a barrier against the light, a shield or an enclosure for divine radiance was created. When it comes to the emanation of the worlds, we call this *tsimtsum*, reduction of divine light. In the realm of *sefirot* we call it *gevurah*, divine power. ("Y-H-W-H God is sun and shield" [Ps 84:12]. Y-H-W-H represents *hesed*; "God" [*elohim*] represents *gevurah*, the shield that hides the sun.)[147]

So *hesed* emerged first, stretching forth without end. Then came *gevurah*, its opposite [the divine light], reduced and hidden. From the union of these two came the third quality, *tif'eret*. *Tif'eret* represents harmony, the mutual inclusion of *hesed* and *gevurah*. *Tif'eret* is the [secondary] color that contains opposing colors and integrates them, the sound that includes opposing sounds and commingles them, the intermediary between *hesed*, spreading boundlessly, endless goodness, and [*gevurah*,] unbounded judgment. *Tif'eret* is thus the true measure of everything, represented as "compassion" or "truth."

Fanciful exegetes added that *hesed* is represented by Abraham (the generosity of Abraham, his goodness, his freely given love); thus "*hesed* to Abraham (Mic 7:20), *gevurah* by Isaac ("the fear of Isaac" [Gen 31:24]), and *tif'eret* by Jacob (called "the chosen one among the patriarchs"; the verse "You give truth to Jacob" [Mic 7:20]). "The patriarchs are the divine chariot" because their souls constitute the divine qualities, revealing these powers of God.

Netsah, hod, yesod, the three *sefirot* that follow *hesed, gevurah*, and *tif'eret*, are essentially the completion of the *sefirot*. When the divine will, the divine mind, and the emotional qualities come to a decision, an agreement to act, we have reached *netsah*. The term refers to victory, triumph, strength, a fixing of the will. When all these elements see alike, when everything that *needs* to be done is properly carried forth, the result is *hod*, visible, revealed beauty. But the *hasidim* hint at another meaning: *hod* derived from *hoda'ah*, "acknowledgment" or "gratitude." This is divinity acknowledging itself, as it were. *Yesod* is fulfillment of it all, the concretization of divine power, reality. This is not the reality we see with the eyes of the flesh, but a spiritual, cosmic reification of the divine.

Malkhut, the final manifestation, is both *all and nothing, nothing and all. Malkhut* represents total revelation of the divine forces, a revelation to the person who is aware. You can see the divine will, thought, and qualities as they are revealed in creation. Yet you know that these are not all there is. Beyond all these forces there still remains the absolutely hidden and mysterious One, beyond any hint of knowledge, not pointed to even by the tip of the *yod* of God's name. This reality remains beyond even the most esoteric human thought, even outside the grasp of the thought underlying creation itself. "Even Primal Man [*keter* as manifest in the creative process], brilliantly shining light that it is, remains dark with regard to it." You perceive the ordering of divine powers and feel in some way that there is also a hidden-beyond-all-hiddens. (You sense its *existence*, but know nothing of its *nature*.) All of this comes about through *malkhut*, through the power revealed in creation, through appearance, vision, and revealed actions.

Malkhut—last in deed but first in thought: "Supreme *keter* is the crown of *malkhut*, of which scripture says: 'He declares the end from the beginning'" (Isa 46:10).[148]

This means that the end of the *sefirot* is linked up to their beginning. The final revelation, *malkhut*, is at the same time the deepest origin. Remember that the very essence of the highest *keter* is the joy of creativity. *Keter* is the divine desire to reveal all the powers when that joy was still locked away in its most obscure hiding place. Revealed in its final externalization, that joy is *malkhut*. That feeling of being within divinity is its "desire to rule." When divinity glimpses that final deed from within its first thought, you have *keter malkhut*.

Because *malkhut* is only a revelation of hidden thought, she is referred to as *ma'amar*, "utterance," or *dibbur*, "word" or "speech" (the *Logos* of Philo), just as human speech reveals that which is hidden in the mind. And because she is revealed to humans and we see and feel everything through her, she is the indwelling presence among people (the lower *shekhinah*, Rachel). But since she is finally nothing but an expression of that which is above her, she who receives their influence but does not influence on her own, she is called "the speculum that does not shine." All she shows and reveals is not herself, but the hidden Source. She is the moon who has no light of her own, the beautiful maiden who has no eyes....

Here you have the ten[149] *sefirot*, joined to God like the flame to a burning coal.[150] Their Source is in the most hidden place, and through them and their various permutations (since each *sefirah* contains all other, each of them is composed of ten) and combinations (various aspects and rungs of the *sefirot* as they emanate through the worlds in increasingly specified fashion) the cosmos is ordered. Their permutations in detail are reflected in the names of God, manifest as a hierarchy of powers in the universe and in the combinations of letters in the Torah. Their general meaning is hinted at in the name Y-H-W-H, in the following manner: *Yod* stands for the hiddenmost point, *tsimtsum*, divine wisdom, *hokhmah*. *Heh* represents its spreading forth, the river, *binah*. *Waw* (= 6) is the six *middot: hesed, gevurah, tif'eret, netsah, hod*, and *yesod*. The form of the letter *waw* is also that of a dot over a vertical line, symbolizing the flow from the Source and its being drawn downward. The second *heh* is the final spreading forth, *malkhut*.

The ten *sefirot* are manifest within the soul as ten soul-powers but on the cosmic level as ten divine forces. They are subject to God, serving in His hand like the axe in that of the woodchopper. Since the soul-powers and the cosmic forces are arrayed parallel to one another, we name those cosmic forces in terminology derived from the soul. Further, since the most visible manifestation of soul is as garbed in the body (the body is called the soul's "garment" in Kabbalah), and that which is visible is most accessible to our understanding, we name the *sefirot* in terms of the body's limbs, as follows:

hokhmah is the mind; *binah*, the heart; *hesed*, the right hand; *gevurah*, the left hand; *tif'eret*, the trunk; *netsah* and *hod*, the two hips; *yesod*, "the seal of the body, sign of the holy covenant"; *malkhut*, the mouth (revelation, utterance, speech), "Oral Torah she is called." When *malkhut* is attached to the last *sefirah* that flows into her, she is called "the crown over the covenant."[151]

In the deeper language of Luria: Because the body garbs the soul, all that exists in body must exist in soul as well, but in a spiritual form. Therefore the soul has to contain not only the ten general forces that you can readily see by examining your own self, but a much more detailed inner structure, including 248 subtle spiritual "limbs" and 365 subtle spiritual "sinews."[152] Now since the cosmos is structured parallel to the human soul and its powers, each of the worlds, *sefirot*, and *middot* has to bear within it a complete representation of the human form, including 613 subtle extensions.

For this reason Luria arranges the *sefirot* as a series of countenances (*partsufim*). *Hokhmah*, for example, is not just a particular manifestation within both soul and cosmos but is rather an entire countenance, and a complete body-like form, with most noble, spiritual "limbs," arrayed in a manner parallel to those of the body.

This is the order of the *partsufim*:

The first is the longsuffering countenance (or just *arikh*, "the long"), primal all-embracing form, an externalization of the divine will (distinct from its inner manifestation, "the Ancient"). This is *keter*, bearing all the divine powers still hidden within it. (*Keter* is numerically 620, referring to the 613 commandments of the Torah plus seven added by the rabbis.)

The second is *abba*, cosmic father, supreme *hokhmah*, flowing forth with all the powers contained within it.

The third is *imma*, *binah*, the supernal spreading forth, the receptive *sefirah*, replete with all its specific powers.

Fourth is *ze'ir anpin*, the lesser countenance, the totality of all the divine qualities, *hesed, gevurah, tif'eret, netsah, hod,* and *yesod.* Since the essential structure of the cosmos is manifest through these *middot* (the six cosmic days, the six directions), their totality is arrayed parallel to that of the first totality, *keter*.[153] Thus the "lesser countenance" parallels the "long countenance," a microcosm to its macrocosm.

The fifth *partsuf* is *nukva,* the female partner of *ze'ir.* This is *malkhut,* receiving from all the *middot* and all that is above them, but having nothing of her own.[154] Therefore this *nukva* can ascend only when she is attached to *ze'ir,* the force that flows into her, or to the upper *middot.*

When *ze'ir* and *nukva* are in complete unity, or *when the outer manifestation of the worlds cleaves to its innermost divine Source, malkhut* is joined to her Lover, the blessed Holy One to His *shekhinah.*[155]

Since the divine mind-energies flow through all the *middot,* the union of *shekhinah* also makes for the unification of all the divine forces. This is indicated by the unification of the divine name, Y-H with W-H, in this fashion: *Hokhmah* and *binah* are represented by Y-H. They unite with *ze'ir* and *nukva,* which are W-H. Through what does this union take place? "By means of that hidden and recondite One"—through *ayin,* the Nothing, that divine wonder that flows through them all.[156]

But *malkhut* is not constantly attached to her Lover. Sometimes the external, revealed aspect of the worlds becomes a *thing* or an *extant being on its own,* and thus is *separated* from its transcendent divine Root. Now the whole purpose of *tsimtsum* and of the breaking of the vessels was indeed so that such separation be possible (in order that man, by thought, word, and deed, might reunite them). This means that the essential exile of *shekhinah* took place in the process of creation itself. Afterward *shekhinah* was exiled again and again, through the sin of the Tree of Knowledge, by the totality of all human sin, by Israel's sin and its exile. She is exiled again in every age, by every individual, in every deed great or small, in every act that distances the natural world, the external, from its hidden, mysterious Root.

Because *shekhinah* is far from her Lover, she gives life to all sorts of "shells," to harsh judgments and terrors, but also to absolute evil, both natural and moral. Humanity and all living creatures are then caught up in the web of natural causality, a place in which the wicked can swallow up the righteous. We are like birds caught in a wicked trap set upon them by men.

We have no other alternative, no other counsel, if we want to escape this trap of external causality, than to restore *malkhut* to her

Lover, the external world and the chain of causality to the divine *middot*. We do this by pure and holy thought, word, and deed. When divinity becomes revealed, that entire illusion called nature evaporates. Then we dwell with God our Rock and Fortress, the One who lifts us out of all accident and causality.

But this too results only in *unification*, the uplifting of evil. It is not yet the "sweetening" of evil in its root, after which *no evil remains, but only absolute good, having returned to its Source.* This is brought about not by restoring *malkhut* to her Lover but by returning evil (the source of which lies in *gevurah*, in *tsimstum*, and in the distancing of *malkhut* from her root), the forces of *gevurah, to th*eir highest root in *binah*.

There are three levels of *gevurah* forces: (1) the realm of *gevurah* itself; (2) the root of *gevurah* within *binah* (*binah*, though wholly good in itself, as it broadens and spreads forth [from the single concentrated point of existence in *hokhmah*], contains within it the root of *gevurah* forces that are yet to appear, since it includes and embraces all); (3) *gevurah* as rooted in *malkhut*, since *malkhut* gives life to all, including evil and the "shells." "His *malkhut* rules over all" (Ps 103:19). *Malkhut* carries within it the possibility of separation and distance from the root.

That is why we need to restore the *gevurah* forces, or the evil, to their root in *binah*, the highest source of *gevurah*, where they will be negated necessarily [by the overwhelming force of surrounding goodness]. *Binah* as itself, in its own essence, has no evil within it. You need to submerge yourself in divine *binah*; there you will see no evil.

The *hasidim* believe that all the letters of the holy tongue, and especially the divine names, are not arbitrary but divine and eternal. The letters point precisely at hidden divine forces. To pronounce them (in purity and holiness) is their highest revelation. Thus they believe that the "sweetening" of judgment-forces in their root takes place not by means of elevated, noble thoughts alone, but through the combining of letters and names that accompany them.

When a person wants to be saved from evil, he should concentrate with all his heart—say the BeSHT and his disciples—on the union of the names Y-H-W-H and A-D-N-Y. Y-H-W-H, taken as one, refers to *ze'ir* and A-D-N-Y to *nukva* (*shekhinah*, speech—as in "AdoNaY, open my lips" [Ps 51:17]). You need to commingle these two in the form Y-A-H-D-W-N-H-Y. Alternatively, you may "sweeten" the name *elohim* [referring to divine judgment] by linking it to Y-H-W-H. This is done as follows: The numerical value of ELOHIM is 86. The word *MaH* (What?), having a face value of 45, is also 86 when fully spelled out (*mem + mem + heh + aleph*). You "sweeten" by concentrating on *MaH*, itself a spelling out of the name Y-H-W-H (filled out as *yod-waw-dalet, heh-aleph, waw-aleph-waw, heh-aleph*). This deletes 41 [from the ELOHIM value of 86], so that only the holy name of 45 remains. You then concentrate on "sweetening" the number 19 [the value of the supporting extension letters—*waw + dalet + aleph + aleph + waw + aleph*] in the root letters Y-H-W-H. Only the holy name itself remains, the name of pure compassion.

This is the meaning of "for Your salvation I have waited, Y-H-W-H" (Gen 49:18). "Waited"—*kivviti*—is derived from the same root as "be gathered"—*yikavvu ha-mayim* in Genesis 1:9. All has to be gathered up in the name Y-H-W-H.[157] The *hasidim* possess many such other "sweetenings" in varied permutations of the divine names, but I did not see fit to write them all.

There is one other way to "sweeten":

"The blessed God knows the future and therefore knows that the righteous will pray to Him. But even if He knows that their prayers would not suffice to negate the decree, God does His part. When issuing the decree, God speaks it only in the form of initials, combinations of letters. Thus when the righteous pray to avert the decree, the letters may be recombined for good."[158]

All suffering, all evil and decrees, negative and judging forces, represent a mixing of powers, derived from letters that are in themselves neutral. Those letters could be formed into any combination in the world. "When the *tsaddik* rearranges the letters that constituted the evil decree, the matter is turned toward goodness."[159]

We have presented two general principles of sweetening judgment-forces: that of uniting *malkhut* with her Lover (*ze'ir* or the blessed Holy One) and that of restoring *gevurot* to their root in *binah*. But there is a third way, higher still than the others. You can raise up *gevurah*-forces not only to *binah*, but to the Root of all roots, the divine Nothing, the divine desire.

"*Shekhinah* is called 'the end of the matter' (Eccl 12:13), having spread forth to the final rungs, as in 'His *malkhut* rules over all.'

116

Therefore, 'her feet descend into death' (Prov 5:5). But once you know that 'their end is tied to their beginning,' you can link *malkhut*, the final rung, called *ani* (I am) to the highest place, called *ayin* (Nothing), a reversal of the same letters. This is 'I am the first and I am the last' (Isa 44:6). In this way you nullify evil decrees, and 'all the workers of iniquity are split apart' (Ps 92:10)."[160]

"The letters are themselves reductions [of divine will or presence]. When you raise them back from their reduced form to [their source in] infinity, the judgments are 'sweetened.' Join everything to your thought; unite speech with thought. Then all the needs for which you pray and all your lack will be fulfilled. Lack will be transformed to fulfillment, the bitter to the sweet. (Learn from the bee, who transforms the grasses in her mouth into sweet honey. How much greater is the power of human prayer!) Take this example: A person wants to travel from outside and settle in the Land of Israel. His present desire is to accomplish the journey, but his true desire—the desire of his desire—is to dwell in the Land. Thus did the blessed God create the world by His desire. His true desire was that Israel be created, so that He might take pleasure in its worship. This is called *ra'ava de-ra'avin*, the desire of desires. The same is true when Israel is afflicted by suffering or evil decrees, God forbid. These too are God's will, so that Israel returns to Him and ascends to yet a higher rung, and so onward. This (meaning the final desire, the desire of *teshuvah*) is also called *ra'ava de-ra'avin*, the desire of desires. This is the 'sweetening' of judgment-forces in their root."[161]

JUDAISM AND UNIVERSAL RELIGION

In the Soul's Secret Places:
Religious Experience and Its Manifestations

Translator's Introduction

Be-Hevyon ha-Neshamah, published in the literary collection *Netivot* in 1913, constitutes Zeitlin's response to reading William James's *Varieties of Religious Experience*. James's work was first published in 1902; Zeitlin most likely read it in Russian translation. The *Varieties* was known and much discussed among Russian intellectuals, including Lev Shestov, who had a particularly strong influence on Zeitlin.[1]

Zeitlin is inspired by James to create his own phenomenology of Jewish religious experience. As a religious insider turned outsider and now longing to be inside again, Zeitlin considers himself to belong to the very small group of people who are truly qualified to write on religion. Only one who has lived deeply within a religious tradition can appreciate the depth of feeling, the nuances of symbolic language, and the complex interplay of emotions evoked by great—or even ordinary—religious moments. But only those who have to some degree stepped outside tradition's embrace can distinguish between dogmatic truth-claims and actual phenomenological descriptions of the inner experiences lying at religion's core, those that James had categorized in such impressive ways.

Beginning with the universal human sense of wonder, Zeitlin seeks out a delicate path between the evocative and the analytic in order to find a language with which to approach the inward heart of religious faith. Not surprisingly, he develops the analogy to love, a human state universally accepted as real and yet eluding full description, precisely because its most delicate self will disappear before the cold eyes of "scientific" analysis.

Wonder gives way to astonishment, and astonishment to sacred awe. Here Zeitlin stands silenced, confronting the ineffability of religion's core. All the while, however, he is developing a set of descriptive tools that leads the reader surprisingly close to his goal. But then Zeitlin steps back, almost fearing that he has trodden where one may not. At this point the essay gives way to quotation from the psalms and prophets, the rabbis and the Hasidic masters.

The goal of this first section of a promised longer work—never completed in this form—is a description of revelation, a phenomenon that Zeitlin insists is universal in human religious life, not the unique property of those formally designated as prophets. Here he stands on familiarly Hasidic ground; one can imagine how overjoyed he must have been to see James confirming so much that to him would translate directly back into the popular mysticism of the Hasidic masters. The list he offers, near the end of the essay, of the multiple forms revelation may take and the ways in which Judaism embraces them only leaves the reader hungry for more.

I have written elsewhere[2] on the unacknowledged influence I believe this essay had on the thought of my own teacher Abraham Joshua Heschel (1907–68). Heschel grew up in Warsaw in the years when Zeitlin's door was open to all comers. Zeitlin, who was in conflict with the dominant Gerer *hasidim* in Warsaw, was apparently more welcome at the table of Heschel's uncle, the Novominsker *rebbe* Alter Yisra'el Perlov. It seems highly likely that they were acquainted, although Heschel has left no published testimony to that effect. The opening section of Heschel's theological magnum opus, *God in Search of Man*, is structured in ways highly suggestive of Zeitlin's *Be-Hevyon ha-Neshamah*.

I. THE NEAR AND FAR

After all the countless books that have been written about religion, the scientific study of religion remains in its infancy. Here and there dawn has begun to break, a few rays of light shining through.

But the cloud is still very heavy. Who can penetrate it? Who can roll away the curtain?

The lovers of religion are many, but who can save us from such lovers? Just as "desire has no eyes," so too does love not allow one to see clearly. The pious enthusiast lacks the ability to judge religion scientifically, just as the lover cannot give an objective report of his beloved. Passionate and stormy feelings may breed life and light but not clear perception and objective evaluation.

Religion's detractors are beyond counting. But just as love keeps one from judging, so too does hate. The enemy of religion is even less qualified to testify regarding religion than is its lover. The "science" of religion was created mainly by religion's detractors. But can one who detests ever be objective?

Then there are many who are neither hot nor cold about religion, the indifferent. They neither love nor hate religion; they look upon it as a part of the human drama. They might analyze religion the way a pathologist dissects a dead body. Of course they find nothing. For two obvious reasons, these cannot construct a science of religion. First, they seek nothing in religion. If you don't seek, you cannot find. Second, they lack the essential sensibilities without which it is impossible to approach anything within religion.

These may be good, upstanding people. They may even possess profound intellect and great knowledge. But their absolute indifference bears witness that with regard to religion they are like eunuchs. They can no more pronounce regarding religion than the blind person can attest to color. How can someone who has never seen a new moon attest that the new moon has arrived?[3]

They will say that these "colors" are a matter of imagination. Your religious "moon"—who indeed has seen it? It was seen by people of feeble mind, and they indeed were mentally damaged by it.

Let's assume for a minute that this is the case. The question still stands: How can people who have no approach to matters of the imagination issue judgments about them? If all those who witnessed the religious "new moon" are among those who "gazed and were damaged,"[4] how can one accept the testimony of those who neither gazed nor suffered harm?

Further, let us say that the imagination has some role in religious truths. These truths should then at least be considered creative works.

But how can such world-scale creations be understood or felt by one who has no inclination toward them, one who understands them neither with heart nor mind? Can a person with no poetic sense understand Homer, Aeschylus, Sophocles, Dante, Shakespeare, or Goethe? If a person lacking in poetic sensibility cannot understand poetry, how can one without religious sensibility understand faith?

But this has further implications still. No one can attest to the health or sickness of those who create religion, of the great religious geniuses. In the eyes of ordinary people, any genius may be considered a madman. Most people consider religious geniuses to be mad. The latter judgment is of no more value than the first. Compared to those who stand above humanity, all of us are mere "ordinary people."

A profound student of this discipline, William James, thinks differently. If this "sickness" is the constant companion of religious revelations, the sickness may be considered good. There are certain distinctive mental states that accompany various forms of revelation. A sense of healthiness goes along with ordinary manifestations of life, while those of a certain religious sort are characterized by "sickness." These states are necessary conditions, primal requirements of revelation. They ["health" and "sickness"] neither conflict with each other nor enter into each other's realms. What might be considered a stain or disfigurement to one is not that for the other. A stormy spirit, spiritual leaps and skips, emotional extremes, exaggerated passion, intense concentration, waking dreams, visions and apparitions, shining reflections and others that do not shine, the exultation of the morning stars and the cries of angels, the exuberance of divine joyous love, the dance of the righteous, trembling that makes one's hair stand on end—all of these would be considered not only useless, but indeed harmful, in the life of a person of science. But for those who seek to stand in intimate relationship with God, to reveal cosmic truth, to see the new light, bringing blessing to humanity and crowning it with a new revelation, they are not just useful, but vital. Mohammad acted like a madman. Didn't Socrates also have within him just a drop of that divine madness? Remember his *daemon*. Remember all the "strange" states into which all the greater teachers of humanity have entered. Remember what Lambroso[5] told you in his *Genius and Madness*.

Just as madness does not cancel out genius, so do these strange states, in which the creators of religions found themselves, not negate their creations. Even more: these wondrous states, where the flame that came out of nowhere and burned on its own, where awe suddenly enveloped them from an unknown source, or where the spirit attacked them and grabbed them by the scruff of their necks, where they heard the melodies of the gods, exulted in heavenly joy, or where they suffered the woe of the great depths—all these testify that they are not of this place, that their dwelling is not among creatures of flesh.

So the question still stands. Who, then, can construct a science of religion? Lovers and haters are both to be counted out. The indifferent do not know right from left in these matters. Who can bring in this heavenly crop? Only certain choice persons are qualified to testify concerning religion. They are those in whom the flame once burned but has now cooled down, those left with "a whispering coal still aglow beneath the heap of ashes." They know how faith is born and have experienced its birth pangs on their own flesh. At the same time, they are far enough from the flame to have gained some perspective. Thus they are able at once to serve as witnesses and judges, subjects of judgment and arbitrators, bearers of both subjective and objective truth. There is enough love in their heart for the king's daughter that they once saw promenading by each day, and with whom they were directly in touch. But now they see her from afar and are able to attest to her beauty. Moreover, they are well aware of that distance. They bow before her in the beauty of holiness, and they are taken aback.

But think carefully. I am not talking about those who "studied and turned aside." They are illegitimate as witnesses. The ancients correctly said: "one who studied and turned aside is harsher than anyone."[6] Such people obviously no longer have anything to do with religion. They are either detractors who may not testify or else are so indifferent that their testimony is worthless. Then whom am I talking about? Those who left religion for this very purpose, to be able to stand at some distance in order to be critical and to see it objectively. These hold toward religion "an outward critique and an inward love" (Prov 27:5). They may be distanced from religion but are still bound to it by a thousand cords. They may view the truth embedded within their hearts as something alien to them, but in the end this truth is theirs. To separate from it would be like separating from life itself.

The religious process within these people is like the cosmic process described by German metaphysicians. The "I" (Fichte) or the "cosmic mind" (Hegel) or the "unconscious" (Hartmann) wants to see or know itself. It therefore creates objects, and in this process of graduated viewing of an objective realm it returns to itself, bit by bit, in a more clarified and conscious way. Something like this takes place in the soul-process of those I have described, who are at once both near and far. They view religious truth as though it were something external to them, something that does not touch them. They gaze at it and study its principles and foundations; they can determine what is essential to its very being and what of falsehood and ugliness has become attached to it. Through this pure gaze, direct contemplation, and tough-minded critique, maintained constantly and over a long period of time, they return to their own selves, purified and uplifted.

One more important point: There are currently many among the "enlightened" who are as far from religion as east is from west, but who nevertheless maintain in their hearts some sentimental piety or romantic view of religion. They may honor or glorify "tradition" or hold on to it because of its relationship to nationalism, or because they see religion as a creation of their people. All of these do indeed bear a certain affection for religion. But they cannot be the ones who create a science of religion or who attest to its nature. The only ones who really stand in contact with religion are those who value religious truth in its own terms, who recognize it for what it is, without needing external support, not that of romanticism, nationalism, or any other. Religion's gates are open to all, but its true face is seen only by a chosen few. Religion is the seal of the blessed Holy One, whose seal is said to be truth. It is the holy of holies, not needing to stand as a serving vessel for any other thing held holy. One who treats religion as such a serving vessel diminishes its holiness, darkens its glow, demeans it by alien worship. This poor person may speak of religion without realizing that it has escaped and slipped away from him.

This too: There are many among us who imagine that they used to be religious enthusiasts or great believers. After study and investigation, inspired by science and freedom of thought, they lost their faith. But is this really the case? It seems to me that many of these are mistaken. They imagine that they've lost something very precious, when it's really nothing at all. These people had simply believed in what others had told them. Then they stopped believing. So what? Only someone who really *has* something can lose it. One who has nothing—what can he lose? How can these people have lost a faith that they never really acquired?

Even if there was a time when such people prayed regularly, fasted, and fulfilled the commandments, does this suffice for us to say that they lost some precious treasure? The "faithful enthusiasts" that these people think they used to be really means only that they were attentive pupils. It does not mean they had really acquired faith as a property of their souls. That which the soul acquires is essential to it, something to which the soul is so attached that the two become one. Such a property is very hard to lose through "study and investigation" or because of "science and freedom of thought." If such a loss does take place—and it can happen—then the person himself becomes lost as well. Such a one goes "down to the pit in agony," wailing and causing heaven and earth to wail with him. In any case, he doesn't talk about his "loss" with the ease and coquettishness with which our "enlightened" speak when they talk of the "innocent faith" of their childhood, their "pure tears," and their "loss of faith."

I say that these people, with all the "innocent faith" of their childhood, never had religious experience and are thus not qualified to attest to religion. I claim that these are worse regarding religion than those who had never believed at all. The latter sometimes "know that they do not know." They realize that they have no idea of what faith is. Sometimes they are brazen enough to say: "If we don't know what it is, it must be nothing—emptiness, lies, vanity, a passing breath." But at other times they say to themselves: "There is indeed a God, but One we do not know." They come into the temple of faith like a stranger entering the holy of holies, knowing that he is indeed a stranger in such a place.

But those who think they "lost" their faith, taking pride and glory in that, think of faith in vulgar ways. They assume that they know what faith is, when in fact they have no idea at all. The "faith" that such people once had is really no faith at all, just an ear open to tradition, submission to the will of others, a faith in human stories, customs, and habitual religious practice.

This is why the science of religion has hardly come to be. There is "philosophy of religion," indeed multiple "philosophies of religion." There are various metaphysics of religion. Thousands of books have been written about religion "in a scientific spirit." But one thing is missing from them all—true science. Only one proper attempt has been made in this field. That is William James's wondrous book *The Varieties of Religious Experience.* James is almost the only person who has found the scientific key to unlock religion's gates. He has revealed a great deal to us.

Nonetheless, the eternal gates still stand closed and locked before us. The gates that James opened are those to the outer chambers. The inner chambers he did not see. Who will open up those inner chambers for us?

I stand shaken and awed before the great work achieved by this cold and moderate man of science. But I still remain thirsty. Who will give me to drink from the well of the One?

James has indeed shown me many varieties, exposed me to many gods.

But it is the One that I seek. I whose ancestors stood before Mount Sinai. I, one of the offspring of Abraham, Isaac, and Jacob.

My ancestors, when they leapt into the flames or stretched out their necks to be slaughtered, called out only: "Hear, O Israel, Y-H-W-H our God, Y-H-W-H is One!"

It is to Him that I cry out in times of trouble and distress. I call to Him: "Help me! Support me! Answer me!" He is my banner and my refuge, my rock and my stronghold, my saving joy and my desire. It is for Him that my soul longs; He is the One in whom I hope. He and none other. There is naught beside Him.

From the depth of my pit, the chasm of my sins, from the lowest point of the netherworld, from amid the confounding powers of evil, the hearts turned to stone, from the defiled souls, out of all the world's harshness, cruelty, and wickedness, only to Him do I flee for help.

When I behold the daughter of Jacob as a lamb amid the many wolves, there is only one Shepherd to whom I cry out. How will James's gods save me? They are as many as there are visions, beheld by varying people in so many different times and situations! These many are all foreign to me. How will they save me when I seek the One who is so close to me? Yes, I too have seen "multiple visions." But "He is One amid all the images."[7] What will *The Varieties of Religious Experience* teach me, if it does not attest to the singularity of the One?

I need light. I desire *to understand and to recognize* the religious. The "light" of theology and that of metaphysics have not shown me my God. *The Varieties of Religious Experience* has shown me Divinity. But still, who can construct a *science* regarding the *One*?

I am not able to build a house for my God. My sins are many and powerful. An iron partition separates me from my Father in Heaven. My hopes are pinned on one who will still come and build that house....

I think of myself regarding religion—though my sins keep me far from the light of God's face—as one of those near/far people. If I do not have the strength to build the house, let me at least help by offering a few stones for its construction. Here and there I have gathered stones—some whole, some still incomplete, large and small. I bring them here as a gift to the great builder who is yet to come.

II. WONDER IN THE HEART

I was very happy to find the following fine, profound passage in Berdyczewski:[8]

Heart and brain, mind and emotion, attractions and sensations—do these make up the person? Does humanity consist of these? Do these also comprise the spirit?[9] What is "spirit"? What is the heart and the godly within the heart? What are mind, consciousness, contemplation, and attention? What are the names that humans give to all these, to themselves, and to all we see around us? What are the sensations of self and spirit? What is that thought or poetic impulse that leads to such arousal and longing, calling forth all the person's spiritual qualities? What is spirit in relation to flesh? Soul in relation to body?

All these questions and all that derive from them are held together by a single thread, linked to a single source—the heart and all the wonder that lies within it. All these radiate and flow forth from there. Wonder is the source of countless views and teachings, both obvious and hidden, regarding both person and society. It is wonder—the wonder of man and of his life—that animates all of these. It is not "fear and trembling," nor is it "the desire to live" or to improve life's conditions.

It is the heart's expansiveness[10] that gives life to our inner selves and strengthens our sense of belonging to the world around us. It is she that sings, that thinks, that sets out forms, and that blows the great storm wind that challenges us and sets our course.[11]

But the question still stands: Where does that eternal wonder come from, that sense of wonder within the heart? Of what does it consist? What is its true nature?

I seek to understand that "wonder" or sense of wonderment in Berdyczewski's teaching. I see him thinking quite simply that it is the human *mind* that stands as the source of all the world's great ideas. Indeed, he says there: "Man creates the objects of thought, the concepts, and the desire to know them all out of his mind."

But then the question returns. What is spirit? What is "the heart and all the godly within it"? Whence does *godliness* occur to the human mind, a mind we generally see as bound to earth and earthly things, as though created merely to "work the earth and to guard it" (Gen 2:15)?

Sometimes Berdyczewski himself is aware of this and says that "wonder within the heart" derives "from the human spirit." "Spirit" is a much broader concept than "mind." But I still stand and wonder. What is the source of this spirit? And where does it seek to lead?

If we come to *describe* reality, we will say: "No one rules over the spirit or can hold it back" (Eccl 5:8) or "The wind will blow wherever it desires. You will hear its voice but will not know whence it comes or where it is going" (John 3:5).[12] But if we seek to *understand* it, we cannot be satisfied with such a description. We need to answer the questions: Whence? and Where to? They can tell us a thousand times that "the wind will blow wherever it desires." But does that satisfy us? All we get is one puzzlement in place of another, one *ignoramibus* for a second.

Sometimes Berdyczewski turns poetic: "The sea will freeze over, mountains will be leveled, heaven's face torn open and earth will be swallowed up. God will give wings to the *tsaddikim* and they will fly in the sea of Nothingness. But the human spirit is not erased. 'Nothingness' itself is his creation, a concept of the mind. All who enter the realm of the spirit are nourished by the fruits [of human creativity]. They eat but are not sated. Even he [who creates them] eats of his own fruits and remains unsated. The human soul is not slaked. Wonder does not cease from the heart."

Or elsewhere:

I hid my face in the ground and cried out: "Eternal God! How many myriads of worlds and manifestations have You created! All this for Your glory! Your throne is beyond recounting! Yet for man, the creation of Your own hand, there is no home, no dwelling for him within these endless chamber, no simple four ells in which he can find rest...."

Then I heard from behind me the angel of His presence saying: "O human! It is *you* who created all these; all the palaces are *your* gift to God."

But if it is *truth* we seek, how will all these pretty words save us? "The human being created all the divine palaces." But the human himself—who created him?

The Torah says: "God created man in His image." From Voltaire onward, people began reversing the text: "Man created God in *his* image." They think this solves the riddle of religion. Not quite. Not only the biblical verse requires interpretation; so too does the scripture of Voltaire. "Man created God in his image." Which man? Which God? If the Voltairian scripture refers to the gods man created in the course of his long struggle for existence—gods who do good and ill, who punish and reward, gods of anger and vengeance who fight with one another until the strongest wins, gods who desire and take gifts from people, who seduce and are seduced, who love smooth talk, listen to gossip, get people into conflicts with one another, following the principle of "divide and conquer," gods who envy human success, who eat and drink like humans, even if consuming the bread of heaven and drinking ancient wine, gods who love, like humans, wine, women, and song, who derive pleasure and are assuaged by all these, gods including the goodly and softhearted who cannot bear human tears, but also the hardhearted who laugh at human suffering and who only after extreme self-mortification, when the human is crushed like a worm before them, when he is reduced to nothing, will let him go—if it is of these gods we speak, surely they are indeed human creations, fruits of man's spirit. Even the one God, insofar as He embodies all these qualities, is just the fruit of human imagination. But who aroused man to create a God "Whom the very heavens cannot contain" (1 Kgs 8:27), or the One Who "if man is righteous, what will He give him, or what will He take from his hand?" One before Whom all who dwell on earth are considered as naught? One before Whom countless millions of spiritual realms, each higher than the next, are still seen as nothing? One Whose very most sublime Crown, "even though it is pure, rarified light, is considered darkness before Him"? One before Whom all the endless worlds, all light and goodness, all the shining glow, all their wealth and happiness, all that fills them and hovers above them, is just a single ray of the light coming off His cloak? One that "thought cannot grasp at all," One Who has neither likeness nor depiction, One Who can never be described, elevated and abstract, distanced in countless and ways not only from human thought but from the human spirit? One for Whom even the most refined thought is considered like worldly deed, Who sees all the endless worlds as just a flash and is not captured by them at all, since "He grasps all the worlds but they do not grasp Him"—who aroused man to envision a God like this, if not the spirit of God that lies within man?

Indeed man sees that light, but it does not derive from his own nature, but rather from a hidden source. It is because God's light shines in us that we have a longing and desire for transcendent mystery. Without that light we would create all sorts of worldly culture, but would never seek the "hidden wellspring."

Goethe was right in saying that were the human soul not sun-like, it would not rejoice and exult so greatly in encountering the sun's rays. So too are we justified in saying that were the soul not godly, it would not rejoice and exult so much, it would not press to break right out of its sheathing whenever one begins to talk with it about a secret light, hidden behind endless veils.

Rather–

"For with You is the source of light; in Your light we see light" (Ps 36:10). Because the sublime source flows within us, because the supreme light shines within us, we see light.

When Berdyczewski speaks of the "wonder in the heart" on its own terms, he draws near to the path of faith. But he is greatly mistaken when he identifies "wonder" with "expansiveness." These are really two entirely different phenomena.

Berdyczewski thinks that just as wonder gave birth to inquiry, so too did it bring forth religion. But it was not wonder that gave birth to religion, but *astonishment.*

III. ASTONISHMENT

The difference between wonder and astonishment? Wonder asks all sorts of questions. Astonishment asks nothing. It is like "the one who does not know how to ask."[13] It stands confounded, amazed, blown away, transported. Wonder indeed gave birth to inquiry and all its branches—philosophy and science. Astonishment births religion and its sisters—poetry and music.

The astonished one sees the world and "it is chaos and confusion." As RaSHI says, "he stands confounded, astonished by the confusion within it."[14] The visionary is "astounded by the vision (Dan 8:27)." There is no question here, no inquiry or investigation. There is only being taken aback, accompanied by a great desire to penetrate and go forward, awe and love, joy within trembling.

"I was astonished for a time" (Dan 4:16). You ask something of the sage, but he does not know how to answer. He knows there is an answer to that question, but he's lost it for the moment. He stands confounded and astonished until the answer comes to him, as though from the highest places.

131

I stood "astonished among them" (Ezek 3:15). Sometimes a person sees much activity and endless people, all of who seem strange to him, to the point of great astonishment.

A great man from among our brethren[15] said it well: "They always talk about the natural evolution of the world. But it is worth stepping out of conventional science, if just for a moment, to recall that it would be perfectly *natural* for the world not to exist, neither it nor its evolution."

Really, what is this great clamor that presses upon us in each moment? Why is it there? What goal does it serve? Who or what has need for the eternal shedding of blood that we call "life"? Who or what needs that empty space we call "world"?

If world and life seem "natural" to us, if we invent thousands of philosophical and scientific ways to solve the riddle of the world's existence, it is only because we belong to this world and are unable to turn our minds away from it, even for an instant. We may know how tough and bitter this world can be, but most of us cannot stand outside it, even momentarily....

We look for answers to the eternal questions. Sometimes we try to break the challenge down by means of sharp reasoning; at others we have a go at it more gently. At times we may admit this, saying: "It could be resolved, but only with difficulty" or "This requires much further investigation." But when a person stops seeking *solutions* to these eternal questions, saying: "This world is an extreme wonder in my eyes," he understands that he is seeking *a new way* to solve the cosmic riddle. Such a one bears within him the seeds of a new philosophy (or a very ancient one in new form). But that person draws near to the way of faith only when he feels with his whole being that *the world is strange to him, in an awesome and confounding way. This brings about ceaseless suffering and the grinding of teeth, but yet it draws and fascinates him—because of the sublimity that lies within it.*

Philosophy and science, by their very nature, serve to *justify that which exists.* Once they justified God; today they justify nature, reality, the world. The only difference between Leibniz and contemporary philosophers is that Leibniz was an advocate for the divine will, while today's thinkers advocate for a blind force or a combination of blind forces. Even those who call themselves pessimists find some meaning or value in the world and in life. Even after all the fierce curses they hurl at the cosmos and at life itself, even after all their sky-splitting cries, their earthshaking heresies, they wind up finding in the world some sort of path toward an idea they can embrace, and the world becomes legitimate again. It is a world "understood," "clarified," or "natural...."

In the end both Schopenhauer and Hartmann find a positive way to justify existence. They too support a "natural evolution." According to Schopenhauer, life negates itself by way of natural evolution. The desire to live weakens and diminishes as recognition of life's vanity increases. But a "natural evolution" in itself is justified; life could not negate itself without that "natural evolution." And since in the end, after that long "evolution," life—the source of evil, as he sees it—is negated and condemned, everything does reach its proper state.

For Hartmann, the unconscious finally becomes aware of itself by way of natural evolution. As it does, recognizing all the evil and pain within existence, it returns to nothingness. Thus the process of "natural evolution" and its value are made obvious. Evolution expands evil, but it also expands consciousness of evil, leading to the negation of existence. So in Hartmann too, all winds up as it should be, reaching a proper end.

True, both Schopenhauer and Hartmann seek not the world's existence but its destruction. They see life not in positive terms but as negative. But since the negation they so desire takes place within the world, since "natural evolution" brings about what these pessimists want, the world that contains it has some meaning. Without this evolutionary process, the desire to live would stand forever, the unconscious would remain blind in its attachment to existence for countless generations....

And the one who deepened pessimism—Friedrich Nietzsche—doesn't he too justify this natural evolution, as well as life and world themselves? He sings love songs to "reality," to life, to the source of life, to life's power and eternity. He believes in the "eternal return" and loves it passionately. All the greatness of his super-man lies in his ability to say "Yes!" He knows all about evil and suffering, the vile and the ugly that reach from one end of the world to the other. He *feels the pain of the entire world within himself*, since he stands at its center as the true content and meaning of all life's existence. Yet he says: "Nevertheless! Whatever there is, needs to be." He loves it all because he "loves the *eternal*."

And we—what should we say after them? If *philosophy* can go either way, and if *poetry* too can serve to justify the world, what about the truth? All these justifications of existence are just made up, phony things that people say so as not to face the open pit that lies before them or to chase away both desolation and boredom....

When we see the world unvarnished, not prettied up in any way, it is all simply horrid. With regard to pain, truth lies with Tasso[16]—"a thousand pleasures are not worth a single pain." With regard to value, Karamazov is right—"all the harmony and perfection in the world are not worth a single child's tear."

A world without God is simply a monster. In each moment lights are extinguished, stars fall, great powers turn to naught. Violence, pillage, tearing limb from limb! Doves in the claws of the hawk! Blood, blood, blood! Pain, pain, pain! Cries pierce the wind, tears and wailing! Still worse are the muffled tears; shame, insult, powerlessness. Babes torn away from their mothers' breast, destroyed without any reason. Cruelty and oppression, slavery and degradation. Leaden skies and steely earth; hearts of stone. Alienation, bereavement, loneliness. Cries that aren't answered; weeping that goes unheard. Or no cries, no weeping, but standing frozen in pain. Endless creatures fluttering between life and death. Sword, sword, sword! The war of all against all, the stronger devouring the weak until they too are consumed. Endless hunger; thirst that is never quenched. Those who dare to rise up fall and are trampled like worms. A moment's light against eternal darkness, a moment's goodness amid eternal evil, a moment's joy before eternal pain, a moment's beauty faces eternal ugliness, a moment's purity versus eternal degradation! False justice and iniquity, down through all generations! Rack and ruin, murder and criminality, chaos, contagion and plague, foolish wickedness and evil of every sort. Who could ever add up or give an accounting of all the wickedness, vanity, and ugliness in this world, the one in which everyone is so anxious to see "beauty," "goodness," and "harmony."

Rabbi Hayyim Vital says in his *Sefer ha-Gilgulim (Book of Reincarnations)* that there are souls reincarnated in water, the mill-wheel passing over them in each moment, hacking them to bits, reattaching them, and beating them with torments unto death and the sufferings of hell. Their suffering is beyond measure and beyond telling. "If people knew about this suffering they would weep constantly...."

Where shall we flee from this terrifying world? Suicides flee from this world. But where do they flee *to?* Back to the world. They die for the sake of their very longing for life, their very love of the world. Schopenhauer already took note of this. They do not deny the world they so detest; they in fact affirm it. They despair of life because they did not succeed in *living* as they had wanted....

But that is not the main point. The point is that suicide is no solution, not even an awful one, to the pain and evil of life in the world. Suppose for a moment that everyone listened to this wise counsel, that everyone decided at some particular time to put an end to life by committing suicide. So on one dark day all of humanity dies off. Will this bring redemption to the world? Will evil cease from the world, evil that lies *within the very nature of existence?*

Won't the evolutionary process bring forth another "humanity"? And if not, won't some perhaps even more unfortunate creature emerge? Even if we imagine—and this is completely impossible—that the evolutionary process would cease its creating, and that after all humans put an end to their lives there would rise neither a new humanity nor anything like it, would this negate the evil in the world? Do evil and suffering befall only humans? Isn't the whole world soaked in blood? Isn't the pain of all endless living things, strangled, ripped apart, and violated by all those stronger than them, and they in turn by those yet stronger—is that all nothing? Are the faults of nature—famine, drought, and frost, floods and fire, earthquakes and tremors—so small?

So if in our egotistical fancy we really desire to leave the evil and pain, the ugliness and filth of the world behind us, where shall we flee? Where shall we turn? Where can we go? Primitive man already felt all the horrors and monstrosities of this world. Even before knowing what "world" and "human" meant, he felt with all his senses that something terrible had taken place and was being woven around him, that he had to find succor from someone who stood *outside* the world.

This is not only the most ingenious idea, but also the most ingenious *feeling* that humans have had. I cannot deny that the external side of religion was created by humans' desire for the help of the gods in that struggle against nature. But the inward part of religion— and from its very birth religion had an inner core: love came along with fear, awe before majesty along with fear of punishment—came about because man felt with his full self the need to flee from this world, that there is an existence beyond that in which our lives are lived. It is to that existence that we need to turn in our travail, one that is holy and pure, the soul of our soul, which is goodness and right.

Of course, man did not have a clear sense of this when religion was born. That is why "extraneous fears [punishment, death]" are commingled with the sense of inner awe. That is why we had all sorts of "alien worship," not yet knowing the One. Nonetheless, some faint and hidden feeling was present. The outward side of religion was created by human egotism and the goal of finding favor in the eyes of powerful gods, to keep them from causing harm and getting them to do good. Theology emerged from the eternal question: "Who created these?" "How can there be a castle without an owner?" "Have you ever seen a world without order?" But the inward part of religion—or, to speak more honestly, its very innermost core—has its source in the feeling of cosmic terror and alarm. It is a cry to the world's Father, in that stately phrase—"Out of the depths I call unto You!" (Ps 130:1).

IV. THE FOUNDATIONS OF ASTONISHMENT

Every feeling is simple at first glance, but becomes complex, composed of many sources, once it is examined and analyzed. The feeling of love seems simple enough. But after examination and analysis we see how very complicated and complex it is, how very many sources the wise of all generations have found for love. Look at all the many faces of love that novelists have revealed. Yet many still stand in wonder, asking: "What is love?"

Still further, when we analyze love down to its roots, taking just one of those roots and contemplating it, we discover that it too is hardly simple at all, that it too contains multiple elements, each of which can be broken down into still others, and so on *ad infinitum*.

We cannot always discover the roots of our feelings. Sometimes we can find but a few, but that does not prove that the feeling itself is simple. It rather shows how limited our knowledge is. Surely those who come after us will reveal more such elements, which will be broken down into further components, and so forth.

Not only is every feeling attributable to varied *elements*, but each also has its own varied *moments*. The elements may be found by analyzing the feeling and breaking it into its constituent parts. But the varied moments can be seen only when we examine it from a *historical* perspective.

Let me explain: A man loves a woman. This feeling contains many varied elements: sexual desire, a longing to reproduce, a sense of beauty, jealousy, conquest, the "will to power," the desire to possess, intimacy of soul, fear of aloneness, the love of company, an image of the pleasure he will derive from his children, sometimes a sense of pity for this woman, a feeling that when strong enough can turn into love, sometimes even cruelty and harshness (especially in perverse loves), sometimes the desire to be caused suffering by that woman (masochism), as well as various other elements that this is not the place to list. Isn't it easy to understand that each of these love-elements and others like them is not simple at all, but is derived from various other factors?

Each of those is present in the feeling of love at every moment. Yet when we come to analyze the elements themselves, we have gotten nowhere in understanding how love develops. Love contains not only these elements but all of love's varied moments as well: the cloudy moment, a deep fog, a vague feeling, suffering and hidden desire, a certain secret fear and secret hope, heaviness and lightness together, joy mixed with woe or woe mixed with joy—all these are not yet love, but from within their fog a future love can be discerned. Then there is the moment when love first blossoms. Those buds are delicate and soft; if touched by a vulgar hand they will wither. Next comes the moment when love grows, revealing its first fruits. It continues to bear fruit, and then comes to burn with passion. This is the moment described by Shakespeare:

> Why then, O brawling love! O loving hate!
> O, any thing, of nothing first created.
> O heavy lightness! O serious vanity!
> Misshapen chaos of well-seeming forms,
> Feather of lead, bright smoke, cold fire, sick health,

Still-waking sleep, that is not what it is!
This love feel I, that feel no love in this.[17]

There are various other moments in love's path to fulfillment (this is not the place to list them) and transitions from each to the next. In each moment not all of the elements are equally active, one more, others less. Or we might say that one element dominates and becomes obvious, while others remain more quiescent and hidden. Sometimes it is male jealousy that leaps forth, or the desire for power, or compassion, the desire for spiritual or physical intimacy, and so forth, all in accord with the moments of love, the person's temperament, and qualities of spirit.

The moment of astonishment we are considering, especially in its most elevated and mysterious sense, also contains various elements that are composed of many others, perhaps reaching into infinity. But let us try to analyze astonishment by its elements and its moments. Surely we will not complete this task, describing precisely all that goes into this wondrous feeling. I only want to begin to clarify it, offering some necessary and helpful notes, leaving it to others to go into greater breadth and depth.

Astonishment contains these elements: simple wonder (What is this? Where does it come from? Where is it going? Lots more questions like these). Astonishment is not contained within wonder, but wonder is contained within astonishment as its most simple and obvious component. Beyond wonder, astonishment also includes a certain sudden bewilderment and a sort of great trembling. The bewilderment passes, but the trembling remains. Anything whose origins we don't understand causes us to tremble. We tremble lest some danger emerge from that source, but we also tremble without any particular reason. In the great cosmic religious astonishment, bewilderment and the ensuing tremor are magnified thousandfold. This trembling itself contains many elements, some of them contradictory: fear of the abyss, of emptiness, of destruction, fear of pain and suffering, but also awe before glory, before that which is most exalted, and beyond all these, fear and awe without any reason at all. Beyond wonder, bewilderment, and trembling, with all their various constituent elements, astonishment also contains a sense of self-negation and submission before that strange and wondrous thing

138

that so causes us to tremble and also bears such awesome beauty. Religious astonishment also includes a powerful love and an attraction to that awesome thing. Every abyss, just as much as it pushes away and bewilders, also fascinates and attracts. The great cosmic religious abyss, even more than it bewilders and terrifies, draws one to it by the power of its wondrous rays of light, peering right through that abyss.

Anyone who has tasted of this astonishment in the course of his life, even if just rarely, knows all this from his own experience. There may be lots more elements in this that I don't know how to name or that have escaped me for the moment.

But for those who have never tasted a feeling like this in their lifetimes, I need to bring the testimony of those in whom this feeling beats the loudest. I think that in fact *anyone* is a legitimate witness in these matters, since we are not at present trying to learn any faith or opinion, but only to get a description of the various feelings they have had and that we of little faith have not.

But some may remain stubborn enough to say: "Since I don't recognize the nature of these feelings in themselves, how will I know if the description is accurate or not?" To them I reply thus. If different people, living in varied eras and differing circumstances, report certain feelings, all of them offering similar signs and descriptions of those feelings, it becomes necessary to accept both those experiences and descriptions as part of reality. In general, we are not able to experience everything that has been and will be done in our world. For countless thousands of matters we rely upon the testimony and experiences of others. Why should experiences of the soul be treated as having any less validity than those of the body? If we are willing to accept the witness of one who has tasted a certain food and tells us about it, even though that food has never passed our lips, why should we not accept testimony regarding a feeling we have never had?

Even further: In the end we all, even the most stubborn among us, believe a man who tells us that he loves a certain woman, even if we are too young to have experienced love or so old that we've lost that feeling. We believe someone who comes and tells us about feelings of terrible hatred, even if we can't understand how anyone can hate so fiercely. We understand what a certain murderer or rapist must have felt, even though such feelings are complete alien and despicable to us. Then why are we so stubborn as to disbelieve one who speaks of exalted and profound feelings, especially when they are described with such clarity and precision?

Of Abraham it says: "He took him outside and said: 'Look toward heaven and count the stars, if you are able.' And He said to him: 'Thus will be your seed.'…The sun was about to set and a great trance fell over Abram. Terror and great darkness fell upon him.…The sun set and it turned pitch dark. There was a smoking furnace and a flaming torch that passed between those [sacrificial] pieces" (Gen 15:5–17).

When Esau came in to Isaac after Jacob had taken his blessings and said "I am Esau your firstborn," scripture says: "Isaac trembled, a very great trembling" (Gen 27:31).

Even if we pay no attention to the Kabbalists who say that Isaac is the incarnation of divine fear, even if we ignore the Midrash that says Isaac "saw hell open beneath him,"[18] the plain meaning of the text arouses thoughts in us. Why and over what did Isaac tremble so? His beloved son Esau has come in to him. Why should he suddenly tremble? Not just "tremble," but "a very great trembling." What was the nature of that tremor?

Great trembling always befalls a person who encounters some wondrous, secret, mysterious thing. Isaac had intended the blessings for Esau. But when he saw that they had been given to another, he felt the hand of God moving all as it desired. He saw the divine counsel negating the many thoughts of man. He saw the power of judgment; he saw the gods of judgment speaking to him, and he was taken by storm.

Eliphaz the Temanite describes his own religious trembling this way:

"Now a word came to me secretly and my ear caught a whisper of it. In reflecting on visions of the night, when deep sleep falls upon people, fear called to me and trembling; then all my bones were made afraid. A spirit passed before me and seared the hair on my flesh. It stood still, yet I could not discern its appearance, though its image was before my eyes. I heard stillness and voice, saying: 'Will man be more righteous than God? A human more pure than his Maker?' He puts no trust in His own servants; He attributes folly even to His angels. How much more those who dwell in houses of clay, rooted in the dust, crushed like a moth! Between morning and evening they are shattered; they perish forever without notice" (Job 4:12–20).

There is a feeling of secret astonishment, described here by Eliphaz through the following signs: a fear not of this world, one that comes upon him suddenly and for no apparent reason. This is a fear that man's power is too small to contain. A voice comes out of silence, a voice from across the abyss, the emptiness, the naught.[19] A wondrous light, awesome and holy, revealed from behind the cosmic lattice. Complete negation and absolute submission before that voice, before the sublime purity next to which even heaven's angels are not pure, and surely not we who "dwell in houses of clay."

When Elihu describes all the powers of nature, all its beauty and sublimity, he says: "For this my heart trembled and was moved from its place" (Job 37:1).

How confounding these words must be to the eyes of one to whom this mysterious astonishment remains alien. But how profound and beautiful they are to one who has attempted to look into nature, not as a scientist, not even as a poet or an artist, not even as a religious person who knows only to exalt and praise the wisdom within nature—but as one who stands *beyond* the world and whose glance surveys and penetrates all that takes place within it.

Isaiah thus describes the feeling of astonishment that attacks every human being when the glory of God is revealed:

> For Y-H-W-H of Hosts has a day set out against all the proud and exalted, when all the lofty will be brought low….Then all man's haughtiness will be humbled and exalted persons brought low; Y-H-W-H alone will be raised high on that day….Idols will pass away entirely. People will enter caves in the rock and holes in the sand before the presence of Y-H-W-H and His majestic glory as He rises to dominate the earth. On that day men shall cast aside the idols of gold and silver that they have made to worship, leaving them to foxes and bats. They shall enter clefts in the rock and crevices in the cliffs because of the fear of Y-H-W-H and His majestic glory, when He rises to

dominate the earth. Turn aside from man, who has breath in his nostrils, for what is he worth? (Isa 2:12–22)

Whoever thinks the prophet here is talking about fear of punishment, or divine jealousy or vengeance, is seriously mistaken. Whoever is used to thinking that way needs to stop for a moment and contemplate the phrase "The fear of Y-H-W-H and His majestic glory." There is no anger or wrath here, no sending forth of harmful angels, but the awesome glory of majesty. The loftiness before which all people are brought low, the astonishment of mortals who see the King in His splendor, totally negates all sorts of lies that human tell themselves and one another, including all the cuteness and playfulness with which these lies are adorned. All of these pass away as the light of truth is revealed, a truth not of this world.

We find it said even more strongly by another prophet: "They will fear Y-H-W-H and His goodness at the end of days" (Hos 3:5). What Isaiah left hidden is now expressed simply and clearly by another prophet. It is not punishment that will awaken fear, but goodness. If in the Isaiah prophecy it might be possible to think mistakenly that we are only dealing with ordinary human fear, fear of punishment by a vengeful God, Hosea's prophecy leaves no room for such error. People will see God's goodness at the end of days; it is as they approach that goodness they will fear and quake. It is that goodness that fills us with awesome trembling in the same measure as it fills us with endless joy.

Habakkuk, too, envisioned the "deed of God," and his soul was wrapped about him: "I am awed, O Y-H-W-H, by Your deeds. Renew them in these years! Make them known in these years! In anger, recall compassion!" (3:2–3). When he spoke of all the good God had done for His people and all the good He was yet to do at the end of days, as he saw his people redeemed from a hand mightier than their own, as he saw the sea's roaring waves about to scatter us and the word of God quieting the sea, as he was filled with praise and thanksgiving before God, in that very moment his first and most essential feeling was: "Y-H-W-H I have heard tell of You and I fear!" (3:2).

Daniel saw in his night vision: "Behold there came with the clouds of heaven one like a son of man. He came to the Ancient of Days and was brought near before Him. He was given dominion, glory, and kingdom that all peoples, nations, and tongues might serve him. His rule is an eternal rule that shall not pass away; his kingdom shall not be destroyed" (7:13–14). Here was the good that Daniel had been awaiting; it was the world's redemption and eternal salvation that was revealed to him in this vision. He saw truth seated on the throne and all nations and tongues bowing down before its glory. Yet still—or better, because of this—he describes his mood thus: "I Daniel, my spirit was pained within my body and the visions in my head bewildered me" (vs. 15). Pay attention to "within my body"—the body is only a container for the spirit. When the spirit sees the mysterious, it becomes bewildered and astonished. It seeks to break forth from the physical in order to cleave to that mystery.

But this feeling has not been granted only to prophets and visionaries. Sometimes ordinary people experience it. Even more, great sinners sometimes feel it when they suddenly encounter the God of truth. Daniel tells us about ordinary people: "I Daniel alone beheld the vision. The people who were with me did not see the vision, but a great trembling fell over them and they ran and hid" (10:7). Of a situation like this our ancient sages well said: "Even though they didn't see it, their stars saw it."[20] In our conceptual language this is a great fear that strikes people suddenly, without any apparent reason, a hidden feeling that a living, exalted, awesome, and holy presence dwells in our midst, even though we cannot name it, and neither our minds nor our emotions have any grasp of it.

Of the greatest sinner among the ancients, Nebuchadnezzar, it is told that once he came to recognize that "[God's] rule is everlasting and His kingdom unto all generations. All who dwell on earth are considered as naught; He does as is His will among the host of heaven. Of those who dwell on earth there is none who can stay His hand and say: 'What have You done?'" (Dan 4:31–32).

Beyond these more or less clear and detailed descriptions, scripture contains many more hints at experiences like these. Jacob, for example, dreams "and behold, a ladder planted in the ground, but its top reached heaven....And Y-H-W-H stood above it" to guard him in all his ways, promising to give the Land of Canaan to him and his offspring and to be with him and return him to his land and birthplace. When he awoke, "he was afraid and said: 'This can be none other than the House of God, the gateway to heaven'" (Gen

28:12–17). One might expect that such a vision would arouse only joy in the heart of Jacob, yet it awakened great fear.

Once we recognize the nature of this mysterious astonishment, we are no longer surprised that these positive promises arouse awe or fear. "Jacob was greatly afraid" (Gen 32:8) when he saw his brother Esau coming toward him, accompanied by four hundred men. This despite the fact of having been promised, "I will be with you and guard you wherever you go." Jacob had just encountered (32:2) "a camp of God." We do not need the explanation [that Jacob feared Esau] "because of what sin might cause."[21] Even with no sin or guilt, the person of heart is astonished and dumbfounded when seeing the divine hand.

When Manoah saw the angel, his first natural, instinctive feeling was, "We will surely die, for we have seen God" (Judg 13:22). This was also Gideon's bewilderment at first. Isaiah, who became used to visions and apparitions, was "like a town-dweller who saw the king."[22] Yet his own instinctive and natural feeling was, "Woe is me, for I am silenced, for I am a man of unclean lips, dwelling within an unclean people, and my eyes have beheld the King, YHVH of hosts" (6:5).

In the Psalms we find various references to a uniquely profound and mysterious astonishment. For the sake of brevity, I will recall only this awesome passage:

> Knowledge is too wondrous for me,
>> high above—I cannot attain it.
> Where can I go from Your spirit,
>> and where from before You flee?
> If I soar to the heavens, You are there,
>> if I bed down in Sheol—there You are.
> If I take wing with the dawn,
>> if I dwell at the ends of the sea,
> There too, Your hand leads me,
>> and Your right hand seizes me.
> Should I say: "Yes, darkness will swathe me,
>> and the night will be light for me,"
> Darkness itself will not darken for You,
>> and the night will light up like the day,
> the dark and the light will be one. (Ps 139:6–12)[23]

The *hasidim* say that by the melody put to these words you can tell whether a person is a *hasid* or a *mitnagged* [lit. "an opponent," an anti-Hasidic rabbinic Jew]. The *mitnagged*, when he chants, "Where can I go from Your spirit, and where from before You flee?" sounds as though he is saying "I *would like to* flee from You, O Lord, I would like to hide from Your presence....How frightening You are, how much ill You bring about! I would even run down a rodent's hole in order to be hidden from You....But where can I run?...There is no escape or hiding from You....I would hide myself in death's shadow....I would do all sorts of things in order not to see You, to avoid You....But what can I do if You are so full of eyes?"

The *hasid* says the very same words in an entirely different tune: "Do I *have to* hide from You? Do I need to be sad, to melt away in fear? Wherever I turn, You are there....I meet You every-where....Wherever I am, Your shining countenance brings me joy...." Even in the depths of hell it is possible to come close to God.[24]..."Why should I fear evil when You are with me? Whom do I have in heaven or in hell, at the eastern dawn or at the sea's far end? All is one to me. My God is with me in darkness as in light. My Life, my Soul, my only One, my Love!"

This reading is very nice and deep when taken in its own right. But with regard to the verses themselves, one would have to say that there is something right in the *mitnagged*'s way of chanting them. Or perhaps more accurately, the verses contain *both* of these melodies and indeed rise far, far beyond them. In the poet's wonder it is possible to see at once both the fear of hell and the joy of paradise.

I have quoted the testimony of ancient prophets and biblical authors and not that of the many who have been "born again" or "repented." Similarly, I have avoided the many *confessions* that James included in his work. Even though the witness of these "human documents" is closer to us in time and spirit, in addition to being more specific, I see in these writings more of personal astonishment and fear than I do of the mystical astonishment that includes true fear of God. Even where I find the latter, it seems as naught when compared to the vast amount of personal and worldly concerns. The dream includes vanity; the spiritual grain is lost amid the vast corporeal chaff.

Only a few statements among these "confessions" are truly dear to me:

"As each year rolls by, I constantly ask myself: 'Why not put an end to your life, either by hanging or by some poison pill?' When I am filled with all those thoughts and life experiences, my heart is tormented by a feeling of great pain. I can't give that feeling any name other than 'quest for God.' I declare that this 'quest' is a feeling, not a thought. It doesn't come about as a result of any intellectual process. Just the opposite—it is born of the heart. It is a feeling of fear, of loss, loneliness, strangeness to all, and yet hoping in someone" (Tolstoy).

"All that my eyes see weighs me down as with a heavy burden. Cursed is the earth for me! All the trees, plants, rocks, hills, valleys are in my eyes draped in mourning, oppressed and moaning under the curse. Everything around me seems to have conspired to destroy me.... My heart is strong in recognizing that all is vanity and empty breath, that there is nothing in the world, not even the world itself, that can bring me contentment. That much was clear to me" (Allain[25]).

"My fear was so great"—writes another—"that if I did not sometimes lean on phrases like 'In God I trust' or 'Come unto me, you who struggle and are burdened' or 'I am the resurrection and the life,' I would surely go out of my mind.

"From then onward [from the time he felt the fear of God in its full power], so great a trembling has taken hold of me that for a certain few days I felt not only that my body was trembling and sweating, but my spirit as well. The sense of divine curse hovered over everything, hell's own sin filled me with the shakes from head to toe. Trembling grabbed hold of me. I cried out with a roar from the heart. I wanted only to remove this heavy burden from upon me—but in vain" (Bunyan[26]).

All these words are *close* to that sense of true mysterious astonishment. But examples of that secret astonishment about which I have no doubt I can only find among a few of the truly pious. Take note! It is not the thoughts of the latter that concern me here, not their investigations, their inquiries, or their demands. I seek only their *testimony*, their descriptions of this hidden, deep, yet natural feeling.

Here is my thinking: It is possible to challenge any sort of piety or devotion in the world. You can deny any of their inquiries and all sorts of their "musts." But it is impossible to cast doubt on the *witness* of certain devoted and pious people. You can't deny that these people have felt an otherworldly awe, a fear of God that cannot be contained, that they have seen *beyond* the border, that they have *touched* God.

The simplicity, clarity, and innocence with which these people's holy feelings are described bear witness to their truth, naturalness, and absolute value. Since they all have the same object, described with so much reality, those feelings have not only a psychological, but a great cosmological worth.…

This is how Maimonides communicates to us the essence of his inner feeling of divinity:

> It is written, "'You shall love Y-H-W-H your God' as well as 'You shall fear Y-H-W-H your God.'" What is the path to loving and fearing God? When a person contemplates the blessed Holy One's great and wondrous deeds, endless and beyond measure, he will praise and exalt God, desiring greatly to know the glorious and awesome Name. Thus did David say: "My soul thirsts for the living God!" (Ps 42:3). One who contemplates these things in themselves is taken aback in fear and awe, being a very lowly and small creature, one of small mind before the One of perfect knowing. David further said: "When I see Your heavens, the work of Your hands…What is man, that You are mindful of him?" (Ps 8:4–5)[27]

The reader should pay attention to the way Maimonides lays this forth, to the simplicity and honesty with which he shows how two opposing forces—love and fear—become a single unity. The very same contemplation that brings Maimonides to praise and gratitude, to "great desire," brings about also great fear and trembling, authentic submission, absolute self-negation.

"Someone asked Nahmanides: 'What is true worship of God?' He replied: 'That which brings you to exultation and joy along with terror.'"[28]

147

"The essence of fear and worship of God is as in 'As they grew higher, they grew more fearsome' (Ezek 1:18). The higher a person's rung is, the closer that person is to God, the more he sees God's greatness, the greater is the fear of heaven."[29]

"Awe follows love. The love of God leads one to constantly contemplate His greatness as Creator. This brings one to awe."[30]

True awe is when dread and trembling fall upon a person because of a fear coming from he knows not where. The mind is clarified and tears begin to flow on their own. Without this, even though he may think of himself as loving God, it is really nothing."[31]

And further:

"There are some who pray in sadness, being overcome by melancholy. They think they are praying with awe. Others are convinced they are praying out of love, when they are simply oversupplied with erotic energy.[32] When it is true love of God, and a sense of shame falls over one, alongside a desire to glorify God and all the rest, then it is good. A person is not called a servant of God unless he serves in both awe and love. But this means that the awe must fall over him, not that he arouse himself to it.

"The glory of God is in everything, since God and His glory are One. God's glory and divine Self therefore inhabit everything. A parable: a king of flesh and blood disguises himself in varied garments, going out anonymously among his troops. He does this in order to see and hear what is in their mouths. The clever among them, those who know the king's way, are in awe of him under these circumstances. Though different in a thousand ways, so too the blessed Holy One, high and exalted, hides Himself in many sorts of garb. 'That which He wears in morning He does not wear in evening.' He goes out among His troops and sees and hears all."[33]

"'In the place of joy there should be trembling.' When your mind contemplates the greatness of our blessed Creator, how all the worlds, all the angels, all the palaces declare His glory, how all are filled with dread and trembling— then God lights up your mind and sends this thought to you. You should be filled with joy that you are serving the true God. But this same contemplation should bring you also to trembling. Whom am I serving? Before Whom do I speak? In Whose presence am I seated? Then you will pray with dread, awe, and shame. Even when God is good to you, you should think: 'This great King has taken notice of me and done me these kindnesses.' Then too you will be covered with trembling and great shame. When you become accustomed to this quality, you will attach yourself humbly to the Nothing. Then you will indeed become a dwelling for the most exalted and radiant worlds."[34]

There are two types of fear [of God], as is known: the higher and the lower. The lower is a fear of sin. This is not fear of punishment. That belongs only to people of lesser character; it is not even considered "fear of sin." Fear of sin is of a somewhat higher order. You are afraid of sinning because it is against God's will and you do not want to be cut off or separated from God. You desire only to come close to His presence. This fear, therefore, derives from your contemplating and gazing at God, the way He is the essence and root of all the worlds, both surrounding and filling them all. All worlds, souls, angels, seraphim, and holy beings are as naught before Him. Their existence derives only from the light and life-force that flows into them from their Creator in every instant. From this sort of contemplation you branch off to consider your own lowly state, taking account of how far you remain from God. This leads you to become absolutely despised in your own sight, leading you to a sense of awesome dread, so as not to transgress God's will. All of this is the lower fear, the "fear of sin." But the higher fear reaches beyond this rung. It is being completely obliterated before the exaltedness and majesty. It comes about through contemplating the Creator's own Self, how He is an endless and absolutely simple Oneness, something no mind can grasp, far, far beyond the emanated worlds. There is nothing to which God may be compared! By gazing deeply into this reality in the most subtle way, you may come to be totally negated and not feel your own existence at all. In such a moment it is no longer relevant to say that you "consider your lowly state," because you are completely wiped out, totally lacking in self-awareness."[35]

"The inward fear is a fear mixed with shame, just as you would have in the presence of the greatest person, the most truly righteous one in his generation. This shame is brought about by being in the presence of his inner qualities, not the externals. This is a sublime awe, a contrition before the endless light that is garbed within divine wisdom, the potential source of all existence. Before it, all is considered as naught. But through this self-negation, 'wisdom gives life to those who master it' (Eccl 7:12)....

"But the truly essential awe comes upon one from beyond, awakened from above. A dread fear of God falls upon your heart, in each person to the extent that you can bear, based on your soul's root, the way divine presence has come to be concentrated in it—just enough so that you will not be completely effaced. The quality of this awe that comes from above is much greater than that which you arouse by the efforts of your own soul. It is even greater than the love of God you arouse within yourself by contemplating God's greatness. The difference between them is like that between light and true darkness.

"Once you attain that rung of the awe sent from above, deriving from *malkhut* in the World of Emanation, then you will surely rise up to attain the Great Love, also coming from above."[36]

"The righteous liken the light of God's presence that is over their heads to a light that spreads all around them. They dwell within the light. This causes them to tremble naturally. But they rejoice in that trembling."[37]

One who deeply contemplates these words that we have brought will discern in them various stages, elements, and moments.

The most elementary feeling of true religious astonishment is: "The people saw and were moved; they stood afar off" (Exod 20:16). Or "Can there be familiarity with regard to heaven?"[38]

A more complex feeling can be discerned in Rabbi Eleazar, who cried when he saw the verse: "His brothers could not respond to him, because they were terrified of him" (Gen 45:3). "If the reproof of flesh and blood causes all this," he said, "how much more the reproof of heaven!"[39] Here we have a combination of awe, shame, and the call of conscience.

Still more complex is that awe discussed by Maimonides, where the most exalted awe is joined to great love, submission, and self-negation—all in one.

Beyond that still is the supreme awe described by the *hasidim*, combining love, fear, shame, submission, and total loss of self.

Still higher is the "awe that comes from above," falling upon the self as one already stands beyond ordinary existence, but whose spirit returns to him as it "flows back and forth" (Ezek 1:14).[40]

V. REVELATION

When a person calls upon God "out of the depths," from the depths of soul and spirit, out of profoundest despair, from amid the great and awesome astonishment that comes when we confront emptiness and mortality, some sort of divine revelation takes place....These revelations vary according to the profundity of the call, the measure of astonishment, the rung and purity of the person's spirit. But there is also a degree of grace that flows into the person in such a moment, as he finds favor in God's eyes, as he is crowned by the divine will.

People always think that "revelation" is the lot of just a few exemplary individuals within the humanity species, "prophets," the most highly elevated among human beings. This error, shared by almost all superficial believers, is rooted in a misunderstanding of revelation's true nature. It is almost as dangerous to faith as is its enemy, denial. It leads people to distance God from humanity, and hence also humanity from God.

Once you think that only two or three blessed people among humans have seen the sublime Face and all others dwell in darkness, you will finally come to that evil, dangerous, and poisonous thought that destroys all good intentions: "Y-H-W-H has abandoned the earth" (Ezek 8:12).

True, people still claim to believe and maintain some vague sense that there is a seeing eye, a hearing ear, and that human deeds are all recorded. They seem to have faith in something called providence, saying, for example, that "no one bangs his finger below unless it had been decreed above."[41] But such images tend to hover over the heart without really penetrating into it in a way that would make people really *live* by them.

Most believers seem to depict providence the way Andreyev[42] describes that "someone" in his vision of "Man." Somewhere out there, way far, far off, beyond the bounds of any worlds we might conceive, there is a certain Someone who gazes out and sees every human deed, writing them all down and keeping the account. Andreyev depicts that One as dwelling in the shadows, ashes over His eyes, and writing with absolute equanimity: "A person was born"; "A person died." In the eyes of the faithful, that Someone rules over humans, conceiving them, birthing them, sustaining them, causing them suffering, bringing them death. That One demands certain acts of people and writes down everything they do. But in the end that Someone, in whom all these superficial believers have faith, does not speak to humans, does not express His spirit to them. Neither does He address our ear nor come into any other sort of direct contact with us. Yes, there have been people, and there may yet be two or three in a generation who experience that too. But for the rest of us, that Someone is just an accountant who can never be escaped.

In the end people tire of that eternal spy, even though He may be clean-handed and pure, above all bribery. People are frightened of Him and taken aback; they flee from wherever it is He dwells. Sometimes a person says: "I won't come out right in this judgment anyway, so what am I struggling for?…Whatever will be, will be.…I just can't live in constant fear and trembling.…'If I am lost, so I am' (Esth 4:16). I will certainly never succeed in pleasing this One who is following me around.…What do I need this for?…Let a person go enjoy himself in this world!"

Job raises a point something like this: "If I am condemned, why should I labor in vain? Even if I wash my hands in snow-water and cleanse my palms with lye, still You will cast me in a ditch and make my own robes detest me" (9:29–30).

Nietzsche expressed the same argument in a more modern and charming way: "A little girl once objected: 'Does God see all? Really *all*? Isn't that rather immodest?'"

True faith, that rooted not in habitual behavior nor simply received by inheritance, not constructed out of theological investigations, but based on true, personal, original inner experience, the faith of heart's thirst and soul's fire, has as its object no such perpetual "Spy," just observing and judging. Happily, it is rather a faith in the Source of life, the very Life of life itself, but One who stands in direct relationship and inner contact with those who truly call. This God not only hears and sees what we do, but also the words we speak and the whispers of our hearts, along with that which is hidden most deeply within our souls. This One speaks His word to man, guiding, advising, and leading us to walk in the paths of righteousness, sheltering us in the shadow of His wings, carrying us like the nurse carries his infants, the infant knowing well who carries him.

This is a mutual, shared relationship, that of parent and child, one of empathy, of hearing outcry, of rushing to the aid of those held close. And those close ones are not just prophets, visionaries, and "righteous;" but *everyone* who calls to God out of the depths. Even one who is called a sinner among men may be good and precious in the eyes of God.

Even more: There are those who are truly wicked, yet for some reason unknown to us, understood only by the Knower of Secrets. God nevertheless sends them His blessing and shines His face upon them. God may address such a person, calling him to conscience, reaching out to him in the language of love: "My child! Why have you strayed so far from Me?"

But the one who is closest to God is the very one who seems most distant: the one despised by people, the rejected, the tortured, the persecuted. It is these who are considered nothing, the lowliest, filled with shame, those who are so low in their own eyes as well as the eyes of others that they dare not even ask for anything, let alone make demands. These knock on the eternal doors like the truly poor, or else don't even knock at all, but stand shamed and embarrassed before the holy glory of all that is. It is to such as these that the Master of All sometimes reveals Himself in all His majestic glory.

As a general rule, divinity touches the deepest and truest pain in all of its manifestations. *Shekhinah* spreads Her wings over the most awful and repulsive wounds. She is revealed when we admit our sins or inadequacies, when we cry out in bitter humility at how far we are from God's shining face. When we feel the terrible bitterness, when the soul flickers in silent despair, saying: "It's all over," She is there. At that moment our final accounting of our lives comes up with a "zero" and our heart is ripped to shreds. Then the voice of pain rises up from earth saying: "Please, O God, save me!"

Shekhinah then addresses us in every term of endearment, far beyond that which even the most loving and compassionate mother could express. She consoles us in ways that are beyond the human heart's capacity to absorb. We can only intuit their goodness. She comes bearing the fruit of the holy field of apple trees, carrying the dew that God uses to resurrect the dead, healing herbs from the

Garden of Eden. These she waves over our wounds. Then a wind comes forth from the treasury of winds, a glory that enwraps the soul, bearing whispers from the highest, highest worlds, ever so distant, obscure, esoteric hints, bound up by a thousand seals, and yet in content so close to our innermost hearts. These speak to our souls that are pouring forth, our impassioned spirits, our wordless and inexpressible longings, the very life of our lives and the essence of our souls.

Among plants She is the lily; among birds, the dove. Within Her palace She is the sacred Mother; to us humans She is glory, compassion, and succor from the highest heavens. She aids and protects Her offspring, calling out: "Let the arrow enter Me, but not harm My children!" She comes before the King of Glory and He reaches out to Her with His golden scepter as She pleads for Her children, Her people, those born of Her. Then the King of Glory rises from the Throne of Judgment and is seated on the Mercy-Throne. He abounds in forgiving transgressions and pardoning sinners. His blessing flows forth to every living creature, a kiss from Lover to beloved, the bread of heaven to all those who hunger, holy water for the thirsty, rays of light for those who dwell in darkness; good news for the downtrodden, eternal joy for those who have been mourning forever.

Then we hear "the sound of Y-H-W-H in strength, the sound of Y-H-W-H in glory" (Ps 29:4). Or maybe either "the sound of a great noise" (Ezek 3:12) or "the small sound of stillness" (1 Kgs 19:12)—all in accord with what we are prepared to hear, our own inner character, our desires, the rung of our spirit. Our eye may then behold "a crackling fire" (Ezek 1:4), or "a font of living water flowing forth from the Temple" (cf. Joel 4:18). There may appear "a youth" or "the Ancient of Days, His head white as snow" (cf. Dan 7:9). It may be a "chariot" or "seraphim, living beings, and holy wheels," angels standing within the King's palace or angels holding up myrtle branches within the deep.

What can a person *not* see or hear in such a moment? Eye and ear might behold the sound of many waters, the music of the spheres, the song of the angels, angels immersing themselves in the River of Fire, treasuries of storm, snow, and dew, holy lights, heavens, and palaces, all without limit and without end.

Look! Look! Listen! Listen!

See even that which has no color, no form, reaching beyond anything mind could conceive. See? But then the drop is reabsorbed into the sea, the ray taken back into the brilliant sunlight, the person—annihilated, no longer there.

But if he still lives to tell what his eyes saw and his ears heard, his mind reaching the greatest inner depths—all this would only reinforce all the visions and apparitions that come like a flash, are there and not there, touch and do not touch. The sages already said: "If your heart races, stand back," for that is the place of wonder, of the hidden.

But who knows? Who has been there? The highest, fiftieth measure of wisdom was not revealed even to Moses, even to that uppermost awareness, awareness from within.[43] More precisely, it *was* revealed to him, but as wonder, as beyond knowing, "hidden of all hiddens." "His angels ask one another: 'Where is the place of His glory?' in order to praise Him." "*Moses himself does not know where he is buried.*"[44]

The various appearances and revelations that happen to everybody at certain times are beyond categorization or definition. They just can't be placed within borders, about which you say: "These are exactly what they are, and here are the signs by which to know them. These are the authentic revelations; 'see them and pronounce them holy.'" But to the degree that it is possible to find some sense of order among these things, this is how it seems to me:

1. The voice of God within nature, in the world, in life, wisdom, strength, glory, and beauty; in all that is elevated, in the grace with which creatures are endowed; in the ball of the sun, searing in the sky, and in the most frail of flowers.

2. Symbols. All that happens in the world, everything that takes place in the course of life, all events, deeds, motions, activities, all the coincidences among events and things, our desires, longings, goals, and intentions, our thoughts and visions—all of these hint at some sublime wisdom. They are all "the fallen fruit of Wisdom above." All point toward upper realms, toward God, standing as recombined letters [jumbling but also pointing to the secret] word of God.

3. God sends particular hints to the individual. From these we can learn to set our path, to guard our steps, to walk in the desired way. We can awaken the good, lifting it high above the world, higher than the sky, beyond all the din and clamor of the cosmos, beyond the vain struggle and useless existence of all those who are sunk into worldly things.

4. Dreams, visions of the night. When the soul is deeply at rest and the senses are in a trance, a person enters most deeply into his inward true nature. Then the outer limits of physical existence are set aside and the images the soul has absorbed from the outer world have become nebulous. Sometimes they even pass away altogether, making room for more spiritual and sublime forms. Then one's essential mind is on its own; there is no place for clear consciousness of the external world. Life in this state still bears within it desire and passion, longing and craving, pain, suffering, and joy. But the subjective "I," the "I" of consciousness, the "I" who sees things as they are, the "I" who is trapped in the external realities, all things so clearly defined, has sort of gone into hiding and become inactive. If and when the person, while awake, has been sunk in coarseness and materialism, in sensual pleasure and external thoughts, or in dreams, he enters a *sub*conscious universe, a realm that lies beneath that of clear awareness, reason, and strict accounting, a world that may be rich in apparitions and visions, but one that remains lowly and vulgar, dark and ugly. But if and when the person while awake is engaged in spiritual pursuits of a pure and holy sort, then in dreaming, if only occasionally, he can live in a realm that is *supra*conscious, higher than the conscious mind, one touching upon the godly. Even if you don't see angels going up and down the ladder, you will at least have some sort of sublime and elevated vision. Those holy forms will cause divine thoughts to flow into you from above. Their imprint will remain with you in your waking state as well.

5. The voice of conscience and thoughts of return. There is no day on which the soul does not speak. There is no day in which regret does not enter a person's heart. Even for one who has no such intent, in every hour a thought of return or repen-

tance passes through the heart, even if just as the merest flutter. Perhaps it even goes unfelt, lying upon the heart but not penetrating within.

Where do all these come from? They are fallen, broken letters of pure divine speech, echoes of that faint voice that cries out each day: "Return, O backsliding children!" It is the echo of the soul, herself a princess who cannot bear all the muck of daily living, the echo of a voice that cuts through all the worlds: "Return, O humans!"

We seek out social or "human" sources for the voice of conscience and these pangs of repentance. But why are they so *constantly* present? Whence all this awesome persistence of the desire to return, even in spite of a person's rational will? What is the source of that relentless voice calling "Come back! Come back!"

We try to silence that voice. We scream at it. We try to be "liberated" from it by new and fresh transgressions. We turn our minds away from it, pretending not to hear. Meanwhile we sink ourselves deeper into the abominations of life in order not to hear that voice. But it doesn't stop pursuing us, trying to lead us to our rest. What is it?

More. Let us put aside conscience and the pangs of repentance. Whence the great *fear* that falls over a person about to sin? Whence this feeling that someone is watching his improper deeds? Yes, we do get over this "fantasy" and go on to sin. But in the end, what is this great fear? Is it not the love of God? If a person has ears, can't he hear, above the bubbling heat of transgression: "Stop, My son. Don't do that!"

6. Desolation of the soul and cosmic longings. Where do all these longings come from that tear the heart into so many shreds? Whence all the inner stirring that allows no silence, day or night? Whence the great thirst that a soulful person feels, a *cosmic* thirst that consumes all of a person's moisture, a thirst that all the world's treasures and pleasures, all of its goodness and beauty, could not even begin to quench? What finally stirs the human heart? What is it that we are aiming for? What is our longing? What do we really seek? And what is it that brings about our great sadness, giving birth to a

melancholy that no joy can chase away? Or, even more precisely, one that bursts forth and breaks out of its bounds *especially* at the time of our greatest joy?

In general, what is the source of our restless spirit, our inner wandering, our constant bouncing back and forth? Why can't we rejoice in our labors, be satisfied with our lot? Why does all the space in the world not seem enough to us? Why is it that "no person dies having satisfied even half of his desires"?[45]

We are all so used to this panorama that we have come to consider it natural. But if we should ask ourselves: *Why* is your soul never sated? *Why* are you never filled up? *Why* do you never know rest? What is it that steals our rest? Everything that surrounds us and passes before us has ends and limits. Why are we possessed with aspirations for the endless?

If you should say that the universe itself is without end or limit, I would ask where you got such an idea. Everything that surrounds us and is known by our mind or senses is in fact quite finite. There is no certain proof of infinity in the world. Then where does it come from, this notion we have that the world is endless? Not from experience or thought, but from our own *longings* for eternity, from our desire to see the world go on forever. And what is the source of those longings?

Further, if you pay close attention to the nature of those longings, looking deeply into the most hidden passions of your soul, you will come to know that we are longing not for what is here, but for what is not here. The object of our longings is something we cannot name, something we can't even talk about. Sometimes we make the mistake of thinking that it is for some external object that we yearn. But once we get that object and our longing should be fulfilled, we understand that it was not that which we wanted, but rather something else. We get the other thing too, yet our yearning does not go away. We grapple our way forward through endless passions and desires, yet our thirst is not slaked in the slightest. We wind up saying that it is not something finite that we truly desire, something defined and bounded in its nature, having both beginning and end, but something that has neither, and that keeps pulling us beyond all boundaries, beyond the limits of the human, the natural, and the self-centered, beyond "existence" itself and all that can be grasped....

7. The inner voice. There are people who constantly hear an inner voice within their hearts. "Do this and not that." This is not the call of moral imperative, but rather an inner voice that guides all of one's actions. It is likely that every person contains such a voice, silenced by the loud din of living and our preoccupation of the senses. This inner voice always sounds as though it were coming from without, either demonstrably commanding or berating the person in a way a mother might berate her child. Or it might have the sound of a great sage giving advice to someone weak and stumbling.

A person goes along his way, wanting to do a certain something. Then he takes counsel with his inner guide and receives a clear message: "Stop! Don't do it!" Why is this? The inner voice does not offer reasons, nor does it engage in give and take. It speaks its word, does its deed, and is gone.

It is as though saying to the person: "I've done my part. I warned you; I pointed the way you should go. You have the power to listen or not."

For some people that inner voice within their heart is so strong and clear that they do nothing without consulting it. They ask things of it as one would an oracle; they don't make a move without turning to their "essential self" or "upper I." The truth is that as long as these people really listen to that inner voice and follow it in the way they live, happy and blessed is their lot. When they stop listening, they stumble at every step along the way.

All of us know people whose inner voice is more or less highly developed. It is loud and clear in some who have nothing to do with what might be called mysticism. Sometimes it occurs in people who seem most healthy in body, emotions, and senses. These often include some very practical types, quite far from anything to do with religion.

I once had a neighbor—thus recounts Emerson's faithful disciple Train[46]—as practical and down-to-earth a man as ever was, who would not do anything of import until he first turned to his own inner world, listening quietly to all that was going on there, until he heard a clear statement from his "higher self" saying: Do just this and that....

8. A feeling of divine closeness. Generally people of faith imagine themselves standing before a great King. But sometimes a person *knows* the nearness of an unseen and unknown presence in a way that is truly felt. Sometimes this is experienced in a simple way: some unnamed One, some X, hidden and mysterious, is standing next to me, looking at me, seeing all I do, counseling me, teaching me, leading me, guarding me from all harm. "Someone unseen stands between the two of us." This statement from the Gospel of John offers a natural and primitive expression of this feeling. Among great people of faith this feeling is both deepened and sharpened, but its essence remains as we have said. Who is that someone? Some tend to see it as a spirit, an angel, a heavenly emissary, but sometimes also "the blessed Holy One in all His glory." In any case, that someone comes to us from somewhere hidden and mysterious, yet we sense His closeness as we would that of a friend who sits nearby, chatting with us.

There are multiple levels within this feeling of closeness. Some experience that One as drawing near after inward outcry and heartfelt prayer. Some feel it more constantly: when awake, in dreams, when lying down and when rising up, when engaged in earning a livelihood, in the midst of conversation. For others it is only an occasional presence; sometimes so intensely close as to make one's heart pound, at other times not present at all. There are those as well who only rarely feel that wondrous presence, hearing it approach as it draws ever nearer to them.

9. In the events of one's life: poverty, illness, human suffering.

If a person does not hear the first, second, third, or later signs, God addresses him in a judging way. This is what God says to such a person:

"You have not heeded My warnings or reproachments, nor have you responded to My consolations or offers of hope. Now you will hear My voice from the whirlwind....Now I grab you by the scruff of your neck and forcibly take you to places that are higher and more exalted than your ordinary life. Forward! Go forward, whether you want to or not. I am your Father and Ruler. I am the One who has sent you. Now it is up to you to fulfill your mission. 'By My life, if I will not rule over you with a strong arm and anger poured forth' (Ezek 20:33). Do I delight in your poverty and suffering? You are My child! Your suffering is My own. 'I am with you in distress.' Your lack is Mine; your shame is Mine. ['When a person suffers, *shekhinah* calls out: "How light My arm, how light My head!"'[47]] But if your ears are too coarse to have heard My more subtle calls, you'd best hear this loud blasting one—

"Know that a great hand is leading you. If you didn't know it when I caressed your face, know it now as it pushes you hard with an awful force and you feel the pain—

"It is not your cry of pain that I seek, but your knowledge, your profound awareness of your exalted soul and its *true liberation*—"

When "all else fails," says Luther, "then God takes His heavy hammer...."

10. Ascent of the soul. There are endless types and levels within this. The senses cease to operate. Imagination does its part and the mind cleaves to a point above. Imagination and mind together create wondrous spectacles. Within a few minutes a person can attain what one otherwise cannot, even in seventy years. You walk on and on with your imagination; mind grows deeper and holds fast to its spiritual/divine point, until it goes in this vision from world to world, entering chamber after chamber, proceeding from spirit to spirit, finally coming before God, the God of all spirits.

To this point I have spoken about forms of revelation that are almost *common*. Every person, if the light of his mind is not blocked and his heart not completely dulled, can see more or less of them. Beyond these are much higher forms of revelation. By gradation they include (1) voices, a *maggid* [speaking angel], *bat kol* [divine echo], and others like them; (2) the holy spirit, with its various manifestations and properties; and (3) prophecy of various types and manifestations.

Of these last sorts of revelation, their nature, essence, and origins, their signs, their special moments—as well as all I have described above, attested to not only by great religious teachers and poets of faith, but by the witness of thousands of people who lived in various times and epochs—more is yet to come.

THE LONGING FOR BEAUTY

Translator's Introduction

Di Benkshaft nokh Sheynhayt is the earliest Zeitlin essay translated in the current volume. It first appeared in 1907 in a literary collection called *Dos Yudishe Folk*. It was then reprinted in his collected Yiddish writings, *Shriftn*, in 1910.

This essay belongs to a group of writings between 1905 and 1910 that represents the great transition in Zeitlin's life, one that can be characterized as taking him both from positivist to mystic and from westernized critic of Jewish tradition to spokesman or apologist for it.

In this case the transition is represented by the voices that appear in the essay itself. He opens with a typical early twentieth-century critique of the Jewish tradition, one that was voiced frequently in the circles around Berdyczewski, where Zeitlin had previously located himself. Judaism's aniconic tradition renders it cold and lifeless, anti-aesthetic and repressive of the creative human spirit. By midpoint in this short text, however, Zeitlin is singing the praises of the Jewish aesthetic imagination, one made richer by its repressed quality, exhibiting an exquisite and highly spiritualized sense of beauty. To this end Zeitlin draws on a vast array of sources: rabbinic, Kabbalistic, and Hasidic, showing an impressive early grasp of a wide range of materials.

In tone the essay has a highly romantic resonance, a quality found in many of Zeitlin's works in that period ("The Thirst" is another prime example) that hover between poetry and prose. This tone was somewhat diminished in his prose writing in the post-1910 period, perhaps being siphoned off into the prayer poems that are translated elsewhere in this volume. By the latest part of his career it had returned, and his "prophetic" writings may be seen as directly continuous in tone to these early essays.

I

"Do not make for yourself any statue or image" (Exod 20:4).

The Jewish people have lived with this prohibition for thousands of years. It has taken root in the people's mind and heart, soul and body. It was held great and holy throughout all ages and generations.

"Make no image!" Jewish religion and philosophy have been imprinted by this thought. Everything had to bear the stamp of incorporeality and formlessness.

"For you did not see any image" (Deut 4:15). The Jew had to remember this whenever considering or imagining the divine. The spiritual had to be kept pure, far from anything to do with body, blood, or flesh. It had to be far from earth, heavenly in the fullest sense. It had to soar to the heights, having no intercourse with anything human.

Human nature struggled mightily against this. The body suffered greatly from such an unearthly Deity. The richly endowed Jewish imagination tried hard to become free of it, fighting a long and vigorous battle. But the incorporeal God was victorious.

The defeated body lay feeble and powerless. Out of fear of anything corporeal, any figure or body, Jewish fantasy trimmed its wings. Abstract intellect ruled over all, and only a pale shadow remained of the all-powerful Creator.

But earth and the body do their part. Fantasy joins with them in the struggle against the enemy. They keep trying to draw pictures, to create bodies.

From time to time they let themselves be heard. Recalling their ancient rule, they rise up to demand their rights. They do so in a low and timid voice, with trembling, but still they say their piece....

The great Maimonides claims that anyone who imagines God in any sort of corporeal manner is a heretic.[48] Along comes Rabbi Abraham ben David and says that it is not so at all, that many great people have seen God as somehow embodied, that "many saintly people" have trodden that path....[49]

Rabbi Moses Taku comes and says that the matter is just opposite from what Maimonides had claimed. Using many biblical and Midrashic quotations, he demonstrates that divinity *must* be represented in a somewhat bodily and sensate manner. The fantasy just has to be holy and uplifting, the senses kept pure and innocent. The godly has to be depicted as something of otherworldly beauty, but not as existing without body or form at all. Nothing lives without body or form.[50]

The Kabbalists did theirs, crying out with a single voice that they did not intend (God forbid!) to depict God as a body. They come forth with a hundred preambles, claiming that with all their verbal pictures they intend only pure abstraction. But at the same time they never cease depicting and representing God in all sorts of images. The preambles stand in place, but their fantasy does as well....

It is, as I have said, a feeble protest against the dominant voice, the general opinion. In hindsight, it was the view of Maimonides that remained dominant. That view lies in deepest agreement with the verses "Do not make any statue" and "You did not see any image."

The struggle continued with regard to inward representations, acts of inner creativity. Here fantasy tried to hold its own; here she tried repeatedly to liberate herself from deadly abstractions. But when it came to outward expression, creative compositions in image and forms, the Jewish imagination never succeeded in liberating itself enough to attain a firm standing. The drawing of gods and goddesses was entirely taboo. Human forms were forbidden altogether, to the point where pictorial art was not able to develop among the Jews. It could not even come to birth....

Traditional Jewish art expressed itself very meagerly in architecture, music, and poetry. But when it came to painting and sculpture, it was able to do nothing at all. Religion stood firmly opposed to it, the concepts of Judaism standing in its way.

But then a wonder suddenly took place. As soon as Jews began to take part in general European culture, Jewish works of art began to appear.

How did this wonder come about? Where did all these world-renowned artists come from? How did a people who had for thousands of years driven away every image and form suddenly start producing Antokolskis?[51]

What sort of place do art and beauty have in the people's soul? In what corner of the collective spirit was it hidden and deeply buried? How did it spring forth so suddenly? How do such miracles take place? How is it all created out of nothing?

European culture and knowledge have certainly made an impression upon Jews. Yet the body and soul of these Jewish artists have remained Jewish. They think as Jews and express themselves as Jewish poets. The Jewish soul hovers over the best of their work.

So the question is asked: Where has all this been until now?

Perhaps this is just a small part of the national treasure. Maybe only a few of the people's rays shine through in the Antokolskis, Israels,[52] and Hirszenbergs.[53] Maybe they hardly know how much one can draw from Judaism.

This phenomenon is clarified by the following thought of Friedrich Nietzsche: All the negative instincts that are unable to find outward expression are turned ever more deeply inward. That which people drive away and hunt down gets pushed deeper and deeper into the soul. That which cannot express itself in creative freedom comes to be buried ever more deeply in a single place.[54]

Images and forms, which Jews always looked upon as something negative, came to be hidden deep within their soul. The Jewish spirit, which could not engage in outward creativity, created within.

Being far from nature and from art, living always in pure abstraction, ever fearing any sort of form or appearance, their inner pictures and forms also should have been pale and feeble. But here the inner needs found their own place, seeking out a different corner.

"Drive nature out the door and it will come back through the windows." Jews drove beauty from themselves, chasing away all sensate images. But "nature" began to address them from another place, in the passionate longing for divine beauty. This longing was so large and intense that it had to express itself in force.

A longing for divine beauty (*tif'eret*), for the longsuffering *shekhinah* and her redemption—all this was permeated with the love of beauty, of harmony, of nature, of the beautiful harmonic form. All of this has broken forth in recent times with terrific power.

And this is only the tip of a deep longing. All these Jewish artists actually know only a bit of the Jewish soul. In the Jewish artists of the future it will surely be even greater and more powerful.

Revealing a bit of this Jewish longing for beauty, showing how it expresses itself in *aggadah*, in Kabbalah, and in Hasidism, is the goal of the following chapters.

II

"How was the light created? God wrapped Himself in a *tallit*, like a prayer-leader, and the world filled up with light."[55]

The dark world became filled with divine light. But that light was too brilliant, it shone too brightly. The world had not yet earned or come to merit so magnificent a light. What did God do? He withdrew the light that had shone in those six days of Creation, hiding it away for the righteous in the world-to-come, for future times, future generations.[56]

"Where did God hide it? In the letters of the Torah."[57]

Learn Torah, in other words. Contemplate it. Enter deeply into it. Read the lines and between the lines. Come to understand its secret senses, its mysteries. Reach toward its inner intentions, its cosmic goals and ideals. Then you will glimpse the hidden light, the light of the future.

But there is another place where that secret future-light is hidden. It is in the open fields, the boundless forests.

If your soul is pure, rise up early, early in the morning. Leave behind the city with its commerce and bustle, its shackles and decay, and go out to the wide-open fields. Look with pure and open eyes at God's free and shining world. There too you will see the secret future-light.

See how God's grace is poured forth over all. Everything is so beautiful and mild, so good and pure. Everything bespeaks profound holiness and eternal goodness, unending happiness and peace. Great secrets; distant, distant worlds of the brilliant future!

See! The city will fall. Everything false, defiled, and impure will vanish. Pettiness, narrowness, and dullness will have no place. All will be free and filled with light, great and holy.

"In the distant future not only will all wars and acts of violence be ended, but also all money, business, and property."[58]

Deep, deep future! All of life will become a brilliant light, an eternal song, an eternal dance of the righteous. God and humans will be one, Creator and creatures joined forever. God will go forth dancing with the righteous in the Garden of Eden, and they will see Him openly....

"Seven categories of the righteous will go forth to greet the *shekhinah*. They will shine like the sun, the moon, the skies, the stars, like bolts of lightning, like roses, like the pure candelabrum of the Temple."[59]

See how the earth dies in winter and is resurrected in the summer! Every blade of grass worships God; each one prays and sings.

Pray, O man! Pray together with those pure and lovely grasses. They love you, they long for you, they seek to pray to God together with you.[60]

Each blade of grass has its own special grace, its own unique beauty, delight, and charm. "When the Prince of the entire world saw all those grasses He called out 'May God's glory be forever; may He rejoice in all His deeds'" (Ps 104:31)![61]

Listen! Everything sings a song to God: the day, the night, the sun, the moon, clouds, lightning, wind, dew, rain and water, rivers and seas, springs, heaven and hell, wilderness, field, and forest, trees and stalks of corn, birds, every tiny creature....

"All the trees speak together; trees speak to people. Listen! Everything speaks. The heavenly spheres are naught but music. You only need the ear to hear.

"The human soul was taken from above. Up there it was used to hearing melodies, songs of the angels, music of the heavenly spheres. When the soul within the body hears a tune, it recalls something of those heavenly melodies and becomes greatly rapturous, raised up to God."[62]

Fresh and pure, endowed with godly joy, was the entire world as it came forth from the Creator's hand. God and world were together in their joy.

"O my world!" God said at that moment. "May you always have the grace that you now have before Me!" Beautiful world! Praised be the One who created it by His word.

"'This is the birth-tale of heaven and earth (Gen 2:4).' Their Creator praises them. Who can shame them? Their Creator holds them high. Who can find evil in them? How lovely, how elevated they are!"[63] Beautiful and holy the world was at the hour of its creation. But still more beautiful and holy will it be in the future that is to come!

When the world was created, the God-King wrote a betrothal document for her. But in the coming future the great wedding itself will take place. At the betrothal the King gave certain gifts. But at the wedding, the entire world will be given.

III

The world was lofty and beautiful. But then humans were created. We brought consciousness, longing, and pain into the world. We were bearers of truth and lies, good and evil, beauty and ugliness, purity and defilement, good and bad deeds, wars, battles, jealousy, hatred, anger, insult, coarseness, wild pleasures, and wild emotions.

As humans went onward, life became ever more fearsome and ugly. The entire world became a battlefield, God's Temple transformed into a giant bloodbath.

Humanity went still farther and, finding fault with the world and its Creator, revealed endless deficiencies and miseries. Not only humanity itself was filled with sin and misery, but the entire world. All is as it must be. Blood must be shed forever. Everything needs to be small and ugly. Such is the world. Such is nature.

The world turned frightful. It came to be split apart and fragmented; all came to be needy, thirsty, sensitive, dark, and small. Often it seems to long for something, to seek help. The world desires to be redeemed, but it is also filled with weakness, brokenness, smallness, and paralysis.

It feels as though things could and should have been different. But there is not yet a strong enough will or sufficient cosmic pain to rip through all the chains and break down all the fences. We break through some chains and we put on others; we tear down a few fences but quickly replace them with more. We are afraid of the free, broad, endless skies, the distant, deep, eternal stars.

True beauty reveals itself only occasionally in human life. It is there when the person jumps out of his own skin, when he becomes heaven and earth, when the person becomes nature itself. This takes place only when we forget all our cleverness, our enlightenment, our inventions, when we set aside our passions and our imaginations. Then we can become wholly overwhelmed by God's awareness, by divine feeling and divine will.

This takes place when the person becomes all, and all becomes him. The person himself becomes the mysterious highest, deepest, purest, and most holy being. One such moment took place at the time Torah was given.

First came thunder and lightning. Crashing sounds and storms; the world was filled up. Everything trembled, fluttered, moved, and was uplifted. Something extraordinary and great was being created. Suddenly everything turned deathly silent and waited. The world was sunk into a single thought.

Soon, soon it will come. Soon, soon it will be revealed. Soon, soon it will appear....

Silent, silent. The birds ceased their singing. The seraphim stopped saying "Holy!" The sea did not make a move. People stopped talking. The whole world was utterly silent and the voice came forth saying: "I am Y-H-W-H your God...."[64]

Hearing God's voice, souls left their bodies behind them. God sent forth the dew with which He will resurrect the dead, and they were revived. Angels carried them on their wings, adorning them with all sorts of jewelry. People became aware of all the heavenly secrets and spoke in the tongue of angels.

IV

That beauty that the whole world possesses collectively, but that appears in all of humanity so very rarely, does indeed manifest itself regularly in a few select persons. Fortunate people! The *shekhinah* rests upon them constantly. Divine beauty accompanies their faces in every moment.

Their beauty is not of this world. Everyone who sees them must fall back in astonishment. Everyone feels this to be something super-human, unanticipated, something without parallel that has never yet occurred.

"Jacob's image is engraved on the divine Throne of Glory."[65]

"Angels ascend to behold the higher image and come down to behold its earthly form."[66]

"When Moses was born the house filled up with light."[67]

Jewish legend recounts four great beauties: Sarah, Rahab, Abigail, and Esther.[68]

Rabbi Bena'ah was out measuring caves. He came to the cave where Adam is buried, and a divine voice called out: "You have thus far seen only the reflection of My image. My image itself you may not see."[69]

"Rav Kahana's beauty reflected some of that of Rav. Rav's beauty reflected that of Rabbi Abahu, and his, that of Jacob our Father. Jacob's beauty reflected that of Adam."[70]

"One who seeks to grasp Rabbi Yohanan's beauty should take a silver goblet fresh from the fire and fill it with red pomegranate seeds. Covering these with a crown of red rose petals, he should place it between light and shadow. The glow will reflect something of Rabbi Yohanan's beauty."[71]

When Rabbi Eliezer took sick, Rabbi Yohanan went to visit him. When he arrived, he found Rabbi Eliezer lying in a dark room. Rabbi Yohanan uncovered his arm and the room turned light. He saw that Rabbi Eliezer was weeping. "Why do you weep?" he asked. "If it is because you have not studied enough Torah, we have already taught 'Whether more or less, it is to be for the sake of heaven.' If it is because you are poor, not everyone gets to have two tables. If because you have no children, look—here is the bone of the tenth son I have lost!" Rabbi Eliezer answered: "I wail for your beauty, which will rot in the earth." Both of them became covered with tears.[72]

When Rabbi Akiva saw Turnusrufus's wife, he turned aside and wept. "Such beauty will decay in the earth!"[73]

Jewish tradition speaks of rare beauty in a great many holy people, miracle workers, messiahs, mystics, and *hasidim*. Especially among the latter has there developed a notion of godly beauty. When they tell tales of greatness, wisdom, and holiness, they also speak of the rare beauty of certain holy ones.

One of the ten *sefirot* of which Kabbalists and *hasidim* often speak is *tif'eret*, which comes to indicate beauty and harmony. Beauty and harmony in all—whether in body, in soul, in mind, in moral qualities, whether in poetics, in thought, in speech, or in conduct. *Tif'eret* must appear in all of them, and through it all must be weighed and measured. Everything needs to be considered in its light.

"A person who is not well dressed slights the quality of *tif'eret*." "When a person dresses up and decks himself out, he should have the intent of blessing God's image."[74]

"The soul moves in every limb and every act a person undertakes. Actions follow the soul; the more beautiful the soul, the more beautiful the deeds. The motions of the great *tsaddikim* are so lovely because their souls are of godly beauty. Every person must have his own motions, lit up by a unique soul."[75]

"When great *tsaddikim* teach or study, Torah shines in their faces. When they mention a particular ancient sage, they place themselves wholly before him, as he is rooted in the divine throne."[76]

"There are three steps that stand before you. First you have to rein in your natural desires. In this way you can attain the quality of the fear [of God]. Then you have to break down and uproot all your inborn bad qualities. This will bring you to a higher rung, that of loving God. But that is not all there is. You have yet to come to a third, far higher step. That is the rung of *tif'eret*. To get there you must see that all your deeds and motions are beautiful and uplifted."[77]

"I used to travel to the Maggid of Miedzyrzec," told Reb Leib Sarah's, "not to hear Torah, but to watch how he put his socks off and on."[78]

"All the meditative unions that the Shpoler Zeyde performed did not reach even a thousandth of that which he did when dancing on the Sabbath and Holy Days. He was as light as a four-year-old child. Whoever saw him dance had to return to God, the heart filled with joy and the eyes with tears."

"Once Reb Shalom[79] was seated at the Shpoler Zeyde's table. Reb Shalom sat in a corner, absorbed in his attachment to God. The Zeyde sat in another corner. When the meal was finished, he called out to Reb Shalom: 'Can you dance?' 'No' was the answer. 'Then watch how the Shpoler Zeyde dances.' The Zeyde raised himself up and danced around the room a couple of times. Reb Shalom was amazed. 'Do you see, really see, how the Zeyde dances?' This happened several times, and the Zeyde did not stop dancing. Reb Shalom said to his people: 'This man's limbs are so holy that he performs divine unions with each step he takes.' The next day Reb Shalom did nothing, but only sat and looked at the elderly Zeyde."[80]

"'His eyes shone like the sun and the moon,' Reb Nahman Bratslaver's disciples told of their master, 'especially on the Sabbath and Holy Days.' Anyone who has not seen his inner fire, his holiness, and his beauty, who has not heard the godly beauty of his melodies, has never experienced goodness. Surely their like will not be seen or heard until the messiah arrives."[81]

"On Friday night," a *tsaddik* told of Reb Moshe-Leib Sassover, "he would put on new morocco-leather shoes and begin to dance. All the greatest matters in the world became manifest in his dancing. Each movement brought forth awesome unifications. The room filled up with light and all the heavenly entourage went dancing together with him."[82]

V

The more strict the ascetic practice, the deeper the hidden suffering within. The deeper the suffering, the greater the longing for beauty.

As intense as this longing may be, the ascetic limitations allow it no way to show itself, to create, to find natural forms of expression. It therefore has to take on peculiar forms, move in crooked ways, speaking always in a secretive manner, doing everything "for the sake of heaven." Both pain and faith must be turned entirely inward.

"'Do not turn after your hearts or your eyes' (Num 15:39). Heart and eyes are two agents of sin."[83]

"A person who interrupts his learning to say: 'Ah, what a lovely tree! What a lovely field!' is deserving of death."[84]

You may not follow your heart or your eyes, not cease learning for even a moment. And yet there are blessings to be recited over these matters....

If you are entranced by the sky's pure beauty, you may express yourself with deep feeling in the blessing "Who does the deed of Creation."[85]

When you see the new moon, your heart filled with both joy and sadness, you may sanctify it in blessing, pouring out your heart to your Creator.[86]

When you behold the whole world order, the cycle of the sun, the moon in all its brilliance, the paths of stars and constellations, you may cry out "Blessed is the One who does Creation's deed."[87]

When you stand in awe before the sea, you can express that feeling in the blessing "the One who made the great sea."[88]

God has to be praised for everything: thunder and lightning, wind and trees, seas, rivers, and wild places.[89]

If you go out in the springtime and see trees blossoming, give words to your joy in "Blessed is the One who left nothing lacking in His world, who brought forth all these lovely beings and beautiful trees for the sake of our delight."[90]

While you are permitted to place no pictures in God's house, you are to beautify God's service in every way you can.

"Herod built his Temple out of variously colored marble. He wanted to cover it with gold, but the sages objected. 'Leave it as it is,' they said, 'because the grain in the marble looks like the waves of the sea.'"[91]

"Why is blue the most beautiful of all colors? Because blue is like the sea, the sea is like the sky, and the sky is like the Throne of Glory."[92]

"Bring beauty to God with a lovely *sukkah*, a beautiful *lulav*, a beautiful *shofar, tsitsit*, a beautiful Torah scroll. The scroll should be written by an artist, using proper pen and ink. It should be covered in a silken garment."[93]

Dress in your best clothing when you come before God in prayer.

"Rabbi Hanina used to say: 'Let us go greet the Sabbath queen, the Sabbath bride.' Rabbi Yannai would dress in his best clothes and say: 'Come, O bride! Come, O bride!'"[94]

The ARI would go to greet the Sabbath queen in an open field. Every Friday evening he and his disciples would go outside the town to greet the Sabbath. Then he would set every soul aright, purify the entire world, and bring the final days closer....[95]

The Ba'al Shem Tov conducted himself in the same manner. He would walk about freely in the fields, surrounded by his disciples, uplifting all souls and bringing all of creation into a higher plane of being.

The BeSHT once traveled to the Land of Israel. When he arrived at Istanbul, he found himself tired and ill from the lengthy journey, one undertaken at great cost and in the face of poverty. Then all his special qualities fell away from him, and he was just a simple, honest, poor Jew. All this took place before Passover, and he did not have the means to celebrate the holiday. He sat and waited for God's grace. God sent an important and wealthy man to him, who invited him for the holiday. The BeSHT went with him, and when he arrived at the man's house he beheld great wealth, a beautifully appointed home filled with vessels of gold. Everything was laid out beautifully for the Passover meal. When he saw this, all his lost qualities were restored to him. The rich man was astonished, seeing this poor beggar he had invited turn into a great man.[96]

Reb Nahman Bratslaver attained all his high rungs through wandering about in fields and forests, praising God together with all of nature, calling out the Psalms from within deep caves, sailing alone in a frail vessel on the great river.[97]

But more than in all of this, we see the longing for beauty in the pain endured by some of the righteous, in their sufferings in the course of the eternal struggle with the "evil urge," in the great sadness of that battle.

"The greater the person, the greater the evil urge."[98]

"In the future, God will bring forth the evil urge and slaughter it before everyone's eyes. To the wicked it will appear as slight as a strand of hair, but to the righteous as large as a mountain. Both will weep, the wicked saying to themselves: 'Such a little thing, and we weren't able to overcome it!' But the righteous will weep for joy, saying: 'How large this is, and yet we have defeated it!'"[99]

Yes, they defeat it, but that victory costs them dearly. If they defeat it entirely, they find themselves longing for it.

A few legends describe for us in brief but powerful words the battle with the "evil urge" and [its link to] the eternal longing for beauty. In just a few lines they draw for us the great tragedies of great human beings. We see before us the fire of suffering and men of iron.

Rabbi Matia ben Heresh spent all his days learning Torah in the House of Study. He was as beautiful as the sun, with a face like that of an angel, because he had never looked upon a woman. One day Satan came by and was jealous of him. "What does Satan say? Will such a man never sin?" Satan came before God and asked: "What sort of man is Rabbi Matia ben Heresh?" "A perfectly righteous one." "Give me permission and I will lead him astray." "Do him no harm, but on that condition, go forth." Satan went and placed himself before Rabbi Matia in the form of a beautiful woman, the likes of whom had not been seen since Na'amah, the sister of Tuval-Cain (through whom even angels sinned, as scripture says: "When the divine beings saw the beauty of human women"—Gen 6:2). Satan stood directly in Rabbi Matia's path. When the rabbi saw the woman, he turned around. The woman again came before him. If he turned to the right, so did she; if he turned left, she was there as well. Wherever he turned, she was right there with him. Rabbi Matia called out: "I fear the evil urge, that he might lead me to sin!" What did that righteous man do? He called to the disciple who served him and said: "Go right now and bring me fire and nails." He brought him burning hot nails, which Rabbi Matia stuck into his own eyes. When Satan saw this he trembled and fell back in awe. God said to the angel Raphael: "Go heal Rabbi Matia ben Heresh." The angel came and stood before the rabbi. "Who are you?" "I am Raphael the angel. God has sent me to heal your eyes." "Leave me be. What is past is past." The angel went back to God and said: "Rabbi Matia says thus-and-so." God told the angel: "Go back to Rabbi Matia and tell him that I Myself take responsibility that the evil urge will never rule over him."[100]

There was once a murderer named Resh Lakish. Once Rabbi Yohanan was bathing in the Jordan. When Resh Lakish saw him, he jumped into the Jordan with him. Rabbi Yohanan said to him: "You should devote that strength to Torah study!" Resh Lakish answered: "With your beauty, you should have been a woman!" R. Yohanan replied: "If you repent, I will give you my sister, who is more beautiful than I, as a bride."

And so it happened. Resh Lakish, the great murderer, became a great *tsaddik.* Previously great in his wickedness, now he was great and good.[101]

Of Rabbi Meir, Rabbi Akiva, Palimo, and R. Hiyya bar Ashi we are told that they were unable to withstand their trials. Only out of God's special love for them were they protected from sinning. We are told, by the way, that R. Meir was given this trial because he had laughed at those who were not able to withstand their evil urges. In the case of Palimo, he was sent this suffering because he had mocked the evil urge itself.[102]

Captive women were once brought to Nehardea [the site of a great rabbinic academy]. They were brought before R. Amram the Pious in his upper chamber, and the ladder was taken away. One of them was beautiful enough to light up the entire room. R. Amram grabbed the ladder so firmly that ten men couldn't hold him back. He pulled it up by himself and began to go down it. When he was halfway down he began to yell "Fire! Fire!" The sages came before him and said: "You have brought us to disgrace." "Don't worry," he replied. "Better you be ashamed of me in this world than in the world to come." R. Amram made the evil urge swear to depart from him. A column of fire came forth from him. Said R. Amram to the evil urge: "You see, you are fire and I am flesh, but I am stronger than you."[103]

VI

The highest Jewish expression of the longing for beauty is found in the "exile of *shekhinah.*" While this concept is one that reflects both cosmic and Jewish pain, it also stands as a gateway to hidden beauty.

Shekhinah has been driven forth! All is dark, everything suffers. There seems to be no hope of restoration anywhere. Worry and ailing, destruction and death are what make up human history. New generations mean new rivers of blood to be shed, new struggles, new pain. Each generation has new false hopes and dreams. Both individual and collective lives seem empty and desolate. If the sun shines through for a moment, things then seem a thousand times darker. The more a person tries to make life better or easier, the harder things seem to get. Seek a little happiness, and you find out how deeply unhappy you are. Try to reach for strength and greatness, and each step will show you that you remain small and weak. If you seek truth, you find only more ever-new lies all about you. If your quest is for knowledge, you will see that true understanding lies buried. How great are the world's secrets! How far we are from true awareness!

Shekhinah has been driven forth! All that is holy, beautiful, great, or good, anything that has true value, is in exile. All, all, is in exile. The finest pearls are sunk in the mud. All existence cries out in pain, seeking to emerge from exile, longing for redemption. Evil and defilement rule this world; the coarse, the untamed, the obtuse, the cruel. If anything great or beautiful does appear, it does not last. Even in the moment of its appearance it has no great power. The world seems to have been created only for filth and baseness. Beauty and holiness have no place here.

Shekhinah has been driven forth! If someone wants to cast a light, to bring redemption, he has to suffer inhuman pain. People toss him in the mud, make him suffer unto death, and then besmirch his name and his honor.

Shekhinah has been driven forth! The Jewish people is exiled from its place. For thousands of years it wanders about, punched back and forth, pursued by both God and humanity. All the wild and wicked, murderers and hangmen, wash themselves in its blood. Human beasts fall upon it; filth and disgrace accompany it always. Self-mockery is this people's only response to all its woes. It cannot constitute itself, knowing not when it will be redeemed or who its true redeemer is.

Shekhinah has been driven forth! Godly beauty does not reveal herself. We seek her, but she does not come forth from hiding. The ugliness of human deeds has driven her away. People are not worthy of seeing her, not deserving of such true beauty. They chase after the sensual, seeming or fleeting beauty, but they cannot recognize the ultimate and pure beauty of the Divine.

How blessed are those chosen few who do see Her, the *shekhinah*. They behold Her in her mourning cloak, see Her tears, hear Her voice. They join in Her suffering, mourn with Her, and they wait together for the true redeemer.

When the prophet Jeremiah came forth from the Temple, he saw a certain lovely woman mourning and lamenting. "Who are you?" he asked. "Beautiful as a human being, awesome as an angel." "I once dwelt in peace, but now I have been driven from my place. My children lie in the hands of their enemies. My kings and nobles are bound in iron chains; the blood of my prophets is shed like water. My night's lodging is destroyed. My dear Friend has abandoned me." She goes on to tell Jeremiah, "Pray to your God for the poor, unfortunate ones. Let Him redeem my children from captivity! Why are you silent, Jeremiah? Go call to the patriarchs and to Moses! Let the shepherds save the sheep from the wolf's hands!"[104]

Rabbi Abraham Halevi, author of the book *Tiqquney Shabbat*, lived in Safed. Every night at midnight he would arise and wander about the Jewish streets, calling out: "Brother Jews! You know that the *shekhinah* is in exile because of our many sins. The Temple has been burnt! Rise up! Let us call out to God, whose mercies are great. Perhaps He will hear our prayer and redeem His people Israel." He would scream so loudly that no one could sleep, and they would all rise up to recite midnight laments. Then they would study, each according to his abilities. Some applied themselves to Talmud, others to the Bible, still other to Kabbalah. Then they would call out hymns and prayers of supplication, all this until the morning.[105]

The holy ARI praised this Rabbi Abraham greatly, claiming that he was a reincarnation of the prophet Jeremiah. Once the ARI said to him: "Know that you are fated to die. There is only one hope for you, and if you do it, you will live another twenty-two years. Go to Jerusalem; pray at the Western Wall. Pour out your heart, and you will merit seeing the *shekhinah*." That pious man went to Jerusalem and stood before the Western Wall. He prayed with great supplication and shed many tears. Suddenly he saw near the Wall the form of a woman all dressed in black. In great fear Rabbi Abraham fell to the ground, crying out: "Woe is me! Woe is me for having seen You in such a state!" He cried and screamed much, tearing the hair from his head, until he finally fell asleep. The holy spirit came to him in a dream, dressed in lovely clothes, and said: "Take comfort, Abraham my son, the Jews will yet return to their place." Rabbi Abraham awoke from sleep and took himself back to Safed. As soon as the ARI saw him, he said: "Now you will live, for you have seen the *shekhinah!*"[106]

Rabbi Hayyim Vital recounts in his dream diary: "First I saw a woman before me, lovely as the sun. She approached me and said: 'Why do you weep, Hayyim, my son? I have heard your cry and have come to help you.' She spread forth her hand, and I began to call out 'Mother! Mother! Help me!' Then I saw God seated on a throne, in the form of an elder, His beard white as snow. His beauty was without end. He held me by my right hand and said: 'Hayyim, My son, do not be terrified; have no fear....'"[107]

Rabbi Levi Yizhak of Berdichev once came to the town of Dikla. It was in the period of counting the Omer [between Passover and Shavu'ot]. He arrived there late on a particularly dark and fearsome night. He stood in the middle of the street, having nowhere to spend the night. A certain tanner invited him in. Rabbi Levi Yizhak wanted to recite his evening prayers and count the Omer. The smell was so bad, however, that he was unable to do so. Late that night he went alone to the House of Study and began to meditate deeply on the wanderings of the *shekhinah*. He thought of her distress and pain, of how far she had fallen. He began to weep, so much so that he became exhausted and started to doze. Then he saw an awesome light before him, one so bright that it would darken the sun itself. From the midst of that light there appeared a woman, adorned with twenty-four jewels. Each of these sparkled so brightly that no human could conceive of their light. She said to him: "Be strong, my son. It will all be good."[108]

Rabbi Ya'akov Shimson of Shepetovka was in the Land of Israel. Once he had a vision of the *shekhinah* as a woman lamenting her beloved husband. The rabbi jumped up and said: "It must be that R. Pinhas Koretser has died...."[109]

The Zohar is filled with accounts of the *shekhinah's* love, joy, and suffering. The entire Zohar is a sort of godly romance about God and the Community of Israel, the blessed Holy One and *shekhinah*. He keeps seeking her, and she is ever seeking Him. People separate them. A few glorious moments shine forth, but they disappear quickly. Their joy is filled with hope for the future, when people will become pure and holy. Both universal human suffering and the particular woes of the Jewish people are reflected in this godly longing. But it contains aesthetic sufferings as well.

"On the day the Temple was destroyed and the Jewish people went off into exile with chains around their necks and their hands tied behind them, Community of Israel [*shekhinah*] came forth from the King's palace in order to walk alongside them. Then she said to them: 'I will walk first, mourning my home, my husband, and my children.' When she saw her destroyed house, the blood of the pious spilled there, and the holy tabernacle burned, she let out such a cry that everything ceased, both above and below. The sound of her voice reached the King, who then wanted to return the world to primordial chaos. All the hosts of angels came down to comfort her, but she would accept no consolation."

The inhabitants of the Holy Land cry out: "We have no mother! Woe, woe to us! Woe to you! We need to mourn, to pour out our bitter hearts before those who feel our pain with us. Every day we go to our mother's bed, but we do not find her there. We ask about her, but no one answers us. We inquire of her bed. 'Not here.' We ask her chair. 'Fallen.'

"We seek out her chambers, but they swear they know nothing. We ask the earth. 'No signs, no footprints.' We ask the [Temple] roof and are told: 'She was springing from roof to roof, all the while mourning and bewailing us.' We inquire of the paths and trails, and they tell us that they did see a woman weeping bitter tears over her children, but they have no idea where she has gone....Let us mourn and kiss the earth where she once walked....Let us kiss the place where she once was seated....Let us kiss the wall of the holy Temple with heartrending tears...."[110]

"In the lower Garden of Eden there is a hidden, secret place that nobody knows. In it there lie a thousand glorious palaces. No one but messiah ever goes into them. All of Eden is filled with divine chariots carrying the righteous, and messiah oversees them all. On Sabbaths, new moons, and holidays, messiah goes into those hidden palaces. Within them lies a secret, completely unknown place called Eden. It is impossible for anyone to conceive it. Messiah circles it round about, until a certain place is revealed to him, one that is called the bird's nest. In that place are depicted images of all the nations that do harm to the Jews. He enters, lifts up his eyes, and sees the patriarchs entering the desolate Temple-site. Then he sees Mother Rachel weeping and God comforting her. She still wants to accept no consolation. Then messiah raises up his voice, and he too begins to cry. All of Eden trembles and all the righteous there weep as well. Heaven itself, which lies above this Eden, begins to shake, and the tremors reach the Throne of Glory...."[111]

"The King, angry at His consort, has driven her from His palace. When He goes to seek her, He finds her lying about in ashes. Ah, what glory she will have! What great love will the King show for her! He will take her by the hand and lead her into the palace. Then He will swear never to be separated from her again."[112]

"How blessed is the community of the Zohar! When the King calls back His consort, He will ask who set her adornments so beautifully. Who set the crown upon her head? Who was it that dressed her in her garments? No one knows better than this community how to adorn the bride!"[113]

"King David said: 'Turn toward me and be gracious to me' (Ps 25:16). Does God have no one more lovely than David, that He should turn particularly toward him? But there is another David, a higher one, who stands over multiple heavenly hosts. When God wants to have compassion for the world, He looks toward that heavenly David. Then his face shines with light, and so do all the worlds. His head is gold, graced with sevenfold golden adornments. Out of great love God says to him: 'Look at Me! How lovely are your eyes!' When those eyes look at God, His heart fills up with love and compassion. As the love begins to burn with strength, God says: 'Turn your eyes away for a while; they burn Me with their fire.'"[114]

"In one of the palaces there lies a golden crown, a most dear and glorious thing. No one now can behold it. It is filled with precious stones and it awaits king messiah. When messiah goes up into the tower, an eagle stands on either side of it. As messiah ascends, the eagles hold up the crown. As he begins to read the Torah, a doorway opens up and a dove flies forth, the one Noah sent forth from the ark. Then messiah puts on the crown. When he goes down, he returns it to the eagles."[115]

Much more is told about the thousands of flying palaces in which messiah dwells. The cherubim there spread their wings; birds never cease to sing. Holy letters fly about, the heavens hanging over them. The heavenly spheres make their music, grape arbors grow alongside flowing streams. Water fountains are surrounded with pearls and diamonds. All sorts of fire and light are to be seen there, and all sorts of sweet voices are to be heard. Messiah is followed about by the cherubim, the heavens, the spheres, the flying eagles, the fire, and the water. All listen to him as he rules over all the heavens, all the inner chambers. There are diamond pillars standing there, shining in every color. The gold is burnished, shining in fiery light. The aroma of every spice wafts forth; the place fills up with incense. Everything sings, chants, prays to God—for the Jews and for *shekhinah*....[116]

VII

In the classic rabbinic *aggadah, shekhinah* is a way of referring to God Himself. It occurs, however, primarily in the sense of God dwelling within, or standing in relationship with, the world. *Shekhinah* loves and leads toward the good. Sometimes *shekhinah* is used in discussing God's dwelling within Israel, enlightening them, suffering along with them, consoling, helping, purifying them, making them holy.

The *aggadah* becomes so used to thinking of *shekhinah* bound to the world or to the Jews that it eventually comes to portray her as something divine but not quite God. In one place we can even find the expression: "*Shekhinah* said before the blessed Holy One."

The more poetically or lyrically the *aggadah* speaks, the more it expresses its own heart, the more clearly the feminine character of *shekhinah* shines forth. We have seen in the passage quoted above that she appeared to Jeremiah as a woman in mourning.

In Kabbalah this is more clear and explicit. *Shekhinah* is simply termed a "queen," a "matron," a "lovely maiden." The Zohar and all works of Kabbalah are filled with accounts of "the union of blessed Holy One and His *shekhinah*."

What do they mean by these terms? "Blessed Holy One" is the "lesser countenance," comprising the six qualities of *hesed, gevurah, tif'eret, netsah, hod,* and *yesod. Shekhinah* refers to the single quality called *malkhut.*

But this too clarifies very little. In order to make it clear, we would have to lay forth the fundaments of Kabbalah. This is not the place for that. Briefly, however, we may note that the "lesser countenance" refers to the qualities through which God conducts the world as they stand on their own, in their divine glory. *Shekhinah,* or *malkhut,* refers to these qualities as they come to be discovered or expressed in the world. *Shekhinah* is often referred to as "speech" or "word," because language reveals that which is hidden within thought. *Shekhinah* is thus divinity revealed.

Sometimes, however, "blessed Holy One" refers only to the quality of *tif'eret* [or divine beauty]. Then "the union of blessed Holy One and *shekhinah*" bears a more aesthetic meaning. Contemplating the expression aesthetically, it really means "divine beauty united with earthly beauty." *Tif'eret* would designate the purity of divine beauty, while *shekhinah* would refer to an all-worldly beauty. *Tif'eret* has nothing to do with this world; *shekhinah* is with the world, of the world, and completely in the world.

The world was once completely united with God. Then all the upper worlds were filled with joy and gladness. Divine beauty shone brightly, openly, and clearly, for everyone and within everyone. Everything was elevated and refined. Then there was indeed a "union of the blessed Holy One and His *shekhinah*," the union of God and world, divine and human, heaven and earth. But there are also times when the world is dark, sunken down, distanced from its Creator, locked into itself, cut off and alienated. Then *perud,* or "separation," takes place. *Shekhinah* is cast away from the blessed Holy One. One feels a longing; one senses something missing. But one cannot approach God; we are too distanced, too separated.

Then *shekhinah's* suffering is very great. Beauty seeks out its godly root; it longs to be uplifted, redeemed. She is sunk deeply into this world. Earthly darkness surrounds her; worldly chains bind her. She is captive to the world and cannot be healed; she is unable to free herself from her distress.

Indeed, her pain is great. But the greater the longing for godly beauty, the more free the world comes to be. The longing grows so great that the chains, bit by bit, begin to fall away. Bondage starts to break down; wings begin to grow. Pain is transformed into longing, enduring passions of the heart into images, images that draw one closer to divinity. Then, slowly, *shekhinah* begins to find her freedom and the union can take place once again. At first it is day by day, moment by moment. But then it grows more and more until hope begins to shine forth, the hope of the great day that is coming ever closer.

Sparks of holiness, sown and strewn throughout the world, are to be found everywhere, even in the most impure and defiled places. You only have to seek them out, gather them up, and draw them together. They must be sought wherever they are, so that they may be imaged forth into a great whole picture, brought forth in an act of creation. That great divine picture is a complete being, a godly organism. It becomes a new "chariot" or container for divinity. The world becomes purer and higher, brighter and lovelier.

How does one gather up these sparks of holiness? How and where does one seek them out? How do you make diverse things into one? That is the business of Lurianic Kabbalah and of Hasidism. But Hasidism has its own profound insight regarding matters related to beauty. A very deep part of Hasidism is the raising up of "alien," or wicked, thoughts. That is a dangerous path, according to some Hasidic spokesmen. The rabbi of Liadi recommends against getting involved in the uplifting of alien thoughts. Those writings that devote much attention to this subject, he says, misconstrue the intent of their master the BeSHT.[117] Rabbi Nahman of Bratslav calls upon the greatest *tsaddikim* (or the very greatest one, who is in the same category as Moses and the messiah) to be much concerned with this. But for the rest of us he has another principle: Do not enter into argument with your temptations. For those who well understand the BeSHT's views, it is clear that he saw the uplifting of impure thoughts as one of his most central teachings.

In order to understand this properly, one needs at least general familiarity with the BeSHT's view of good and evil. The whole world is divinity; God and world are one. Nothing exists outside of God. All, all is divinity: what you hear, what you see, what you feel, what you think. The godly is indeed everywhere—in good and in evil, in joy and in pain, in high and in low, in great and in small, in beautiful and in ugly. In one place it may be obvious; elsewhere it is hidden and locked away. But in fact it is equally present throughout.

All, all, consists of letters of the Torah, permutations of God's thought, various appearances of a single reality. All are limbs of the same body: the great God-King revealed throughout the world. All belong to Him, and He belongs to all.

But if all is divinity, how can one really speak of the bad, of evil, sin, ugliness, or impurity? If God is equally everywhere, how do we make distinctions? Can we then say that this is good and that is evil, this is kosher and that is forbidden, this is pure and that is defiled? Is all not the same? Are all the letters [of a single alphabet] not the same? Are all limbs [of a single body] not equal?

If the BeSHT had conceived of God as did Spinoza, he would have had to join him in saying that all concepts of good and evil, perfection and imperfection, are entirely human inventions. Pure divinity has nothing to do with them. Because humans have no perfect ideas, it seems to them that one thing is good and another evil. The cosmic essence, nature, or God is neither good nor evil. Human beings love, take pleasure, suffer, live, and die. God remains unaffected.

But the BeSHT, even though his thought is pantheistic, like Spinoza's, and he too perceived the oneness of God and world, conceived the matter in an entirely different way. God and world are one, but God is not bound to [that is, limited by] the world. The world altogether is a sort of illusion, a kind of hiding of God. If God willed it, it would cease to exist. The world, on one hand, is divinity itself. On the other hand, it is a creation, a work of art, a masterpiece. As a creation, the world has its own goal toward which it comes nearer from time to time, rising higher and attaining greater purity.

Spinoza's God is lifeless, a pure idea. The BeSHT's God is one that lives, strives, grows, and blossoms. It suffers and writes poetry, it thinks and creates, in all that tears at the heart, in all the soul's desires. The BeSHT's God is in man, even in his shortcomings and his miseries, his sins and his pettiness.

But the BeSHT also cannot share the claim of those who say that evil has no real existence at all. Why not? Evil does have a reality. We feel it. Wherever we turn, we see its influence; at each step along our way we hear its heavy breath. How can that which has no real existence cause us so much pain and suffering from cradle to grave, hardly giving us a chance to live?

The BeSHT thinks about it this way: Evil is the lowest level of the good. It is not the opposite of the good. It is the very same stuff as goodness, but in a much lesser concentration. Because people do not see the bit of goodness that lies within it, they call it evil. Everything in the world contains varied levels of reality, from highest to lowest. Goodness also contains many levels. In the highest of these, the goodness is very great; in the lower, it is a weaker presence. In the very lowest, there is only the smallest bit of goodness. But something of goodness is in fact present everywhere. Without this nothing can exist.

Evil thus has a reality, but it exists as the lowest level of the good. It too can be uplifted.

Now if you broaden and deepen this assumption, you will come to understand quite well how we must go about our encounter with evil. We cannot tear evil away; we cannot uproot that which God has created. We simply need to lift it higher, to raise it up. All that is found in those lower levels can be raised up higher. When it is found on those lower levels, it is called good.[118]

On a single tree one may find many types of fruit: ripe and unripe, overripe, and even wormy. It is all of a single matter, but from it one make products that are better, worse, or completely bad. When these products fall apart, only little shards or fragments remain. There is no "opposite" here, but only varying levels of the same reality—some more perfect, some less so, and some completely imperfect.

In the BeSHT's language it is expressed this way. Every worldly love, every worldly fear, is a fallen divine love or fear. Every bit of earthly beauty is a bit of fallen godly beauty; so too earthly wisdom. What is a person to do? We have to accept the world as it is. We have to contemplate and imagine each thing as it is, but we also need to take it back to its root. We need to make every love a divine love; every fear must become a divine awe; every beauty must be carried back to divine *tif'eret*.

Contemplating and imagining that divinity is present in each thing, we then leave the thing behind and immerse ourselves deeply in the divine presence. This means perceiving the special godly "something" in each thing. But then we leave behind the "something" and go after the totality, the principle, the essence. In that way each thing is uplifted and made divine.

You perceive beauty and desire to understand it in a coarse and sensual way. But think deeply. Right here, in that which so draws me and overwhelms me, there lies something divine. Within the beauty I see there is something of a higher divine beauty. That is the main thing, the godly that lies within. What value is there in a single ray when the whole sun lies before me? Why a single drop, when a whole ocean stands before me? I must turn my love to God, for that embraces all.

Thus a person journeys from visible beauty to divinity. Everything small and sensual disappears; all becomes pure and holy.

A tale told by an earlier Kabbalist, Rabbi Isaac of Acre, well explains Hasidic thought: "Once the king's daughter came forth from immersing herself in a stream. A simple person saw her and said: 'Ah! If only you were mine!' When the princess heard this, she answered: 'There! Over there in the cemetery.' The simple man did not understand, but he began to walk toward the cemetery. He sat for days and nights in that place, contemplating the king's daughter. He still maintained the hope that she would come and meet him there. He waited for some months, but she did not appear. He compressed all his senses, his imagination, and his thoughts into this single passion. He saw only the image of the princess before him. Bit by bit, he began to forget every human concern. He forgot everything he had ever seen, felt, or thought. Living so completely alone and devoted entirely to this one idea, he eventually forsook the sensual image of the princess's beauty and began to grasp it spiritually. Surrounded by this spiritual beauty, he began to live in godliness. After a time he became a great saint."[119]

From great passion to the life of the spirit; from spiritual living, to God.

PRAYERS:
SONGS TO THE ETERNAL

Introduced and Translated by Joel Rosenberg

Love and Anguish: On the Poetry of Hillel Zeitlin

The heart is an organ not much bigger than two joined hands, yet it can contain a deity larger than the universe. Hillel Zeitlin understood this paradox well, and his prayer poems are both a celebration and a complaint of its realities. His conversations with God are a lover's discourse: ecstatic in their sense of divine saturation of the world and the believer; and bitter, even indignant, in their profound disappointment over divine abandonment of the faithful. In few poets have bliss and torment alternated so rapidly and so intensely—indeed, almost synonymously. To love God is to chide God with a frankness that can only exist between intimates. To feel divine presence is also to stew in divine silence. To exult in divinity's Creation is to recognize the unredeemed state of the world. The people Israel is shown as a perennial offering to the unfathomable purposes of the Almighty, yet paradigmatic of a wider human destiny. The divine abandonment of a people is tantamount to an orphaning of the world. In one remarkable prayer (#15), an almost verbatim translation of a prose poem by nineteenth-century lapsed Catholic freethinker Hugues Felicité Robert de Lamennais, Zeitlin speaks in the name of "all the families of the earth whose dawn of freedom has not yet arisen."

In their worldly sweep and prophetic address Zeitlin's *Tefillot* (Prayers) resemble the gnarled, syncopated, and visionary strophes of Walt Whitman's *Leaves of Grass*, and in their meditative intimacy they anticipate the 1933 Yiddish prayer lyrics of Rabbi Abraham

189

Joshua Heschel's *Der Shem Hameforash: Mentsh (The Ineffable Name of God: Man)*. As Heschel would be, Zeitlin was open to a multicultural universe and thus knew how to frame the problems of the Jews as part of a predicament for humanity. Zeitlin, for his part, had an intercultural reach that embraced, among others, ancient and recent Christianity, Buddhist spirituality, Nietzschean philosophy, and the heritage of freethinkers over many centuries. If God is everywhere, divine revelation is not the exclusive property of a single people, nor even the province of belief, as such, but virtually an inborn faculty of the biosphere. Even the trees are wrapped in prayer shawls.

And yet, the poet's connection to his people—to actual, historic Jewry—is unabashedly earnest and crystalline, his poems' tincture of tradition intensive. Texts of Jewish tradition flow into the poet's consciousness as a seamless whole and are as ready at hand as one's breath or heartbeat. Hebrew Bible, Talmud, Midrash, Kabbalah, and Hasidism function here as organs of perception more than as textual allusion. The rhythms of Jewish exclamation or invocation ("God great and holy!" "How long!" "Arise and save!" "If not now, when?") inflect these poems throughout. In calling on ancestors and shepherds of the people Israel ("you who slumber in Hebron") to plead on behalf of twentieth-century Jewry, the poet casually traces the Kabbalist's map of divine emanation. The wordplays endemic to Hebrew lore and literature become a means of navigating the shoals of spiritual loneliness. The rhetorical question (over four hundred of which punctuate the Book of Job) is the basic currency of thought in these poems. Events of the Jewish present or recent past (Ukrainian pogroms of the World War I era; the desecration of Jewish graves in Vilna; Arab riots against the Jewish Yishuv) take their place in a long history of martyrdoms and violations of the people Israel. At the heart of these prayers is the elemental "Why?" that had infused the plea of the psalmist and the ash heap's Job. But Zeitlin repeatedly shapes this question into a demand for something more, again something world-embracing in its scope: an unmasked Divinity, a new gilding of the mountaintops of Zion, a decisive showing forth of eschatological redemption. The sufferings of the faithful are only a preface. But to what? As he well knew, Zeitlin was situated at a vortex of catastrophe, the greatest crisis of modernity's advent, which, in the inter-wars era, was only gathering breath for another, more torrential raging. He senses he will not survive it (and indeed he did not) but is determined to exit the world as a servant of divine will. But what *is* that will, and where does it tend?

It is worth noting that Zeitlin was not charitable toward the Arabs of Palestine, whose 1921 riots claimed the life of Zeitlin's friend, novelist Y. H. Brenner. Despite the complexities of Zeitlin's attitudes toward Zionism (see Arthur Green's Introduction to this volume), Erez Yisrael, the Land of Israel, was for him "our home" and "our mother," and this, alas, did not allow him to make room for a rival nationalism on the same ground. So, in his poem responding to the riots and Brenner's death (*Tefillah* #16), he invokes poetic hyperbole and biblical metaphor in calling the rioters "forest beasts of men" and "wild asses" (the latter applied to Ishmael in Gen 16:12). Zeitlin was otherwise open to the heritage of Islam, as other writings of his attest, in the same way he sought for models of prayerful address in Christian and post-Christian writers of several eras, and, despite the brutalities dealt out by Polish anti-Semites, could base one of his prayer poems on a prose work by Polish national poet (and philo-Semite) Adam Mickjewicz. But a similar spirit toward Palestinian Arabs does not inhabit these poems, a matter that reflects the bitterness of the historical hour and the rapidly burgeoning expectations of Jewish national aspirations in Palestine, toward which Zeitlin was otherwise, for other reasons, ambivalent.

Throughout these pages the poet repeatedly submits himself for scrutiny by the God he addresses, channeling Rabbi Nahman of Bratslav (through Nahman's disciple, Rabbi Nathan of Nemirov) and frankly admitting that "at times, oh, at times, [my heart] burns with a lust for this world." Nowhere is such confession more pained than in a poem written on the occasion of his fiftieth birthday, in which he invokes multiple hyperboles of rabbinic and Kabbalistic idiom: "For truly, I've blemished the root of my soul, I've damaged the channels, I've sealed off the wells, I've rejected divine abundance....I touched holy worlds up above and cut down Eternity's plants." The last reference recalls the rabbinic tale of Jewish heretic Elisha ben Abuya, who, in beholding the mysteries of heaven, "cut down the shoots"—a phrase suggesting either the metaphysical sin of causing division in divine unity (however one might imagine that act) or the more socially visible scandal of corrupting the next generation, convincing young Torah scholars, say, to leave off their studies and take up a worldly trade. Zeitlin's language remains traditionally emblematic, and so we would be unwise to plumb it for specific biographical content. The ocean, the abyss, the depths of She'ol, the cemetery, the cell of a prison, the state of uncleanness—such is the terrain of spiritual forlornness repeatedly invoked by the poet. It is essentially gnostic language, the cry of the orphaned soul trying to recover its royal lineage, its near-forgotten kinship with a *deus absconditus*, a hidden divinity, while straying about in an opaque and alien world. Yet it is a world that has aroused the believer's lusts! Such is the paradox of what Zeitlin calls "the creature's truth," and so the creature who prays here offers up, for whatever it is worth, the damaged goods of its own spirit because "I can't give You more than I have." In such a context the spirit audaciously nurtures the fervent hope that, whatever its infirm state, or even in that very same broken condition, it can become, speedily and soon, a tabernacle for the divine Presence. Not for nothing is the holiest site in Jewish custom and belief the ruins of a Temple wall.

Two major strands of Hasidic tradition have flowed into the poet's imagination. On the one hand is the contemplative Hasidism of the movement's eighteenth-century founder, Israel ben Eliezer, the Ba'al Shem Tov (or BeShT), and his early disciples, for whom divinity was an all-encompassing and all-inhabiting presence, a Being whose fullness and abundance were accessible in the state of *devequt*, the serene attachment to divinity cultivated by self-surrender and contemplative prayer. Zeitlin seems to approach this state for moments in his poetry, though only rarely for the space of an entire poem. More often, his mood resembles that of the BeShT's great-grandson, the aforementioned Rabbi Nahman, who drew on the crisis-ridden Kabbalah of the great sixteenth-century mystic Rabbi Isaac Luria, for whom the "empty space" in divine plenitude, made necessary for the world's creation, became the source of primordial catastrophe and the state of spiritual alienation that forever after has afflicted seekers of God. For Reb Nahman, this was something resembling "the creature's truth" referred to by Zeitlin. It was the premise for a life of faith (*'emunah*), whose strength was derived not from the serene contemplation of *devequt* but precisely from the "empty space," from the conviction that somehow, despite all lack of reassurance, divinity yet remains there, like the residue of oil or perfume that continues to dwell in a bottle that has been emptied. In such a state the spirit offers its own dumbness and paralysis, its own torment and yearning, as a gesture of devotion. And so, the poet calls upon God to make of him an instrument of divine will. In his birthday poem Zeitlin repeatedly speaks of having been summoned back from She'ol (which, in the logic of gnosticism, could as easily be the world of the living as the underworld of the dead, for the purpose, he hopes, of giving life to others in the same state, serving in the role of spiritual healer, companion, or herald).

The translations in the following pages have striven to eschew both the literalism of a verbatim rendition and the false simplification of a popularizing redaction. (Fortunately, Zeitlin's Yiddish version of these poems was often simpler, less verbose than the Hebrew, and could be consulted when needed.) Where helpful, I have indicated wordplay parenthetically, but sparingly. I have also added parenthetic citations of scripture or Talmud (the abbreviation B.T. = Babylonian Talmud; the symbol > means "based on") in the numerous places where Zeitlin makes allusion to them, but I have not cross-referenced these to possible citations elsewhere in the tradition. I have, in places, preserved Zeitlin's representation of divinity as male, particularly in his address to God as Father, though in other ways I have muted pronouns and metaphors of maleness for God. In truth, the Jewish mystical tradition on which Zeitlin drew had a doubly gendered sense of divinity, but rendering divine gender in this manner would only prove a distraction to the modern reader. In one respect in particular I have adopted a practice that I pursued as translator of *Kol Haneshamah*, the Reconstructionist prayer-book series: the Tetragrammaton (YHWH), which, to the devout Jew, has always been taboo to pronounce by its letters, was traditionally substituted by a word most often translated as "Lord," which, of course, is a male metaphor. (In truth, "Creator" would probably be more accurate.) Instead, wherever the equivalent of the Tetragrammaton is encountered (typically rendered by Zeitlin as a Hebrew letter 'ד, symbol of the number "4"), I have chosen to substitute, in small capitals, some epithet of divinity appropriate to the context, such as The Almighty or The All-Merciful, or O Gracious One, or the like, an artifice that conveys reasonably well the notion that divinity has many faces or guises.

In 1931, Zeitlin published a Yiddish version of his poems, *Gezangen tsum Eyn Sof* (*Songs to the Boundless One*), which includes Yiddish renditions of the poems from *Tefillot*, plus a number of new poems, among them a remarkable supplement under the subtitle *Meshiakh Tefilles un Shekhinah Gezangen* (Messiah prayers and *Shekhinah* songs). The new lyrics in Yiddish are among the finest in the whole collection and demonstrate Zeitlin's skills in a variety of poetic modes, including rhymed couplets and quatrain stanzas. In one instance, his song "*Yedid Nefesh*," he creates a Sabbath song in the same rhyme, stanzaic scheme, and spirit of the familiar song by that title in the Sabbath prayer book, but with wholly new content. Another poem, "Tiefster Vuntsh" (deepest wish), based on a medieval hymn by the Spanish Jew Moses ibn Ezra, builds in its rhymed couplets toward an extraordinary vision of the personal afterlife. Because of the blissful and ecstatic conclusion of this poem, it forms an appropriate conclusion to the whole collection and has therefore been moved from its original place.

Such a conclusion would not be as resoundingly effective had we not possessed in abundance, throughout the collection, the turbulent ocean of Zeitlin's inner world—a place of shipwrecked sailors, tormented prisoners, broken vessels, mazelike byways, rapacious predators, and the mission of one called back from She'ol. It is hard to read these verses and not identify in some way with the spiritual itinerary on which he takes us. These lyrics capture the tumultuous mood of Zeitlin's supremely dangerous era and encompass both the depths and the heights of a soul that is keenly self-aware.

Prayers (*Tefillot*)

1. From Anew

Great and holy father, source of all who come into the world,
You create Your world, Your child, all Your children, once again, in
      every second.
Were You, for but a moment, to withdraw the love of Your Creation,
all would turn to nothingness and void. Yet You pour out
upon those born of You, on all Your creatures, streams of blessing
each and every moment.

Again, the morning stars appear and sing a song of love to You,
again, the sun goes forth in strength and sings a song of power to You,
again, the ministering angels sing their song of holiness to You,
again, all souls, in thirst for You, sing out their pining song to You,
again, the grasses sing a song of yearning as they rise before You,
again, the birds sing out a song of joy to You,
again, abandoned chicklings let out their orphan cry to You,
again, the trees put on their prayer shawls and lead all in prayer to You,
again, the fountain whispers out its prayer,
again, the poor, wrapped only in their need, pour their meditation out
      to You
their souls, their prayer, pierces the highest heavens to ascend to You,
again, their bodies crumble to bits before Your Glory,
but again, their eyes are ever raised to You.

With but a single ray of light from You, I am penetrated by Your aura,
but a single word uttered by You, and I arise again to life,
but a single stir from Your eternal life, and I am saturated with the
      dew of youth,
for do You not create anew all that is?
Create me, then, anew, O my parent—me, Your child, life renewed!
Breathe into me from Your nostril's breath,
and I shall come to life anew,
the life of childhood renewed!

2. The Holy Ones

Upon hearing the news that on the New Moon of Iyyar, 5680 (April 19, 1920), intruders were casting out the bones of the sacred dead from their graves in the [Jewish] cemetery of Vilna and burying horses in their place

God great and holy,
God great and holy over all of Israel,
I, a sinner, I, the impure, I, the lowly, I, a broken one,
come to pray before You, Holy of all Holies, purest of the pure,
loftiest of the lofty, most steadfast of all rocks!
For whose sake do I pray before You?
For those who have walked before You all the days of their lives,
who have breathed and moved about only for You,
for those who have not forgotten You even for a second,

195

whose lifebreath went out only to make holy Your great name.
It is *our* sin that that the holy ones are now defiled,
it is our sin that now even Your precious servants find no rest,
it is our sin that the bones of Your holy ones are now cast out from
their graves.
Bodies that were a dwelling for Your holiness are being cast out
—Your dwelling place defiled!
Bodies that were a sanctuary for Your presence have been made
impure by evildoers
—Your sanctuary rendered unclean!
Bodies that were a chariot riding toward You are made objects of
shame and mockery
—Your chariot shattered!
Now, the bones that once, touched by Elisha's bones, had come to life
[2 Kgs 13:21] are being cast out from the grave.
And now, men who are pigs come here and throw away the bones of
these, Your sacred dead.
They throw them from their graves and bury horses in their place.

Yet You, dear God, keep silent? Do You hold back? You suffer this to
happen? You do not shake the heavens and the earth?!
Yes, it is true our sins have grown abundant. But what have these, the
pure, the beautiful, the holy, done to You to deserve this?
If not for our sake, act on their behalf!
Your redemption surely shall arrive,
Your lovingkindness surely shall be revealed,
Your Name shall be made great and holy
when You raise up again Your dwelling place,
Your sanctuary,
Your chariot.

3. The Gate of Tears

Day and night, I cry out before You,
day and night, I cry out before You,
and there is none to answer.
My inmost depths cry out to You,
and there is none to answer.
The hidden pinpoint of my soul is yearning for You,
but there is none to answer.

While once, in days of old, when I would seek You,
in my weeping, and cry out to You,
I seemed to get an answer.
But now, great walls divide us, me from You,
like gates of iron bolted shut,
and yet, by the tradition of Your holy teachers, You have declared:
"All gates are closed up but the Gate of Tears" (B.T. Berakhot 32b).
But now even these gates are closed and locked.
There's none to open them!
"Hope for THE ETERNAL ONE! Your heart be strong and full of
      courage!" (Ps 27:14).
"If you have prayed but not been answered, pray once more!" (B.T.
      Berakhot 32b).

Until my final breath of life, I shall not cease from pouring out my
      prayer to You,
My final breath of life shall be but song and prayer!
My final breath of life, caressing of Your spirit!
My final breath of life—a droplet in the ocean, a wisp of wind, a ray of
      sunshine—it shall be a breathing of the breath of Your Eternity.
A white dove comes to rest upon my window sill—and oh, may it
      bring news of Your redemption!
A light wind blows upon my face—and oh, may it bring me Your
      greeting!
A surge of light breaks forth into my room—and oh, may it reveal a
      vision of Your peace!

4. Purify Me

By the hand of Your holy teachers, You have declared:
"The one who comes to purify is given help." (B.T. Shabbat 104a)
But oh, how often have I knocked upon Your door,
upon Your pure, eternal gates,
and there was none to help!

Who is the one who helps? Who is the one who can assist? Who is the one
      who gives support?
They grab us by the tufts of hair upon our head and thrust us force-
      fully through
      the gateway of uncleanness.
They cast stones upon us, and sink us into an abyss of sin, into a muck
      of mire, into the depths of She'ol.

Shall it be said: "We have no care for You"? "We have no bond with
  You, nor with Your purity"?
But why, then, have You created me? Why do You bestow on me Your
  gift of life? Why have You breathed into me Your animating breath?
If You care not for me or what I do, why have You placed me on this
  earth?
Am I not Your emissary like everyone who bears the breath of heaven?
Why, then, don't You give me strength or power to achieve what I was
  sent to do?
Why do You not give me strength or power to drive out of my path all
  that disturbs my mission—the desire of the flesh, my narrowness
  of spirit, all my melancholy, and my torment, and my stumbling?
Why isn't my will entirely bound in holiness to You? Why do You let
  me act against Your wishes?
Is not Your breath of life a force that purifies and refines? Does not
  Your lifebreath emanate from Eden? Don't the waters of Your
  fountain flow from the inmost room in heaven's Temple?
And so, from where comes to the world the taint of life?
From where come the desires that are not for You?
From where, the longings that are but for dust and ashes?

Your right hand can console me. Why, then, do You bring me down?
Your spirit lifts me up. Why, then, do You sink me into dusk?
My heart calls out to You. Why, then, do You push me far from You?
Whenever I come nearest to You, You keep walking far away from me.
Whenever I approach You, You drive me away, and persecute me, and
  push me out.
And is my wrongdoing so great? Have my transgressions been that grave?
And if they've truly been that grave, can You not find it in You to forgive
  them,
You who lift all worlds, and everything that lives, and all the generations?
And if I have become unclean, are You not the Ocean that washes
  clean every impurity?
And if my spirit has grown dark, are You not the sunlight that can
  penetrate all darkened corners?
And if I have grown weak, and if I have grown fragile, and if I have
  been beaten down, are You not the Stronghold of Eternity?

If I am but a droplet from Your Ocean, let me fall into the mouth of God!
If I am but a ray from Your great Sun, may I again return to it!
Light of the Boundless One! I open up the crannies of my soul before You.

So, may You encircle them, surround them, enter them, and penetrate
them thoroughly.
Light of the Boundless One! My life is Your life; my light, Your light;
my breath, Your breath.
Light of the Boundless! Become one with me. Cling close to me.
Enable me to dwell amid Your heavens while I live upon this ground.
Let me cling unto Your spirit while I live inside my body.
May I cling unto Your radiance from the depths of my abyss!

5. Midnight

In the depths of night. All silent. All asleep. My heart remains awake.
I am awake. You are awake. Let us dwell together!
I pour my meditation out to You, You pour out Yours to me. We listen
to each other's voice. Come, let's cling together for all time!
This time, I don't cry out to You. I don't ask anything of You. I am
with You. You, with me.
Shall I sing my song to You? Shall I trumpet all that roars aloud inside me?
Shall I pour my tears' libation out to You?
My song and call You haven't wanted. My tears and sighing You
haven't sought.
Why should You need my tears? Why should You need my sigh? All of
me is Yours already.
Why should You need my petitions? Why should You need my pleas?
All of me is Yours already.
Why should You need my longings? Why should You need my
desires? All of me is Yours already.
Why would You need words? Why would You need utterances?
Come to me here. Enter me without a word being said.

6. I and You, and Nothing Else but You

A prayer of R. Meirl of Apt, with several modifications

Supreme power of the world! Here am I, in Your hand alone, like clay
in the hand of the sculptor.
Were I to strive with strategies and schemes, and all who dwell on
earth stood at my right,
if even the angels and seraphim wished to save and support me,
if even all worlds of heavenly light, the highest of worlds up above,
were emanating mercy upon me,
without Your power and help, I would have no redemption!

And if any in the world would wish me harm, but You in compassion cast
    a favorable eye, and from Your holy abode should grant me good,
then pleasant shall my portion be! My salvation shall arrive, my source
    of help shall be revealed.

What do I ask of You, then? Please be my help, O Master of all worlds,
    and may my eyes be open to behold the truth of it, and may Your
    faithfulness be steady in my heart continually, never to depart,
and may I never, in thought, or utterance, or deed, serve anything but
    You.
Help me, please, give help to me! The splendor of Your greatness, may
    it never, from my thought or from my heart, depart.
Let Your life shine forth in each and every moment,
though puny is my worth among Your deeds.
What value do I have among all things You have created?
I am nothing set against the world that You have made.

Help me, please, give help to me, for my heart is ever joyous at Your
    presence, You who created me for Your glory.
And may Your love burn in my heart continually,
and may You emanate upon me from Your wisdom,
Your greatness and Your might before my eyes,
though I am small in value and devoid of understanding.

Help me, please, my source on high,
so that all You do with me might give delight to me.
May I never reap confusion from serving You in truth,
may no one envy me, nor I, the lot of any other,
may I never have desire for anything beside Your will.
Show me, I pray, Your laws! Let me, Your servant, do them, clear and
    pure of heart,
with joy, humble of spirit, and with love for Israel, Your people,
and may Your Name be made holy in me.

7. Compassion

O God, the God of Israel,
who am I that I should pray to You about Your children?
Who am I that I should merit praying to You about the children of
    Abraham, Isaac, and Jacob?
Who am I that I should set my prayer before You about Your great and
    holy people, the people Israel?

Who am I and what am I? A poor creature, wretched, a vessel brimming
    with disgrace and shame!
A mere shard amid the broken clay of earth! A worm among the
    worms that crawl about!
Who am I to come in hope of stirring up the greatness of Your love?
Who am I that I should come to waken Your compassion for this flock
    forlorn and straying?
"A great and holy people," and, for all of that, "a flock forlorn and straying"!
Great Your people, great in bearing up Your burden, raising Your banner
    up forever,
struggling for Your holiness, for Your holiness's truth.
And for all of that, "a flock forlorn and straying," a flock that's lost, a
    flock that's scattered, a flock brought forth for slaughter.
O great and holy Father! Have compassion for Your children!
O great and holy Shepherd! Have mercy for Your flock!
I am not fit to pray for them. But I can bear no more their burden—
    this heavy load of mine.
I can no longer bear their suffering—this suffering of mine.
I am not fit—no, surely, surely, I'm not fit.
But act, I pray, this time, for one who *isn't* fit, for one who is worth
    nothing…
For have You not a treasure hidden and concealed? A treasure house
    of gifts unmerited?
Bestow, I pray, such grace on me! Be gracious unto me, O my Creator,
    from that place!
Just take a little lovingkindness from that treasure house—and spread
    it out upon the many tens of thousands of Your people,
upon the many millions of Your children!

8. And If Not Now, When?

If not now, Creator, You who dwell on high, then when?
If not now, when all the world is hovering between life and death, then
    when?
If not now, when all the earth is in travail, and cries out in her pain
    like one who's giving birth, then when?
If not now, when humankind is wallowing in its blood, and drinking
    blood, and sinking into blood, then when?
If even now Your kindness will not come, then when? If even now
    Your help doesn't arrive, then when? If even now Your light won't
    shine, then when shall it appear?

Are they too few for You, the sacrificial altars we, Israel, Your children,
array before You with our blood?

Are they too few for You, the many tens of thousands of the victims
offered up to You?

Are they too few for You, the hundreds of holy communities slain by
murdering tyrants?

Are they too few for You, the tens of thousands of Your children who
gave their lives in making Your Name holy?

Are they too few for You, the cries of children stabbed and defiled
while their parents watched?

Is it too small for You, the immense pain that by now fills the heart of
everyone of Israel, even as they strive to find relief for it, to quiet
it, to drown it in the depths of their desire?

Isn't the wordless cry thousands of times greater than the cry
expressed in words?

Isn't it like this by now, the cry from every heart?

And all the world? Doesn't it now cry *to You?* Is it not to You that it
cries out? Isn't it to You that it aspires?

Is it not to You it cries out in the weight of its wrongdoing? Is it not to
You it calls in tremor and convulsion?

Is it not it to You it calls under the burden of its blundering and malice?

Truly, human beings have strayed afar, so far, from You. They can't
reach up to You.

They forgot the way that leads to You. They forgot Your name.

But in pursuing happiness, is it not You they seek?

In searching for life's substance, is it not You they seek?

In searching for the truth of life, is it not You they seek?

Whether sooner, whether later, won't they surely come to You?

Why do You forsake them, letting them stray so far from You?

Why do You forsake them, letting them wander many days amid their
folly?

Why do You forsake them, letting them wander many days in their
idolatries and in the depths of their uncleanness?

How long will You hide Your face? How long will You conceal behind
a mask Your rays of splendor?

Reveal Your face! Take off the mask! Let You be shown unto Your
children!

Say to them: "Here am I, whom you have sought and haven't found!"

Reveal, I pray, to all the world, Your word:

"Here am I, in whose hand your life, your happiness, your truth are found. Come to Me!"

9. We and the Children of Nineveh

This prayer to prayer #12, and more generally the material beyond, are suggested by allusions in the book Keter Shem Tov *("Crown of a Good Name").*

You said to Your servant Jonah, son of Amittai:
"You have pitied the gourd, over which you have not labored and which
    you have not grown, which exists one day and in the next is gone,
and should I not have pity for Nineveh, the great city, which has within
    it more than one hundred twenty thousand people who do not
    know their right hand from their left, and also many cattle?"
    (Jonah 4:10–11)
Truly, we, the children of Abraham, Isaac, and Jacob, are we not like
    the children of Nineveh?
And if our sins, as well, are now grown great and heavy, don't we cry
    to You, just like the Ninevites, with all our strength?
If we don't tear our clothes in penance, don't we tear our hearts?
For whom and for what are we being killed and slaughtered? Is it not
    for You and for the holiness of Your Name?
You have pitied "Nineveh, the great city," for "more than one hundred
    and twenty thousand people," and why don't You pity us, Your
    children, who are millions upon millions?
We, too, "do not know our right hand from our left."
We do not seek rescue either from the "right" or from the "left." In
    You alone is our salvation.
We see our help and our redemption only in Your power, in Your
    authority, and in Your love, and in Your truth and Your
    endurance, to which is bound our own.
Will You forsake us, O Creator?

10. We Were Slaves…

"When You acquire a Hebrew slave, six years shall he labor and in the
    seventh he shall go forth unconditionally free" (Exod 21:2). And
    when shall we go free?
You further said: "And you shall sanctify the fiftieth year, and declare
    freedom in the Land for all of its inhabitants. It shall be a Jubilee

203

for you, and each of you shall be restored to what you had, and each of you shall be restored unto your kin" (Lev 25:10).

And when will You declare freedom for *us?* When will You restore us to what we had?

See how many Jubilees have been, in which we have been sunk into the dark, in poverty, and in indignity, and in oppression. When shall we be freed? When shall we find redemption? When shall Your light appear to us?

You further said: "And when a person strikes the eye of his male servant, or of his handmaid, so that it will be destroyed, he shall send them forth in freedom, as a compensation for the eye. And if he cause to fall a tooth belonging to his servant or his handmaid, he shall send them forth in freedom, as a compensation for the tooth" (Exod 21:26–27).

And we, Your servants, whose every limb You've crushed and shattered in our dark and frightful exile, when will You send us forth in freedom?

Will You demand from human beings justice, You who trample us underfoot?

Will You demand of human beings that each must free his servant, yet close us up in a dark imprisonment thousands of years?

It is now thousands of years that You have poured Your wrath upon us. Is that too few?

It is now thousands of years we haven't had a single moment's peace. Is that too few?

It is now thousands of years we've gone from chains to chains, from prisons to prisons. And is that too few?

You further said: "And if the slave should surely say, 'I love my master, and my wife and children, I shall not go free,' his master then shall bring him to God's presence, and bring him to the door or to the doorpost, and shall pierce his ear with an awl, and he shall be his slave forevermore" (Exod 21:5–6).

Are we like that ear-pierced slave? Have we, too, said: "We love our master, we will not go free"?

Do we not aspire toward freedom, toward liberty? Can't we break through to go forth from the pit of prison, the imprisonment of exile?

Can't we break through to burst the chains of slavery in which You have imprisoned us since the day that we were exiled from our Land?

11. The Sound of the Shofar

"My innards, oh, my innards! Oh, how I writhe in pain! The walls of my heart! My heart's in turmoil, I cannot be still. For you, my soul, have heard the shofar's blast, the call to war.

"Calamity upon calamity is heard, for all the land is plundered, suddenly my tents are ravaged, in but a moment my curtains are torn. How long shall I see military banners, and hear the sounds of war?" (Jer 4:15).

Riots upon riots, slaughters upon slaughters. Our life is lost and our possessions up for grabs. Our name subjected to insults and curses. Our honor trampled under every foot. Weeping without remission, groans wherever we turn. Hands are weakened, knees are buckling, spirits bowed.

How long will the earth cry out in pain and not give birth?

How long will we see flags of war and hear the horns proclaiming war?

When will we behold *another* banner—"the banner to the nations"? (Isa 11:12).

When will we behold *another* shofar call—"the Messiah's shofar"?! (1 Sam 2:10).

12. "The Blessed Holy One Prays"

Master of the Universe! Pray, You Yourself, for Your children. You Yourself, please, stand as our word. Please, be our advocate.

"If he has one to represent him, one against a thousand..." (Job 33:23). If there is no one representing us—who is like You, a worthy advocate for us?

Who is like You, who knows our suffering, our wretchedness, our shame? "The Blessed Holy One prays" (B.T. Berakhot 7a).

If "those who can pray are finished and gone," who besides You can pray for our sake?

We truly had someone who knew how to fall before You in prayer for forty days and forty nights on our behalf. Where is he?

We've grown exhausted, and are weary. Our tongue has no words. The well of our tears has gone dry. Like those who can't speak, we stand here before You.

"The Blessed Holy One is Israel's heart."

You are our heart. You are our aspiration. You are our final hope. With You, we are everything. Without You, we are nothing at all.

13. The Deeds of Lovingkindness of the Ancestors and a Redeemer for the Children

From a prayer in the book Hemdat Yamim (Delight of Days), *with numerous abridgments and modifications*

Master of the Universe! Who can count the names of the multitudes of Israel who have, with their blood, made holy Your Name?

How can Your heavenly altar contain the abundance of sacrificed souls? What's going on there with so many ashes, of those who have been burned for Your sake?

Is there a place on Your garment of purple (*porphyria*) not yet stained by the blood of Your children who stand at the periphery (*mefarperim*) between life and death? Why isn't their blood brought up to Your altar to make null and void all our sins?

Will it truly serve justice that cattle and sheep blood be accepted by You, while the blood of Your children is shed unreceived?

What laying on of hands is this, O God of all gods, by which You support hands to shed the blood of the innocent, hands busy oppressing those busy with Torah, empowered to destroy the holy sheep of Your flock? (> B.T. Betzah 20a–20b).

And what is this silence You hold toward the peoples who heap their abuse on Your Name, abusing the name of Your children who are slaughtered and slain for Your Oneness?

Why, in Your might, do You give power to the thorn but not the wheat? The system is awry: the cult prostitute (*qedeshah*) is there for the eyes [to behold] (> Gen 38:12–19), but holiness (*qedushah*) is trampled underfoot.

How are Your sheep, once gentle and soft, now like those dead in darkness eternal?

How are Your grape clusters, once succulent and tasty, now scrawny and thin, and blasted by wind from the East? How long will the flame of Your wrath set them burning?

Have the waters departed from the canals of Your love? Have the thirteen streams of Your mercy gone dry?

Look down from the heavens on Your community of innocents, stretched out in prayer at Your palace's threshold, their heart torn asunder, impoverished, in turmoil, as they moan in their unquietable yearning. Give ear to their pleas, give heed to their prayer and their search. Is it not a trifle, given the greatness of Your love?

And if our sins (*'avonoteynu*) have answered (*'anu*) for us, and a cloud (*'anan*) has beclouded us (*'innenenu*) and come between us and You, send forth Your merciful wind to disperse it, and in the sunshine of Your justice may it melt.

Shine forth Your wondrous glory, power of Eyn Sof, the Infinite, to reveal the brilliance of Your deeds of love, the bright, ancient white of fullness divine. Let their luminous rays now shine upon the crimson anger of Your judgment.

Let a mercy sublime be revealed in all Your powers, as they descend in their glory to illumine with brilliance the face of a refulgent full moon (> Song of Songs 7:3). Let her arise to Your Being's uppermost channels, as the crown of our ancestors' merit.

Awaken, you who slumber in Hebron, come forth from your graves, rise to the splendor of the Throne of Mercy, to arouse the remnant of this precious flock who struggle in the grip of all those who do them harm. Plunder and punishment are brought down upon them, mortal abuse puts your people to test. "If they're driven hard for but a single day, all of the sheep will die" (Gen 33:13).

Arise, beloved Abraham, and stand before THE LOVING ONE. Remind divinity of the Covenant Between the Parts (Gen 15:9–16), and please say the following:

"Don't give Your beloved children into the grasp of lions and wolves! And if my children sinned, transgressed, or wrought iniquity and are sentenced to die by the fire, remember, please, how I offered my own life to a fiery furnace, to be burned for the honor of Your Name, and how I sanctified Your Name throughout the world. Let my burning stand in place of theirs."

Arise, Isaac, you who were bound as sacrifice, pour forth your meditation and your tears to our all-merciful Creator, and please say the following:

"If my children sinned, transgressed, or wrought iniquity and are sentenced to be killed, remember how I stretched my neck out for the knife, to be slaughtered for the honor of Your Name. Let my offering-up stand in place of theirs."

Arise, now, Jacob, perfect one, and implore the presence of the Splendrous One of Israel (*Tif'eret Yisra'el*), who hears all prayers—pray for the children of the flock, your flock, who moan and groan amid suffering and captivity, oppression and misery, undergoing humiliation at the hands of Esau, and please say the following:

"How long, O GRACIOUS ONE, will You forsake and push away my

207

children, for whom I sacrificed my life, sullied and defiled at the hands of Esau and Ishmael, my foes! 'I fear them, lest they come and strike me, mother and child alike' (cf. Gen 32:12).

Have compassion for the scattered sheep of Israel, children of Abraham, Your beloved, children of Isaac, Your offering, and 'the children with whom You've graced Your servant' (cf. Gen 33:5).

And if my children sinned, transgressed, or wrought iniquity and are sentenced to exile, please remember my own suffering and exile when I went forth from my father's house. 'By day a scorching heat devoured me and a frost by night. My sleep had fled from my eyes' (Gen 31:40). Let now my exile stand in place of theirs."

Arise, now, Moses, faithful shepherd, and feed the children of your flock, they who now pasture in a land filled with night, and can't bear the crises and shocks day by day. The light of Israel is now darkness, as they're attacked and tormented, the targets of mocking by those who dwell in comfort.

I pray, O mightiest of shepherds, you who were like a father to Israel, and, when they sinned in the wilderness and suffered distress, you stood in the breach, averting the wrath of murderous divinity: be now for us a sheltering rock in our land of captivity, and implore THE ALL-MERCIFUL, and say:

"Do not destroy Your people, Your inheritance, whom You, in Your greatness, have rescued!

Remember how You ran before them like a horse in the wilderness, so their foes would never strike them nor destroy. How can You now destroy them in their captivity, as they run from marauding lions and destroying eyes?

'Look down from heaven and see, regard this vine, the shoot Your right hand planted!'" (Ps 80:15–16)

Arise, now, King Messiah, behold the community of THE GOD OF COMPASSION, utterly abandoned to the hands of innumerable foes. "With whom have you left the few of the flock?" (1 Sam 17:28) Awake, demand justice from the Creator, and say:

"Today I am 'one who suffers, well-versed in disease…one smitten, afflicted by God…like sheep led to slaughter, like a ewe mutely suffering her shearers to shave' (Isa 53: 3, 4, 7). 'Is my strength that of rock? Or is my flesh bronze…that You decree for me bitter events?' (Job 6:12, 13:26). And see, now, my children, in the lands of their foes. What good did it do, my own suffering and illness, to atone before You, to atone for my children, and still they are captive and scattered?

I pray, Righteous One, remember the good deeds of David, Your servant, my chains and my torments and woes."

Save, now (*hatsilah-na'*), Your eminent ones (*'atsileykha*), who are
sunken (*tsolelim*) in great depth, among a mixed multitude of
nations. Bring them out of their darkness and back to their
birthright, to find restoration in the Almighty's realm. For it is
their possession.

Let the merit arise before You, of Your righteous and great-souled,
who are slain and burnt and strangled for the oneness of Your
holy Name, and the merit of Your holy Messiah.

"Behold, divine protector, look upon the face of Your Anointed One"
(Ps 84:10).

"Let our eyes behold, in full beauty, the one who will rule over us"
(> Isa 33:17).

Crowned with the crown of crowns, and adorned with the Presence's
splendor!

14. Arise, and Save Us!

*The framework for this prayer I have taken from the prayer of [Polish
national poet Adam] Mickjewicz at the end of his book about the
[Slavic] Polish diaspora.*

You are our Father, who brought out Your people from slavery in
Egypt and brought them into the Holy Land.

Return us to our motherland!

For the sake of our Redeemer, our righteous Messiah, who will raise
from their graves those who sleep in the dust, please bring back
our motherland to life!

For the sake of our fathers, Abraham, Isaac, and Jacob, who were
tested, instructed, and called to Your service in that Land return
us to our motherland!

O Archangel Michael, who watches over our nation, stand in prayer
and in pleading for our sake!

O Elijah, our Covenant's angel, you who come "to restore the hearts of
the parents to the children, and those of the children to the parents" (Mal 3:24), please come and plant peace in our midst.

The young man "ruddy-cheeked, [bright-eyed,] and handsome"
(1 Sam 16:12), the one who, in former days, widened and made
great our kingdom, let him once again wage battles for us!

"David, King of Israel, lives and endures!" (B.T. Rosh Hashanah 25a).

209

Awake, now, from your slumber, lead your people, command them for battle, in your strength!

O God, God of our ancestors, the strength of Samson, Gideon, and Jephthah plant in our midst!

The strength of the Hasmonaeans, Bar Kokhba, and Rabbi Akiba plant in our midst!

The spirit of Yohanan of Gush Halav and all other guardians of Israel plant in our midst!

The holiness of Rabbi Shim'on bar Yohai, the wisdom of Rabbi Meir, and the devotional spirit of Rabbi Judah plant in our midst!

For the sake of those tortured and slaughtered by Nebuzaradan and Nebuchadnezzar, arise and save us!

For the sake of those tortured and slaughtered by Antiochus, arise and save us!

For the sake of those tortured and slaughtered by Vespasian and Titus, arise and save us!

For the sake of those tortured and slaughtered in the days of Hadrian, the days of our destruction, arise and save us!

For the sake of those tortured and slaughtered through all our centuries of exile, arise and save us!

For the sake of those cast into the fires of the *Auto da Fé*, arise and save us!

For the sake of those mangled in the dungeons of the Inquisition, arise and save us!

For the sake of those who hid in caves to worship their God, from fear of the Inquisition's executioners, arise and save us!

For the sake of all our martyrs, the holy ones of Israel, who were tortured by the Crusaders, arise and save us!

For the sake of all our martyrs, the holy ones of Israel, who were tortured by all the Chmielnickis, the Gontas, the Petluras, the Makhnos, and the Balakhoviches, arise and save us!

For the sake of all the tens upon tens of thousands of holy ones slain and slaughtered, tormented and persecuted in the Ukraine, arise and save us!

Messiah, O scion of David, our righteous Messiah, throw off with force the chains on your hands, bind up your loins, call on the name of your God, arise and save us!

15. Out of the Heart's Oppression

From Paroles d'un croyant *(Words of a Believer) by [Hugues Felicité Robert de] Lamennais*

From the depths of our distress, we call to You, O God!
Like living creatures who lack the means to feed their children, we call
    to You, O God!
Like a ewe whose offspring has been stolen, we call to You, O God!
Like a dove in the beak of a hawk, we call to You, O God.
Like a hind in the claws of a panther, we call to You, O God.
Like an ox in the grip of a marauding beast, we call to You, O God.
Like a wounded bird that's been chased by a dog, we call to You, O God.
Like a sparrow exhausted, who falls into the sea and goes down in the
    waves, we call to You, O God!
Like wanderers astray in a drought–ridden desert without any water,
    we call to You, O God!
Like shipwrecked sailors who wash ashore on a desert island, we call
    to You, O God!
Like someone at night who beholds in a graveyard a terrible vision, we
    call to You, O God!
Like a father who has been robbed of the bread he intended to feed his
    hungry children, we call to You, O God!
Like an innocent who's been cast by the wicked into a prison dark and
    dank, we call to You, O God!
Like slaves under the rod of their masters, we call to You, O God!
Like one innocent of crime in a time of oppression, we call to You, O God!
Like the people Israel in the land of their servitude, we call to You, O God!
Like the children of Jacob, when the king of Egypt cast their children
    in the Nile, we call to You, O God!
Like the twelve tribes of Israel in Egypt, when, day by day, their labors
    were increased and their bread was lessened, we call to You, O God!
Like all the families of the earth whose dawn of freedom has not yet
    arisen, we call to You, O God!

16. "My Distress I Shall Tell in Your Presence…"

When the news arrived of the riots in Jaffa and the deaths of pioneer builders, including [writer] Yosef Hayim Brenner

My Creator, my Creator!
It is very bad for me. I am very much in pain. The burden of my suffering

is very great. I cannot bear it. I have no one to turn to. None to
help. None to give support. Yet You stay silent. You give help to
our foes. You wipe out Your children. How long? Until when?

We run to our house. We run to our mother. We run to our Holy
Land.

We've said: Our mother will console us. We've said: she will wipe off
the tears from our face.

We have come to our house. We have come to our mother. And there,
too, we find our foes. We go from slaughter to slaughter. And
where is our rescue? Where is our salvation?

From the land of slaughter, from Ukraine, our children ran to You, ran
to Your Holy Land.

By the sweat of their brows, they sought to water it, but You have
watered with their blood the thirst of our cruel foes for murder.

Shall I pour out before You my torments and my troubles? Where
shall I find words to express all this?

But what need have You of my words? What can I express to You that
You don't know already, without a thing being said?

You know everything. But as for us, we know nothing. We don't know
why for many centuries You have allowed Your children to fall
victim to the knives of legions in the lands of exile. And for those
who fled back to You, only to fall, they too, beneath the knives of
Arabs in our Holy Land.

And even *he?* He who sought You out through sufferings so frightful
and could not reach You, given that he saw only the afflictions
of his brethren, but *Your* compassion he never saw; he who
walked about with such great truth before You, even though,
from the weight of his despair and pain, he sometimes forgot
Your Name, and even fought mightily, sometimes misguidedly,
with those who spoke Your Name; he whose heart never did
know joy, being ever filled with the sorrow and trouble of Your
children—this man, Yosef Hayim, who so much loved, who
so abounded in the power of love, why have You cast away
his life? Why have You handed him over to forest beasts of
men to tear him apart? Why have You let merciless wild asses
quench his lamp? Why was that skull shattered, which had
been so filled with light?

No! No, I cannot any longer bear all this. Your words provide no
bandage for my wounds.

"Your words of consolation"—but how can Your words of holiness console me?

They shall surely say: "There is no birth without blood." Why must the blood of innocents be shed and shed again? While the polluted blood, the blood of murderers, will reign throughout the generations?

God great! God holy! Let a new thing be heard from Your mouth!

Let a new light gild the mountaintops of Zion!

Let it suddenly be revealed! Let it unexpectedly be seen! "Let the redeemer quickly come into the palace—the master we have waited for" (Mal 3:1).

May a great lightning bolt flash suddenly in the world! May a great rain of blessing come to Your servants, to them who yearn and thirst.

In one hour, in one moment—suddenly—

Let Your Name be made great and holy in the world!

Yitgaddal ve-yitqaddash shemeyh rabba' ...

17. The Far and the Near

You have said through Your sweet psalmist: "Near is THE REDEEMER, to all who call, to all who call to God in truth!" (Ps 145:18).

Do I not call on You in truth? Does not my very blood call out to You? Does not every particle of my soul cry out to You?

And what is the truth You seek? Shall I not say: it is Yours? By Your own truth, Yours, the Infinite?

Am I not Your creature, and do I not call out to You, in every sense, the creature's truth? Don't I call out to You with the same truth You represent as the Creator?

And when I, Your creature, am also a creator, don't I create by Your power? And how is mine the truth that belongs to the Creator of all things?

I cry to You with all the strength You've given to my heart, with all the pain and turmoil, with all the fire and desire, with all ability and wisdom, with all the understanding and the knowing in my soul. From where could I have a truth greater than this?

And if You are not true to it, what truth do You ask from someone who calls out to You only from this?

And if You truly seek out a person who's nothing before You—who, besides You, knows there's nothing else but You?

My truth is unworthy in Your eyes, so You are not near me when I cry. Do You mean to demand truth greater than I have?

213

How can I muster such a truth if You haven't given it to me?

I give You my body, and all my soul, and all that my spirit desires. I can't give You more than I have.

And if You deem it too small, make larger my soul, make richer its strength, expand its borders, so it might provide You more.

Develop, expand, and deepen this vessel, in order that You might have more.

Enlarge and enhance the truth in my heart, so with truth reawakened I might sing to You once more!

18. Between Fires

From Liqqutey Tefillot (Collected Prayers) *of Rabbi Nathan Sternhartz (R. Nathan of Nemirov), with changes and abridgments*

My Father, my Father! You know my heart has burned with the flames of a mighty blaze. You have seen the inferno of my heart.

You know that sometimes my heart will be kindled, and kindled only for You.

But at times, oh, at times, it burns with a lust for this world.

I wander from fire to fire. From a fire for heaven to a fire for flesh and blood.

I stray from Your fire of holiness to the fire and brimstone of hell.

Yet I escape from the fires of Gehenna, and run with all strength to Your fire of truth.

I wander and stray between fires—Oh, how can I flee from their midst?

And "I fear lest the great fire consume me" (> Deut 5.22).

Both the fire of my love for You and the fires of my flesh, I can't bear them, I cannot endure.

I wander and stray in a desolate land, in which I can find no respite.

Here I am, like a ship torn apart in the sea.

I go up to the skies, I go down to the deep, I go up and go down, I go down and go up, from ocean to ocean, from wave unto wave, and none quenches the fire of my soul.

From the depths of the sea, I cry out You: Oh, save me, I pray, may You save!

Send me Your spirit, Your spirit of holiness, Your spirit of rest and release.

Let the spirit of God hover over my heart, so that it might find peace and relief.

Let the spirit of God hover over my heart, that it might endure
　　heaven's fire.
Let the fire not burn up the vessel that holds it!

19. Kindness, Kindness!

Also from Sternhartz's Liqqutey Tefillot

Please, ANCIENT ONE, give counsel to me, give mercy to me, give
　　thorough salvation to me!
Bestow upon me the wonder of life, so I'm not like one dead while I
　　live.
Grant me kindness unmerited, despite my base deeds and my confusion
　　of mind.
Have pity, have mercy, I pray, on my spirit that suffers in pain.
Let Your compassion be stirred for my pinpoint of good, lest it sink
　　into evil's depths.
Let Your compassion be stirred for the spark that is in me, which has
　　come from the light of Your fire.

My heavenly Father!
You who pity the humble, You who listen to the poor,
You who behold the misery of the oppressed, who hearken to a cry
　　from the bottomless depths of She'ol,
is there anyplace from which You would not hear a groan or a sigh?
Do You not hear my groan and sigh from the depths of my pit?
Have pity, I pray, for one so sore of spirit as I, for one so dejected as I,
　　for one such a fool as I am, for one sapped of strength such as I!
Whatever in me that is good is captive in the prison of the world and
　　of time.
Thousands upon thousands of partitions, iron walls, one enclosure
　　after another, surround me,
thousands upon thousands on the lookout for me, so many who lie in
　　wait. They don't allow me a moment's relief.

Oy, me, oy! How bitter is my lot!
Oy for the days and the years spent breaking barriers, only to see them
　　rise up again!
To You I've cried out, to You I have called, to You, so full of compassion.
Turn Your ear to me and hear. Open Your eyes to me and behold my
　　desolation!

215

20. The Longing of Spirit

Suggested by phrases from Rabbi Yedayah ha-Penini; by a prayer from the book Hemdat Yamim (Delight of Days); *and by a passage from the* Tokhehah (Reproof) *of Rabbenu Bahya ibn Paqudah*

Say, now, O my soul, to God:
Am I not Your daughter, the daughter of a king?
Why have You exiled me from the royal courtyard, to glean in the field
    and to search out food by the sweat of my brow?
Why have You sent me from the evening stars to embrace the garbage
    heap? I know well my pedigree, my ancestral house. But I do not
    know who sent me here.
Why have You shamed me, my father? So I'd be smothered with a veil
    and pass out?
What have You done to me, pitching my tent so far from Your abode,
    to dwell among strangers unknown?
Why have You sent me to Azazel (> Lev 16:8, 10, 26), I who am
    heaven's gazelle? My hoof is untested in earthly terrain.
My protector has sold me, my Maker enraged me—given me dust for
    my food, clods of earth for my tongue—so that I now have
    thunder in my heart.
My father has spat in my face, caused me shame and disgrace.
I've been stolen away from a place of fulfillment and glory (> Gen
    40:15). And here I can do nothing to restore what I have lost.
What have I here? I am poor and in turmoil (> Isa 54:11), exiled and
    banished, for I am unclean, I have strayed far away from my
    Master. And I go after evil, through whose thickets of shame I
    am drawn.
Oh, where has my splendor departed? Where has my glory turned
    away? How has my face grown so dark?
How is it I go forth, my hands to my head, dressed in black clothes,
    and draped in a mantle of mourning, and all who look upon me
    now flee?
Why have You flung me away like a rock from a sling, and not bound
    me in the cradle of life?
I've been snipped from the source of awareness, wrenched away from
    the fountain of wisdom, brought away from the site of the holy,
    taken out from the citadel of the brave.
Oh, why have You sent me to pasture in ashes, sunk in the depths,
    yearning for You and melting away in my tears?

21. How Much I Have Yearned

Based on a passage from St. Augustine's Confessions, *with abridgments and changes, and removal of passages not in the spirit of Israel*

I desire to cling to You with all my heart, no longer to know dearth
and pain.
My life is filled with Your bounty, for when You fill my spirit, You
make lighter its load.
In me still struggle old joys, by which I am moved to tears, and
present-day mourning, in which I rejoice, and I don't know
which will prevail.
Oy, me! Have mercy on me, O my God!
Oy, me! I haven't concealed my wounds.
You are the doctor, I am the patient. You, full of love and compassion.
I, impoverished and sorrowed.
What is the life of a human, if not to be full of trials, without rest for
one single day?
When I dwell in my troubles, I yearn for elation, and when I'm filled
with joy, I worry about trouble.
Between yearning and fear, is there no rest, is there no joy, where a
person can live free from trial?
Oh, woe and alas for the joy of the world chased so swiftly by fear, for
all its delights have been poisoned!
Oh, woe and alas for the pain of the world with its vacuous greed and
heavy distress, which shatters one's fragile forbearance!
Is not all of my hope dependent upon Your abundant compassion?
Allow me to fulfill Your will. In turn, place Your will in me.
Still do I wander in darkness, but already Your sweet voice enters in
me. It calls me back to my home.
Behold, I am like a pilgrim on foot, whose journey ahead is still distant. Look how he yearns for his destination, for the place that
his journey intends.
Surely, I go…
I hear the voice calling me.
How much I have yearned for the abode of Your holiness,
receive me, I pray, O my Father, into Your palaces' midst,
for I am the work of Your hand.

22. Attachment to God

From the song of Simon the Theologian found in Martin Buber's book
Ecstatic Confessions—*with changes and abridgments and removal of*
passages based on Christian dogma

Come, now, to me, You whom my soul has desired, and desires still.
Come, now, solitary One, the solitary God, for I am alone, as surely
    Your eyes can see.
Come, now, to me, You who've made me alone, despised and
    abandoned in Your world.
Come, now, to me, sole desire of my life, You who have strengthened
    my yearning for You, the like of which has never been seen.
Come, now, to me, my breath, my very life, come, now, O solace of my
    soul. Come, now, to me, sole beauty or joy that I've ever known
    in my life.
I thank You for this, that without transformation, without any change
    or reversal, You have remained one with my soul, and that in
    being the God Most High over all, You are to me all, and in all.
Your spirit, a bread hidden and concealed, but never consumed—how
    much it will cling, truly does cling, to the lips of my soul, and
    cross all the banks of my heart.
I thank You, my God, that You are to me a day without night, a sun
    without dusk.
You have no place to hide, for Your glorious Presence fills all worlds.
You have no place to hide, for what sort of place could contain You?
But what ten thousands of ten thousands of worlds can't contain, the
    human heart can hold.
Let, now, my heart be a place open to You. Let, now, my heart be Your
    palace of holiness.
Come, now, into Your royal palace. Come, now, into my heart. Dwell
    within me, and I within You.
Please do not separate from me, even for a moment, all of the days of
    my life. And when the day of my death shall arrive, let me
    remain within You, O life of all life, You who rule over all.
Please don't forsake me for even a moment, lest while we're apart my
    enemies find me and fall on my spirit to swallow it up.
Be, now, my refuge, a source of all strength, Your tabernacle placed
    within me forever. May I be fulfilled with the happiness of it,
    even when I am in torment, and saturated with Your life, even as
    I die.

Place, now, in me Your abode, and I'll be enabled to defeat any king. For You are my bread and my drink. When I'm wrapped up in You, I experience hours of rapture no human tongue can express.

My tongue has no word. What happens in me, my soul may behold, but it's something it cannot pronounce.

It comprehends fully the things that it sees and even may try to express it. But the words for it fail, they remain inaccessible. One truly beholds what cannot be seen, something that hasn't an image. It has no complexity, it is most elemental: the greatness of boundless divine.

The soul beholds fully what has no beginning, what has no end, and what has no realm in between. And whatever it sees, it knows not how to express.

You are the fire by which all lamps are kindled from one end of the world to the other. And the fire is never exhausted.

You are the single, primordial lamp. Your light cannot be divided. All the world's separate lamps draw their strength from Your light, and by Your light they are guided.

Behold You are here, O great, primal light. You are eagerly seized by my naked heart, and I cannot provide it a name.

I have chosen for myself to keep silent. But the wonder of You, awesome in splendor, gives emphatic command to my mouth and my pen, telling me: Speak! And write!

Here He is, in my abode. Here He is, within me. Here He is, in His palace. Here He is, in my heart. The One who inhabits all worlds!

I am resting upon my bed. Because God is in me, behold, even me, I'm transported beyond all worlds.

To the One to whom all belongs, the One who endures forever, I dare to declare: "I love You, O God," and I can do so, because God loves me.

I am sated to the full with expectation. I am wrapped and covered in its shawl. And when I am one with my God, I soar up above the skies.

I know so well, and for sure, that the matter is true in this way, but it is beyond my comprehension: where goes my inner world at such times?

I know that I surely have seen what no mortal being can see.

I know that the One who is hidden, exalted above every creature, has taken me into itself, into the shelter of its hand, and behold, I'm beyond all worlds.

I, an ephemeral being, see within me my eternal Creator, the life that never goes astray.

At such a time, the thing comes alive, in my heart and also in heaven:
the light is One, both here and beyond.

23. On the Threshold of the Sixth Day

*On the occasion of my fiftieth birthday, in the month of Sivan
(May–June), 5681 (1921)*

Five "days" I have lived in Your presence, fifty years of the "week" of
my life—five decades of the seventy years of the typical human
life.
On the threshold of the sixth day, I walk before You—the threshold of
the sixth decade of life. On the threshold of the Sabbath eve of
my life's days.
Give me the strength to run before You, on this, my Sabbath eve, that I
might stand before You on my Shabbat.
Give me a youthful vitality, a firmness of character and holiness of will,
to repair on this, my Sabbath eve, the sins of my earlier days.
For truly, I've blemished the root of my soul, I've damaged the chan-
nels, I've sealed off the wells, I've rejected divine abundance.
For truly, without knowing, I touched holy worlds up above and cut
down Eternity's plants.
For truly, I've distanced myself from Your presence, like all who pass
through this vale of tears.
For I've grown far away from You, yet You haven't gone far from me.
For I've gone astray, and You have always looked for me.
For I've gone astray, like a sheep that is lost, and You called me sud-
denly and I heard.
For You called to me and I turned to You, and I was able to come back
to You.
I walked after You, but my knees often stumbled, from walking too
much in alien fields.
For truly, I walked after You even while straying, in days I spent hiding and in days of the strength of my youth.
For truly I've grown weary with the toil of my life, and You haven't yet
shown me Your good, You haven't yet made known Your ways.
But I truly continue to walk after You, and I stumble and rise, I
stumble and rise.…When will You lift me, my Creator, so that I
shall not stumble anymore?
When will you gird me with strength, so I shall not cease running
after You, even for a moment?

For truly, I've found You. But why do You hide?

For truly, I've found You, but I, to my woe, suddenly push You away.

For truly, I've found You, but why is my flesh not cleansed in Your holy fire?

For truly, I've found You, but why are there hungers and yearnings still in me that aren't a desire for You?

Whom else do I have, in heaven or in earth, but You? Why do I still wander and stumble?

For see, when I fled from Your face, You would seek me, but now that I seek You, You're like one who flees me!

Have I truly fled from Your face before now? I *imagined* I was fleeing Your presence. But can one escape from God?

Can one escape from God's soul of all souls, from divinity's life of all lives?

But You have established a mystery in You, whereas I had imagined You'd grown distant from me and I had grown distant from You.

And You have numbered all the moments of my life. You have made known to me, God, what You have made known.

You have allowed me to fall into a She'ol of despair, that I might come out and bring others from there. You have allowed me to taste the taste of death, the taste of doubt without end, in order to live and give life to others.

You've allowed me to fall in the depths of the ocean, so that my pain might grow, so my cry might grow louder, so my yearning for You might grow stronger.

You've allowed me to fall into pits of uncleanness, so I'd know and be warned, and give warning to my brethren.

Is such what You've done for me? Why have You left me to my soul?

You who know my sitting and my rising (> Ps 139:2), don't You yet know that my feet are sometimes liable to fail?

For like the lightning bolt that cracks before my eyes, Your light may sometimes disappear,

And I'm left alone with myself, amid a darkness immense, until I multiply my cries to You, from the midst of the dark where I dwell.

If You have done thus to me, if You have cast me into She'ol, so that I might arise, and bring many up with me, if I fulfill Your will. and enact Your word, then pour out Your light on me, fill with it all that's within me.

As I enter a day of great toil, let me, I pray, carry out Your command that has called me from the depths of She'ol.

Let Your spirit rest on me. Let Your counsel make me wise. Let Your will be my will.

221

From *Songs to the Boundless One*

Translations from the Yiddish

Over There, Over There...

There, over there, a Wall still stands. How my soul aspires to that place!
There, over there, a House once was placed. Where, O where, is that
House?
There, over there, God's song has been heard. Where, O where, is that
song?
There, over there, God's light has shone. Where, O where, is that light?
There, over there, God's fire has burned. Where, O where, is that fire?
There, over there, God's people has lived. Where, O where, is that people?
Souls, tearful and mournful, hover about at that Wall. Fly there, my
spirit, over there, over there.
A cup in the heavens, filled up with tears. Include my tear, as well!
May a breeze on the Ninth of Av's night carry my sigh to the store-
house of sorrows.
You souls who are wandering over old, beloved graves, what do you
hear? What news do you bring?
Has the Father remembered His children? Does He bring them back
to His table?
Is Israel's mother consoled? Has God's Presence thus been redeemed?
Has the Hind of the Dawn already appeared? Have the first rays of
daylight already arisen, driving out the darkness of night?
Does one hear at the desolate Wall the song of the cherubim renewed?
Does one not behold the wandering birds, bringing the news of
redemption?
Can one not already see, on Zion's mounts, first traces of our Messiah?
Does not one already hear from that place the shofar's summoning
sound?
Our ancestors who slumber in Hebron, do they hear, do they feel our
troubles and our pain?
Do they weep, do they pray for their children, cast aside and dis-
persed, who have wandered about as orphans in grief, for, by
now, some two thousand years?
Do they hear the last cry, the ultimate groan, the howling of pain with
no words?
Do they know of the hope reawakened, the ray of light that into dark
cellars now shines?

Abysmal depths are our woe. But heaven's heights, our hope reawakened.
　　Do they reach over there—our lament, our relief?
Transport me, my soul, to that holy Wall's site, to those hovering spirits,
　　to generations of voices, the echo of time.
Let us see, let us hear, at that site of our hope:
there, where a House once stood, let us see a cornerstone laid;
there, where God's song was once heard, let us hear a new song for the
　　Forthcoming Age.

The Descendant of David

Star to star declares: He lives! He is there!
Cloud says to cloud: He hovers in the air!
Wind says to wind: Bear the child, bear!
Dawn says to dawn: It's day everywhere!
Mountain says to mountain: He stands, he stands!
Road says to road: He walks in the Land!
Dust says to dust: His steps, do you hear?
Wind says to wind: His spirit is near!
Grass says to grass: Silence, be still!
Wood says to wood: Get ready to fulfill!
Sea says to sea: Leviathan quakes!
Heaven says to earth: Your bridegroom awakes!

Waiting for God's Arrival

From a prayer in 'Or ha-Hayyim (The Light of Life)

May it be Your will, our Father, our King, our Friend, Light of our soul,
　　Light of our spirit, Light of our lifebreath, that by virtue of the
　　Covenant that You once made with us, Your children, Your servants,
　　and by virtue of Your Thirteen Attributes of Mercy—which never
　　turn back empty from You!—You'll call to mind our ancient love
　　for You, our age-old fidelity, and rejoice in us, as in those great,
　　ancient times, bringing back Your Presence to its former abode.
We can no more bear Your separation from us than the body can
　　endure its separation from the soul.
Our bodies yearn, our souls exhaust themselves in waiting for
　　redemption from Your Presence, Your *Shekhinah*.
We pray to You, we cry to You, O divine Name, O Father merciful,
　　may You take pity on Your *Shekhinah*, who languishes in exile.
Give help, holy Name, to your *Shekhinah*, let us be reunited with Your

223

love, so sweet and and precious to our soul, to our spirit, to our
breath of life.

May our King re-enter His celestial palace. Amen, and may it be God's
will!

What Is Become of the Eternal Tree?

From a passage in Netsah Yisra'el (Eternity of Israel), *where the great Maharal [Rabbi Judah Loew of Prague] departs abruptly from quiet contemplation into effusion of soul and prayer*

Can one take account, can one give account, can the thought be com-
prehended?

The heart is struck dumb when one calls it to mind. Had we not lived
through it with our own bodies, it seems to me as if it all is parable.

But how is this?

Had we not been the children of Abraham, Isaac, and Jacob, even had
we been the wildest of the wild, the strangest of the strange, had
the Glory of Israel's God not been revealed to us, and the light of
God's Torah not shone for us, could anyone believe such things
could befall us?

If, moreover, we are indeed children of Abraham, posterity of Isaac,
tree of Jacob, seed of Holiness, root of Truth, how could such a
thing be known to happen—that which has become of us?

A tree that's planted by a river, a stream flowing from Eden, whose
roots are sunk into the deepest ground, whose branches spread
to all directions in the world—how could anyone in the world
have moved it from its place?

This people to whom was revealed eternal love, to whom were given
laws and statutes no other people was given!

This people, to whose children God had spoken, and before whose
maidservants God's Glory was revealed!

This people, for whose sake, God—in whose eyes even the heavens
were not pure enough and to whom even the angels were found
lacking—descended from His Chariot amid flashes of lightning,
and, to the whole world's wonderment, took a seat on the earth!

How, amidst God's holy abode, or before the Throne of Glory, amid
the highest of all eternal places, could the impure have entered?
How could God be conquered by heathens? How could they
have plundered divine treasures and given them away to alien
gods?

How could they have divided up for judgment the holy martyrs, condemning them to lashes, exile, slaying, burning?

And oy, oy, how many times it has been!—that the dove can find for its foot no place of rest, nor even refuge for itself on unclean ground!

There is no nation that has not imposed its yoke on us, has not oppressed or suffocated us, and once they have been sated with our blood, has not spit us out from their land.

Even if God were to make a new heaven and new earth, there would be no land to settle in nor any place of rest for the children of the living God.

People ever chase us out: "Get out, you filthy ones! Don't touch them, anyone! Let's make new laws to deal with them!"

The Torah of God's servant, Moses, has commanded God's children to clothe themselves in beauty—a crown upon their head, a holy seal placed by their heart, their clothes the color of the Throne of Glory. But today, a foreign hat is placed on their head and an alien seal on their heart, and, in place of Glory's clothes, a yellow patch.

Were all the rivers made of ink, and all tree branches pens, and all the heavens parchments, and all people in the world were scribes, they'd still fail to capture our troubles and woes, which surpass all of nature and all worldly laws.

And You, O holy Name, our God, if You are still our Father, whose great Name is still proclaimed over Your children, why is Your holy, awesome Name dishonored by Your children's state—they to whom it is said in taunt: If you are the children of the living God, why has God hidden His eyes from you all these years, while time and again you are led like sheep to the slaughter?

If our ancestors and we have sinned, we are still placed at Your mercy, and You can snatch us from the world with Your own hand. Why would You give us into foreigners' hands, letting Your Name be dishonored through our fate?

For this, our prayer is spread out before You, and unto Your Throne of Glory. Have mercy on us! Save us from the hand of strangers! At least, let us not be made the butt of laughter and ridicule among the peoples!

Beloved of Soul

A free poetic rendering of the Sabbath song "Yedid Nefesh"—rhythm, sound, and much imagery throughout are my own

225

O splendrous King of all, O world's grandeur and might,
a song are You, dear God, a dream that arrives by night.
I thirst for You, Beloved, how I pine away for You,
I stand before Your Palace's door, Oh, let me now pass through.

My spirit, sick with yearning for Your restoring love,
Oh, lead her by the waters of Your healing stream above.
Oh, guide her toward Your will, to serve at Your behest,
that she might, in Your Presence, set her woe at rest.

Oh, You who are mine in joy, You who are mine in pain,
just let me kiss the hem of Your garment's exquisite train.
Let me bow down to Your Glory as Your Chariot passes through,
Oh, grant me just one fleeting glance at Your Splendor's regal view.

You who are my Master, You, O Father mine,
Without You, how can I exist, how can life be mine?
Oh, see, behold, oh, see, how your child aches for You.
Oh, rise, yes, come, arise, come quickly into view!

Let Earth proclaim the joyous news: that You at last have come!
Already has the hour struck. We call to You: Welcome!
Even now they're spreading out Your spacious Tent of Peace,
God's Glory now will shine on us its freedom and release!

The Mother

Based on strophes in Rabbi Moshe Alshekh's Midnight Song. *A free poetic rendering—rhythm, sound, and certain images wholly my own*

Where has your companion gone away?
Has he vanished in the sky?
Exile's captive, on foreign ground,
He languishes, in shackles bound.

His princely crown has fallen down,
His purple garment now is torn,
Stolen from his palace site,
His army struck by serpent's bite.

226

A cry arises over woodland trees,
The angels sighing bitterly,
The sheep are straying in the field,
Oh, where is their protector's shield?

What does God's Presence say?
Oh, my head, Oh, my crown!
And there is One who says:
I'm going down, I'm going down!

I'm going where my children go,
Into exile, to the dark below,
I'm going where the sinners go,
To mitigate their exile's woe.

Now clothe yourself in sackcloth black,
Run through the streets and marketplace.
Father, father, what's this you do?
Mother, mother, where are you?

I am with you, I am with you,
What you are suffering I suffer, too.
For your misdeeds is Mother banished
For your misdeeds, Her voice has vanished.

From Where Will Come My Help?

Turn, turn, turn and convulse—
All's in disguise, everything false.
Cold, cold, oh, it's so cold—
Where am I in this world?

Nowhere a path, nowhere a way,
Nowhere a night, nowhere a day.
Nowhere an earth, nowhere a sky,
All is but waste, all is decay.

We wander about, exhausted we stray,
Where are You, O King? O Father, we pray.
Where are You hidden? Where concealed?
Don't you hear of our woe, our need to be healed?

Around on all sides, all is darkness, repression,
Around on all sides, all evil oppression.
Oh, how can one find a pathway to You?
How to reach You? If only I knew!

Arise, come out, oh, why do You hide?
Throw back Your cloak of dissembling disguise!
Break through walls of chaos; give ear to our cries,
Open up all the gates with light for our eyes!

Oh, drive away now the dark clouds of gloom,
bring out for us now the light of Your love.
And may You at last Creation's clothing assume,
Give answer, O dream—our King from above!

Deepest Wish

Based on the first and last part of [Moses] Ibn Ezra's Baqqashah
(Prayer), with modifications of form and content

For You my flesh, for You my blood,
for You my love, for You passion's flood,
for You my staying, for You my going,
for You my being, for You my life outflowing,
for You my seeing, for You my hearing.
for You my turning, for You my appearing,
for You my today, for You my tomorrow,
for You my joy, for You my sorrow,
for You my thanks, for You my song,
for You my sound, for You my clang,
for You my cry, for You my shout,
for You my speech, for You my being mute.
From You my shape, from You my form,
from You my longing, from You my storm,
from You my breath, from You my embrace,
from You my build, from You my face.
I am the altar, I am the bull,
I am the sacrifice for my sins to the full.
You are mine while I live, You are mine when I die,
to You my suffering calls, to You my needs cry.
As from a woman in childbirth does my pain to You pour,

like an unhappy pauper, I knock on Your door.
May You be my stronghold, be my embankment,
Bring near to You my prayer, behold my lament.
I without You—all mine are the woes,
I without You—a straw the wind blows.
Press through a wall to the place where I stand,
stretch out to me Your loving right hand,
give light to where I walk on the way,
give renewal of spirit to my night and day.
Drown my misdeeds in the sea of my tears,
raise my prayers up, above heavens' tiers.
When You read of my sins, please render them null,
When my repentance arrives, please accept it in full.
And when my last hour in the end presses in,
let me not flog myself long because of my sin.
And when I shall from this world's gates depart,
may Your angels greet me with an open heart.
May they escort me into Your palaces sublime,
and set my soul free from exile's grime.
When my spirit shall enter into Eden's blissful space,
let there flow upon me *Shekhinah*'s light and grace.
And may my shelter be inside Your hidden light,
my spirit drenched in awe as I behold Your Face's sight.

NOTES

Foreword

1. [Zeitlin in 1934 wrote a review essay on the Piasecner's *Hovat ha-Talmidim*. It is reprinted in the posthumous expanded version of *Sifran shel Yehidim*, pp. 240–44. A. G.]

Hillel Zeitlin: A Biographical Introduction

1. The most important studies of Zeitlin are the full-length biography by Shraga Bar-Sella, *Between the Storm and the Quiet: The Life and Works of Hillel Zeitlin* (Tel Aviv, 1999) [Hebrew], and several Hebrew articles by Jonatan Meir. Meir also published several essays of Zeitlin, accompanied by a lengthy introduction, in a Hebrew volume entitled *Rabbi Nahman of Bratslav: World Weariness and Longing for the Messiah*, published in the Jerusalem scholarly series *Yeri'ot* in 2006. The only prior work in English is the unpublished doctoral dissertation of Moshe Waldoks, *Hillel Zeitlin: The Early Years (1894–1919)* (Brandeis, 1984). This introduction makes grateful use of all of these sources as well as Aaron Zeitlin's memoir, *Mayn Fotr*, included in HZ's *Reb Nakhmen Braslaver* (New York: Matones, 1952), pp. 11–47. A bibliography of Zeitlin's writings, composed by E. R. Mal'achi, appeared in *Ha-Tekufah* 32–33 (1948): 848–76, with the supplement in the following volume, 843–48.

2. *Ketuvim* 2 (1928): 28–29. Also appeared in *Ha-Do'ar* 7 (1928): 29.

3. Zeitlin's memoir was published without notes. All footnotes to this piece are mine. A. G.

4. 1742–1822, scholar and Jewish communal statesman.

5. 1780–1857, rabbi of Gomel, leading disciple of the first two HaBaD rabbis.

6. R. Shalom Dov Baer of Rechitsa (1866–1920).

7. R. Menaham Mendel Schneersohn (1789–1866).

8. Fishl Schneersohn (1887–1958), psychologist and novelist.

9. All classic writers of the nineteenth-century Hebrew *haskalah*.

10. Religious philosopher and apologist, Spain, fifteenth century, author of *Sefer ha-'Ikkarim*.

11. Religious philosopher and mystic, key figure in the Berlin *haskalah*, 1753–1800.

12. Philosopher of Jewish history, leading figure of the Galician *haskalah,* author of *Moreh Nevukhey ha-Zeman*, 1785–1840.

13. Monye Bokal (d. 1886), founder of the *'Am 'Olam* movement for Jewish agricultural settlement, a predecessor of the Territorialists.

14. John William Draper (1811–82), Anglo-American scientist and intellectual historian. My thanks to Jonatan Meir for this reference.

15. Dimitri Ivanovich Pisarev (1840–68), radical social critic.

16. Nikolai Gavrilovich Chernishevsky (1828–89), Russian social thinker.

17. Nikolai Aleksandrovitch Dobrolyubov (1836–61), Russian literary critic.

18. Nikolai Konstantinovich Mikhailovsky (1842–1904), journalist and revolutionary democrat.

19. Joseph Hayyim Brenner, Zeitlin's youthful friend, well-known Hebrew writer, killed in Arab riots of 1921.

20. Volumes 5–8 (1899–1902). The entire work was reprinted in Zeitlin's *Ketavim Nivharim* (Warsaw, 1910).

21. 1900.

22. *Ha-Zeman* 1 (1905); *Masu'ot* 1 (1919). The *Masu'ot* piece is in part a revision of Zeitlin's earlier enthusiasm for Nietzsche.

23. Included in his *Ketavim Nivharim*, v. 2 (Warsaw, 1911).

24. *Sifrut* 1 (1908): 67–84.

25. *Sifrut* 2 (1908): 33–82.

26. *Sifrut* 4 (1910): 141–60.

27. Russian religious philosopher (1866–1938). Of Jewish origin (originally Schwarzmann), Shestov was attracted to the mysticism of Russian Orthodoxy, recasting it in contemporary philosophical language.

28. *King Lear,* Act 3, Scene 2.

29. Zeitlin was married to Esther Kunin in 1896. She too came from a HaBaD family, living near Gomel. They had three children. The eldest, poet Aaron Zeitlin, was born in 1898. The two younger children were Elchonon, whose memoir *In a Literarishn Shtub* was published posthumously (Buenos Aires, 1946), and a daughter, Rivka.

30. A special section of the Zohar.

31. This concluding note seems to indicate that Zeitlin was interested

in settling in Erez Israel following his visit there in 1925. It is unknown how serious these intentions were, or whether they ever constituted a concrete plan.

32. Y. H. Brenner, *Mi-Bifnim*, pp. 334f.

33. *"Yosef Hayyim Brenner: 'Arakhim ve-Zikhronot."* He-Tekufah 14–15 (1922): 617–45.

34. *Baruch Spinoza*, pp. 135f.

35. *"Di Benkshaft nokh Sheynheyt"* (translated below), original in Zeitlin's *Shriftn* (Warsaw: Velt-Bibliotek, 1910), p. 34.

36. See Nicham Ross, *A Love/Hate Relationship with Tradition: Neo-Hassidic Writing at the Beginning of the 20th Century*, doctoral dissertation, Ben Gurion University, 2004.

37. S. Bar-Sela', *Beyn Sa'ar Li-Demamah*, p. 136.

38. V. 4 (1919): 501–45.

39. Reprinted in the volume also entitled *'Al Gevul Shney 'Olamot* (Tel Aviv: Yavneh, 1965), pp. 169–93.

40. Eliezer Schweid, "Prophetic Mysticism in Twentieth-Century Jewish Thought," *Modern Judaism* 14, no. 2 (1994): 139–74.

41. *Davar la-'Amim* (Warsaw, 1928), p. 13.

42. On these efforts and groups, see J. Meir's introduction to Zeitlin's Bratslav writings, p. 22, and the sources discussed in note 107.

43. It was precisely Zeitlin's insistence on linking these two impulses, the scientific and the spiritual-prophetic, that caused Gershom Scholem, an avid reader of Zeitlin in his youth, to distance himself from Zeitlin. Scholem, wholly committed to the scientific enterprise (in his case the historical-philological study of Kabbalah), had great suspicion of anyone who maintained this view. See the letters quoted by Meir in his introduction to Zeitlin's Bratslav writings, pp. 13f.

44. Here one sees especially the closeness in spirit between Zeitlin and Rabbi Abraham Isaac Kook, who was working out his own blend of Jewish mysticism, universalism, and Jewish national-religious rebirth. On the parallels and connections between Zeitlin and Kook, see J. Meir, "Longing of Souls for the Shekhina: Relations between Rabbi Kook, Zeitlin, and Brenner," in *The Path of the Spirit: The Eliezer Schweid Jubilee Volume* (Jerusalem, 2005), pp. 771–818.

45. J. Meir, "Zeitlin's *Zohar*: The History of a Translation and Commentary Project," *Kabbalah* 10 (2004): 119–57 [Hebrew]; and A. Green, "Hillel Zeitlin and Neo-Hasidic Readings of the Zohar," *Kabbalah* 22 (2010): 59–78.

46. Originally published in the New York *Morgn Zhurnal* v. 46 #13,650 (29 Av, 5706/1946).

Hasidism Then and Now

1. *"Aufgaben der polnischen Juden," Der Jude* (1916–17): 89–93. The passage is translated into Hebrew by J. Meir in the introduction to his edition of Zeitlin's essays on Bratslav (Jerusalem: Yeri'ot, 2006), p. 13.

2. Subtitle: "Pages for everyone who wants to save himself from the falsehood that is currently drowning the world."

3. [All notes below are mine. A. G.] BeSHT is an acronym for Israel ben Eliezer, the Ba'al Shem Tov (1700–1760), the mystical teacher and wonderworker around whose example the Hasidic movement emerged.

4. R. Eleazar Rokeach of Worms (ca. 1165–c. 1230) and R. Yehudah he-Hasid of Regensburg (c. 1150–1217) were the central figures of the medieval Rhineland mystical circles known as *Hasidey Ashkenaz*.

5. R. Hayyim Ibn Attar (1696–1743), a contemporary of the Ba'al Shem Tov, was a well-known Moroccan Kabbalist and Torah commentator.

6. Eleventh-century pietist in Spain, author of the classic *Duties of the Hearts*.

7. Zeitlin is writing in the context of modernity in general but specifically refers to the aftermath of the First World War and the social and political transformations that followed.

8. It is noteworthy that 1924 was the year Stalin succeeded Lenin in leadership of the Soviet state. Events in Russia were very keenly on the minds of Warsaw's Jews.

9. Revision of a translation first made by Rabbi Zalman Schachter-Shalomi.

10. *Likkutey 'Ezot* by Rabbi Nahman of Bratslav.

11. This fifteenth principle was added by Zeitlin in the Hebrew version in *Sifran shel Yehidim* (1928).

12. I have composed these three chapters in the language of the Zohar, as befits their mysterious thought content [HZ; all other notes by A. G.]. These three chapters are addressed to Yavneh members, or perhaps to an elite core within Yavneh that Zeitlin called *Beney Hekhala* (Children of the Palace).

13. Zeitlin is here playing on the seeming connection between the Hebrew roots BNH (build) and BWN (contemplate, understand), the place-name Yavneh, and (below) the personal name Benayahu. See Zohar 1:6a–b.

14. B. T. Ta'anit 16a.

15. Zohar 1:6a–b.

16. *Yihudim,* or "unifications," are the essential secret practices of Kabbalah. Usually they involve the joining of the *sefirot* or *partsufim* in a particular configuration, often having to do with a particular spelling out

of the letters of the divine name Y-H-W-H. Bringing them together in a contemplative exercise thus forms a particular "unification" of God's name and affects the related cosmic forces.

17. B. T. Yoma 21b, referring to the fire on the Temple altar.

18. This is Zeitlin's wishful extension and universalization of *ahavat yisra'el*, although he has recognized above that it belongs more to the future than the past.

19. From *Patah Eliyahu*, a passage from Tikkuney Zohar recited in the Sephardic and Hasidic prayer services.

20. This and other structural and numerical parallels between the inner divine self, the Torah, and the souls of Israel are widespread in Jewish mystical sources. The point is that each of these three dimensions must be kept whole if the others are to be preserved.

21. The obscure phrase *mafrid aluf* in this verse is widely interpreted as *mafrid alef* (bringing about separation within the One).

22. Mishnah Sanhedrin 10:1.

23. Rabbi Tsadok ha-Kohen of Lublin (1823–1900), Hasidic master and original thinker and author. See his *Takkanat ha-Shavin* (Jerusalem: Mekor ha-Sefarim, 2002), 14a and elsewhere.

24. B. T. Tosafot to Menahot 110a.

25. Referring to an ancient legend that the "lower waters" of the second day of Creation called out against the injustice of their being farther from God.

26. I.e., a time when the political situation reveals that the End is near.

27. Zohar 3:75a.

28. B. T. Berakhot 32b.

29. Zeitlin seems to have lost track here and does not mention the fourth party. Might it be the Zionists, concerned with the Land?

30. Meaning uncertain. See B. T. Zevahim 89a.

31. Yitzhak Landsberg, later known as Yitzhak Sadeh, emigrated from Poland to the Land of Israel in 1921. He became the founder and first commander of the Palmah, the famous defense force of the pre-state Jewish community that formed the basis of the Haganah, the Israel Defense Army, during the War of Independence.

32. Nehemia Aminah, one of the founders of the Po'el Mizrahi, the religious socialist party in the Land of Israel.

33. These seem to be Heisherik and Steinsaltz, mentioned in the preceding letter.

34. While the intended further chapters did not appear, Zeitlin did indeed cover these subjects in later writings. On HaBaD and Bratslav, see especially the two posthumous Yiddish collections *Introduction to*

Khassidism and the Way of Khabad and *Reb Nakhman Braslaver,* ed. Aaron Zeitlin (New York: Matones, 1952). The final chapter, "The Hasidism of the Future," is represented here as Zeitlin's "Call for a New Hasidism." The first discussion of this intended work is found in a 1907 letter from Zeitlin to Joseph Klausner, editor of *Ha-Shiloah,* quoted by J. Meir in his edition of Zeitlin's articles on Bratslav, p. 15n52.

35. [1815–88. His book *Shalom 'al Yisra'el (Peace upon Israel* {Zhitomyr/ Vilna, 1868–73}) was the first positive evaluation of Hasidism by a modern writer and was seen as marking the end of a century of fierce battles over Hasidism's legitimacy. This and all subsequent bracketed footnotes by A. G.]

36. Dov Baer of Miedzyrzec, *Likkutey Amarim,* "Introduction." [This book is also called *Maggid Devaraw le-Ya'akov.* The critical edition is by Rivka Schatz-Uffenheimer (Jerusalem: Magnes Press, 1976). The passage is on p. 5.] I will bring quotations from Hasidic literature *as they are,* except when wording needs to be changed due to improper usage.

37. He means to say that it cannot be grasped by the outer soul, but only by the soul within, its innermost part, its godliness.

38. *Likkutey Amarim* #56, pp. 83f.

39. [Based on a widespread play on words already found in the earliest Kabbalistic sources, intentionally misreading *me-ayin* to mean "from Nothing" instead of "from where?"]

40. R. Menahem Mendel of Vitebsk, *Peri ha-Arets, Tetsaveh* (Kopyst, 1814), 11a.

41. *Likkutey Amarim* #60, p. 91.

42. *Likkutey Amarim* #78, p. 134. That which the author of *Peri ha-Arets* calls "being" his master, writing in *Likkutey Amarim,* calls "Nothing." This will come as no surprise to one familiar with Hasidic writings. There are often contradictions in the use of terms, and not always even between different authors. For our purpose, however, the idea is essentially the same.

43. *Sha'arey ha-Yihud veha-Emunah* by R. Aaron of Starroselje (disciple of R. Shneur Zalman of Liadi), *Kelalut ha-Yihud,* 27b. [*Pele'* or "wonder" is *aleph* spelled backward; *aleph* is frequently taken to represent *keter,* the primal One behind the process of emanation.]

44. R. Abraham ben David of Posquieres, in the introduction to his commentary on *Sefer Yetsirah.* I have joined his words to those of the *hasidim,* even though he preceded them by many generations, since the *hasidim* base themselves on him with regard to Being and Nothingness.

45. R. Israel Ba'al Shem Tov, *Keter Shem Tov* (Brooklyn: Kehot, 1972), p. 31 and elsewhere.

46. *Peri ha-Arets, Bereshit,* p. 9.

47. *Likkutey Amarim* #120, p. 197.

48. *Tanya*, Chapter 42.

49. [He can also withdraw it back into himself.]

50. See *Kitvey Kodesh* 5b, and many other sources. A distinctive explanation of *tsimtsum* is found in HaBaD writings, but that will have to be elaborated elsewhere. Here we offer only general headings, fundaments accepted by all Hasidic systems.

51. *Likkutey Amarim* #60, p. 89f., quoting Zohar 1:234b.

52. Ethics #4–5.

53. *De Profundis*.

54. *Or Torah*, (printed with *Likkutey Amarim*), p. 192

55. [Rabbi Elijah of Vilna (1720–97), the great opponent of Hasidism.]

56. R. Mordecai of Chernobyl, *Likkutey Torah, Sixth Instruction* (New York, 1954; reprint of Lvov, 1865), p. 4b–c.

57. R. Meshullam Feibush Heller, *Likkutim Yekarim* 54 (ed. Jerusalem, 1974), p. 10b.

58. *Likkutey Amarim* #200, p. 325.

59. *Me'or 'Eynayim, Likkutim* (Jerusalem, 1999), p. 340.

60. R. Israel BeSHT. [Source not identified.]

61. R. Shneur Zalman of Liadi, *Tanya*, Part II, "*Sha'ar ha-Yihud veha-Emunah*," Chapter 1, based on the BeSHT.

62. Ibid., Chapter 3.

63. [Commenting on the *Kedushah* liturgy of the Sabbath service.]

64. R. Mordecai of Chernobyl, *Likkutey Torah* (New York: Israel Wolf, 1954), p. 77.

65. [Based on Deuteronomy 30:14.]

66. Avot 6:2 (*Perek Kinyan Torah*).

67. *Keter Shem Tov* (Brooklyn, 2004), cf. pp. 79f.

68. Ibid.

69. *Me'or 'Eynayim, Pinhas*, p. 202.

70. Ibid., 200. [Human emotions, which may have physio-psychological bases, are in fact reflections of mysterious cosmic forces, the "qualities" of the Creator.]

71. Ibid., p. 201.

72. R. Nahman of Bratslav, *Maggid Sihot* (*Sihot ha-RaN* #52, commenting on the verse "Tell of His glory among the nations" [Ps 96:3]).

73. R. Ephraim of Sudilkow, *Degel Mahaneh Ephraim, Va-Yera'* (Jerusalem, 1963), p. 19, in the name of his grandfather the BeSHT.

74. R. Israel BeSHT, *Keter Shem Tov*, p. 112 and elsewhere.

75. R. Elimelekh of Lezajsk, *No'am Elimelech, Lekh Lekha*, ed. G. Nig'al (Jerusalem, 1978), p. 35.

76. *Peri ha-Arets, Bo*, p. 50.

77. [*Hesed* in this context is usually rendered as "abomination"; the Hasidic text is reading it as "love."]

78. *Me'or 'Eynayim, Pinhas*, p. 202, in the name of the BeSHT.

79. Ibid.

80. In the name of Rabbi Nahman of Bratslav—from *'Alim li-Terufah*, #310.

81. R. Ze'ev Wolf of Zhitomir, *Or ha-Me'ir, Noah* (ed. Jerusalem, 2000), p. 12.

82. Ibid., *Lekh Lekha*, p. 16, interpreting *Tikkuney Zohar* #30, p. 74b.

83. *No'am Elimelech, Va-Yera'*, p. 40, in the name of the Maggid of Miedzyrzec.

84. *Or ha-Me'ir, Hayyey Sarah*, p. 39.

85. R. Abraham ha-Mal'ach, *Hesed le-Avraham, Lekh Lekha*, p. 32.

86. R. Shne'ur Zalman of Liadi, *Commentary to the Siddur*, pp. 152f.

87. A summary of *Tanya*, Chapter 5.

88. *Likkutim Yekarim*, 20b.

89. Ibid., in the name of R. Meir of Przemysl. Others quote it in the name of the BeSHT. I quote this as the BeSHT would understand it.

90. [These are Kabbalistic symbols for evil and the fallen sparks. The "kings who died" is based on the narrative in Genesis 36. The number of 288 fallen sparks represents four times 72, the fullest spelling out of the name Y-H-W-H, also pointing to the word *meRaHeFet* (hovering) in Gen 1:2.]

91. [Zohar 3:135b.]

92. [Here we see the strong influence of Nietzsche on Zeitlin and the latter's attempt to link it up to Hasidism, or to use Hasidism as a brake on the Nietzschean assertion. The "will to power" (that is, the manifestation of self) does indeed lie at the heart of existence, but as the self-manifesting presence of the Creator within all that exists. Denying this and taking that selfhood as one's own, using it as a form of individual self-assertion, is the root of all evil.]

93. *Midrash 'Aseret ha-Dibberot* 1 (*Bet ha-Midrash* 1:63).

94. [Based on 2 Sam 14:14.]

95. *Keter Shem Tov*, p. 8.

96. R. Jacob Joseph of Polonnoye, *Toledot Ya'akov Yosef, Tazri'a* (Jerusalem, 1962), p. 316. The "female waters" refers to awakening that comes from "below," from the human, from the earth. ["Know" in the verse is being read with a sexual edge, as in the biblical "Adam knew his wife Eve" (Gen 4:1).]

97. From the BeSHT's commentary to Psalm 107.

98. The BeSHT. See *Degel Mahaneh Ephraim, Massa'ey*, p. 222, *Teshu'ot Hen*, selections on *Mishpatim* (Jerusalem, 1966), p. 63 and elsewhere.

99. *Ginzey Yosef, Va-Yetse'* (Jerusalem, 1960), p. 130.

100. Ibid., in the name of R. Mendel of Premiszlany.

101. B. T. 'Eruvin 13b.

102. R. Jacob Joseph of Polonnoye, *Ketonet Passim.*

103. *Peri ha-Arets, Be-Har,* p. 83.

104. *Meʾor 'Eynayim, Mattot,* p. 206.

105. *Or ha-Ganuz La-Tsaddikim, Va-Ethanan* (Warsaw, 1887), p. 42.

106. [Referring to the rabbinic quip "I dwelt—*GaRTY*—with Laban, but kept the 613—*TaRYaG*—commandments."]

107. *'Arvey Nahal, Va-Yera'* #9.

108. *Meʾor 'Eynayim, Lekh Lekha,* p. 30.

109. R. Hayyim Tyrer of Czernowitz, *Shaʾar ha-Tefillah,* Chapter 8.

110. Distilled from *Or ha-Meʾir* on the Song of Songs, in the name of the Maggid of Miedzyrzec and *Likkutim Yekarim,* 13. [The passage goes through six of the seven lower *sefirot,* interpreted as moral categories in Hasidism: love, fear, glory, triumph, gratitude, and attachment.]

111. [*Middot* (sing. *middah*) is an extremely difficult term to translate. Literally "measures," it often refers to ethics or ethical conduct—in Yiddish a *bal mides* (= *middot*) is an ethical person—but in the Hasidic context it can also mean "emotions," based on associations with the seven lower *sefirot* and their human emotional counterparts. "Qualities" or "attributes" are also frequently appropriate renditions.]

112. *Keter Shem Tov,* p. 38, based on "Pharaoh drew near" (Exod 14:10) and elsewhere.

113. Ibid.

114. [B. T. Berakhot 17a.]

115. *Orhot Tsaddikim* [an anonymous ethical treatise, fifteenth-century Germany] *Shaʾar Yirʾat Shamayim,* p. 238. I have brought this quotation from a much earlier source because it is entirely in the spirit and style of the *hasidim.*

116. *Noʾam Elimelech, Lekh Lekha,* p. 35.

117. Levi Yitzhak of Berdiczew, *Kedushat Levi* (Jerusalem, 1958), *Bereshit,* p. 3.

118. *Noʾam Elimelech, Kedoshim,* pp. 330f.

119. *Sippurey Tsaddikim.*

120. *Meʾor 'Eynayim, Shemot,* p. 105.

121. *Likkutim Yekarim,* in the name of the BeSHT.

122. *Meʾor 'Eynayim, Hukkat,* p. 196f.

123. The "Holy Letter" by the son of the *Noʾam Elimelech.* Included in G. Nigʾal's edition of *Noʾam Elimelech,* p. 603 [R. Eleazar of Lezajsk].

124. *Tzavaʾat RYVaSH.*

125. Ibid.

126. *Or ha-Ganuz la-Tsaddikim, Mishpatim*, p. 44.

127. R. Shne'ur Zalman of Liadi, Commentary to the *Siddur*, in a note on midnight vigils. [This is the HaBaD approach, intellect controlling the emotions and hence human actions.]

128. *Tanya*, Chapter 16.

129. *Peri ha-Arets*, The Holy Letters (letter #12), p. 167.

130. *Tanya*, Chapter 49.

131. *Tanya*, the Letter on Repentance, Chapter 4.

132. Based on various passages in *Tanya*.

133. *Keter Shem Tov.* [Cf. *Degel Mahaneh Ephraim, Devarim*, s.v. *ba'aravah.*]

134. [The text is playing on *shivyo*, "*his* captivity." Learn from him; take captives as he does.]

135. *Keter Shem Tov*, p. 75.

136. R. Abraham Kalisker, The Holy Letter.

137. [A quotation from R. Isaac Luria's table hymn for the third Sabbath meal.]

138. *Keter Shem Tov*, p. 75.

139. R. Jacob Joseph of Polonnoye, *Tsofnat Pa'aneah, Va-'Era* (ed. G. Nig'al), p. 75 and elsewhere.

140. It is impossible to understand this "sweetening of judgment forces" until you know the order and nature of the *sefirot*. I therefore turn to explain this, according to books and authors but also following my own understanding. This will also serve better to clarify some of the points discussed above. [Here Zeitlin gives a brief account of the ten *sefirot* (lit.: "numbers," stages of divine self-manifestation), the essential symbol system of classical Kabbalah, as well as other Kabbalistic terms as presented in early Hasidic sources, based largely on the HaBaD version of these teachings.]

141. [This is the opening phrase of the Zohar on Genesis.]

142. [These terms, derived from the *Idra* sections of the Zohar, are widely used in Lurianic Kabbalah. They refer to the earliest and most obscure stirring of the drive toward self-revelation within God. The term *Longsuffering* indicates that the first arousal within God, even preceding the thought of creation, was that of pure compassion for all creatures that were to emerge from the process.]

143. R. Moshe Hayyim Luzzatto, *KeLaH Pithey Hokhmah*, Chapters 7 and 12 [paraphrased].

144. [The fact that *Adam Kadmon* (Primal Man) is a parallel symbol to *'Atika* (the Ancient One) is a way of saying that the human was the goal of creation from the start.]

145. R. Moshe Hayyim Luzzatto, *KeLaH Pithey Hokhmah*, Chapter 4.

146. [A relationship with a God who is all *hesed*, free-flowing love and beneficence, would put humans in the passive role of receivers alone.]

147. [Adapted from the opening chapters of *Tanya*, Part 2.]

148. [From *Patah Eliyahu*, a passage from *Tikkuney Zohar* recited in the Hasidic liturgy.]

149. The *sefirot* are ten, even though the count here, including both *keter* and *da'at*, is eleven. Sometimes *keter* is not listed as one of the *sefirot*, being *above* them all. Some counts do not include *da'at*, since it is only an effulgence and firming up of *hokhmah* and *binah*. [The *sefirot* must be ten, a tradition going back to their first mention in *Sefer Yetsirah*. Every list will count either *keter* or *da'at*, but not both. Hasidic sources usually begin with *hokhmah* and list *da'at*.]

150. [An image taken from the opening paragraph of *Sefer Yetsirah*, the earliest source for the term *sefirot*.]

151. [This is a euphemistic way of saying "the corona of the phallus." When *yesod* and *malkhut* are fully joined, she is depicted as an extension of his own bodily self.]

152. [These reflect the bodily structure of 248 limbs, not coincidentally parallel to the 248 positive commandments of the Torah, and 365 sinews, parallel to the Torah's 365 prohibitions.]

153. [It is through the *middot* that the forces hidden as pure potential within *keter* now come to be manifest in the dimensions of time (the six "days") and space (the six "directions").]

154. The sefirotic indications within the name, according to Luria, are as follows: the tip of the *yod* points to *arikh*; *yod* is abba; *heh* is *imma*; *waw* is *ze'ir*; the final *heh* is *nukva*.

155. Sometimes the term *ze'ir*, or "blessed Holy One," is applied to *tif'eret* alone, since it, as Truth, includes all the other qualities, embracing all.

156. This is the meaning of the traditional Kabbalistic formula that is recited before performing a *mitsvah*.

157. See R. Joseph Bloch, *Ginzey Yosef, Va-Yehi*, Selections, p. 201, as well as several passages in *Tsofnat Pa'aneah*.

158. *Rav Yeyvi* on Psalm 18 (Ostrog, 1808), p. 44b. [Evil events— plagues, persecutions, natural disasters—result from divine decree. The righteous have power in their prayers to avert the decree from being carried out in its harshest form. This prayer-power is another sort of "sweetening" of evil, one in which God himself takes part!]

159. R. Gedalia of Linitz, *Teshu'ot Hen, Va-Yetse*, p. 33.

160. *Tsofnat Pa'aneah*, etc.

161. *Or ha-Ganuz la-Tzaddikim, Be-Shalah*, pp. 41f. (abbreviated). [The discovery that misfortune is a result of the divine will, brought in

order to arouse repentance, will lead to a "sweetening" or acceptance of that misfortune in the worshiper's mind.]

Judaism and Universal Religion

1. [See *William James in Russian Culture*, ed. Joan Delaney Grossman and Ruth Rischin (Lanham MD: Lexington, 2003). The volume includes essays by Alexander Etkind, "James and Konovulov: The *Varieties of Religious Experience* and Russian Theology between Revolutions," and Brian Horowitz, "Lev Shestov's James—'A Knight of Free Creativity.'"]

2. [Arthur Green, "Three Warsaw Mystics," in *Qolot Rabbim: The Rivka Schatz-Uffenheimer Memorial Volume*, ed. R. Elior and J. Dan, vol. 2 (Jerusalem, 1996), pp. 36ff.]

3. [Zeitlin is making metaphoric use of the ancient way of proclaiming the new month on the Hebrew lunar calendar, when one who witnessed the first sliver of new moon attested before the court.]

4. [Referring to the famous rabbinic tale of the "four who entered paradise," one of whom, Ben Zoma, "gazed and was damaged." Talmud Hagigah 14b.]

5. [Cesare Lambroso (1835–1909), Italian criminologist and theoretician on human nature.]

6. B. T. Pesahim 49b.

7. [The language is that of *Shir ha-Kavod*, a medieval Jewish hymn used in the Sabbath morning liturgy.]

8. [Micha Joseph Berdyczewski (1865–1921), Hebrew thinker and essayist, also of Hasidic background, and a major influence on Zeitlin.]

9. [The Hebrew word *ruah*, here rendered "spirit," also means "wind," especially reflected in the biblical quotations below. But as a translation of the German *Geist*, it also has a broad range of intellectual connotations.]

10. ["Expansiveness"—with a nod to Berdyczewski's indebtedness to Nietzsche—is an attempt to articulate a distinction between *peli'ah* and *hafla'ah* that will become crucial at the end of this chapter.]

11. From his essay "In Ethics and Life." See Berdyczewski, "Lifnot Erev," *Arakhin* (Warsaw, 1899): 88–93.

12. [Quoting the New Testament as scripture is most unusual in Hebrew letters. Later Zeitlin would include translations of Christian prayers in his *Longings for the Endless*.]

13. [The last of the four children in the Passover Haggadah.]

14. [RaSHI's comment to Gen 1:2.]

15. Lev Shestov in his book on Dostoevsky and Nietzsche. [Shestov

(1866–1938) was a religious philosopher and mystic, an important influence on Zeitlin. The book referred to here is *The Philosophy of Tragedy*, 1903. Zeitlin published an appreciation of Shestov in *Ha-Me'orer* 2, no. 10 (1907), 175–80.]

16. [Torquato Tasso, Italian poet (1544–95), author of *La Gerusalemme liberata*, a man of great sensitivity who suffered terrible pain in his later life, including long years of confinement in a madhouse.]

17. [*Romeo and Juliet*, act I, scene 1, lines 171ff. My thanks to Joel Rosenberg for his help in identifying this source.]

18. In Midrash *Bereshit Rabbah* 65, the version is, "When Esau came in to his father, hell came in with him." The *Yalkut Shim'oni* (on Gen 27) offers a similar version. But the source that RaSHI brings ("He saw hell open beneath him") is much more appropriate to scripture's deep intent. It was not Esau who brought hell along with him, but Isaac himself who saw it open before him.

19. I mean beyond what people consider "abyss," "emptiness," or "naught." When seen from the perspective of above, these are true *being*.

20. B. T. Megillah 3a.

21. B. T. Berakhot 4a.

22. [B. T. Hagigah 13b.]

23. [*The Book of Psalms: A Translation with Commentary*, trans. Robert Alter (New York: Norton and Co., 2007).]

24. Rabbi Nahman of Bratslav, *'Alim li-Terufah* #310.

25. [Marcel Allain, French novelist (1885–1969).]

26. [John Bunyan (1628–88), author of *The Pilgrim's Progress*.]

27. *Mishneh Torah, Yesodey ha-Torah* 2.

28. *Toldot Ya'akov Yosef, mishpatim*, in the name of the BeSHT.

29. *Ben Porat Yosef, va-era*.

30. *Rav Yevi* on Psalm 34.

31. *Likkutim Yekarim*, p. 2.

32. ["Melancholy" and "erotic energy" are literally "black bile" and "red bile."]

33. *Me'or 'Eynayim*, selections, pp. 313f.

34. *Kedushat Levi, bereshit*, p. 3.

35. Ibid.

36. The prayer-book commentary of R. Shneur Zalman of Liadi, introduction to the midnight vigil (ed. Vilna, 1912), p. 300.

37. R. Isaiah Horowitz ("The Two Tablets of the Covenant") in the name of Nahmanides.

38. B. T. Baba Batra 16a.

39. B. T. Hagigah 4a.

40. "When one hears the divine voice, containing the source of life, one's soul cleaves to its root. It no longer lives the life of flesh." Nahmanides to Deut 5:23.

41. [B. T. Hullin 7b.]

42. [Leonid Andreyev (1871–1919), Russian symbolist writer and dramatist. Zeitlin seems to be referring to his play *The Life of Man* (1906).]

43. [This is the sefirotic rung associated with the mind of Moses. It is still slightly lower than *binah*, place of the unknown fiftieth "gate."]

44. [A remarkable interpretation of Deut 34:6. Moses himself is the "man" of "no man knows his burial place." B. T. Sotah 14a.]

45. [Kohelet Rabbah 1:34.]

46. [George Francis Train (1829–1904), eccentric American businessman and public figure.]

47. [B. T. Sanhedrin 46a.]

48. [*Mishneh Torah, Hilhot Teshuvah* 3:7.]

49. [*Rabad's Commentary*, ibid.]

50. [Moses Taku, important thirteenth-century rabbinic sage who disapproved of both philosophy and Kabbalah.]

51. [Mark Antokolski (1843–1902), Russian-Jewish artist whose sculptures dealt with both Jewish and Gentile subjects.]

52. [Jozef Israels (1824–1911), prominent Dutch-Jewish painter best known for his striking realist style.]

53. [Samuel Hirszenberg (1865–1908), Polish-Jewish painter and teacher at Bezalel Academy in Jerusalem.]

54. [Friedrich Nietzsche (1844–1900), important German philosopher and philologist. See *The Will to Power*, trans. Walter Kaufman (New York: Vintage Books, 1967), pp. 202–3, 359.]

55. [*Bereshit Rabbah* 3:4.]

56. [*Bereshit Rabbah* 3:6.]

57. [*Me'or 'Eynayim*, pp. 44–45; *No'am Elimelech, Va-Yera'*, p. 40.]

58. [*Likkutey Moharan* 1:13a.]

59. [*Va-Yikra Rabbah* 30:2.]

60. [*Likkutey Moharan* 2:11.]

61. [B. T. Hullin 60a.]

62. [Meir Ibn Gabbai, *'Avodat ha-Kodesh* (Jerusalem, 2004), *Helek ha-Takhlit,* chap. 10, p. 273.]

63. [Based on *Bereshit Rabbah* 12:1.]

64. [*Shemot Rabbah* 29:9.]

65. [*Bereshit Rabbah* 82:2.]

66. [B. T. Hullin 91b.]

67. [B. T. Sotah 12a.]

68. [B. T. Megillah 15a.]
69. [B. T. Bava Batra 58a.]
70. [Ibid.]
71. [B. T. Bava Metsia 84a.]
72. [B. T. Berachot 4b.]
73. [B. T. ʿAvodah Zarah 20a.]
74. [*Noʾam Elimelech, Hayyey Sarah*, p. 52.]
75. [*Noʾam Elimelech, Kedoshim*, pp. 330–31.]
76. [*Noʾam Elimelech, Iggeret ha-Kodesh*, p. 603.]
77. [*Noʾam Elimelech, Lekh Lekha*, p. 23.]
78. [*Seder ha-Dorot mi-Talmidey ha-Besht* (Jerusalem, 2000), chap. 3, p. 54.]
79. [R. Shalom Shakhna, son of R. Avraham "the Angel" and grandson of the Maggid of Miedzyrzec.]
80. *Sippurey Tsadikim meha-Hut ha-Meshulash.*
81. *Maggid Sihot.* Lvov (?), 1850, 25b.
82. [*Maʾaseh Tsaddikim* (Jerusalem, 2000), p. 106.]
83. [*Talmud Yerushalmi* 1:5.]
84. [*Mishnah Avot* 3:9.]
85. [B. T. Berachot 59a.]
86. [That is, the blessing recited over the new moon during *Kiddush Levanah*.]
87. [B. T. Berachot 59b.]
88. [Ibid., 54a.]
89. [Ibid.]
90. [Rabbinic blessing recited upon a blossoming fruit tree each spring.]
91. [B. T. Bava Batra 4a.]
92. [B. T. Sotah 17a.]
93. [B. T. Shabbat 133b.]
94. [B. T. Shabbat 119a.]
95. [*Shivhey ha-Ari ha-Shalem* (Jerusalem, 1981), chap. 8, pp. 100–101.]
96. [*Shivhey ha-BeSHT*, ed. Rubenstein, pp. 361–62.]
97. [See *Hayyey MoHaRaN II* 1:1; *Sihot haRaN* no. 117; *Likkutey MoHaRaN* 65:1–2.]
98. [B. T. Sukkah 52a.]
99. Ibid.
100. [*Yalkut Shimʿoni* Genesis 161.]
101. [B. T. Bava Metsia 84a.]
102. [B. T. Kiddushin 81a.]

103. [Ibid.]

104. [*Pesikta Rabbati* 26.]

105. R. Naftali Bachrach, *'Emek ha-Melekh*. [Parallel attributed to R. Hayyim Vital in Ya'akov Moshe Hillel, ed., *Sefer ha-ARI ve-Gurav* (Jerusalem: Ahavat Shalom, 1992), p. 86.]

106. [Tsvi Hirsh Koydonover, *Kav ha-Yashar* (Jerusalem, 1993), pp. 490–91.]

107. *Shivhey Hayyim Vital*. [Parallel found in R. Hayyim Vital's *Sefer ha-Hezyonot* 2:5, ed. Eshkoly (Jerusalem, 1954), p. 44.]

108. *Ma'asim Noraim Niflaim [Ma'asiyyot Nora'im [!] ve-Nifla'ot* (Cracow, 1896), p. 38.

109. Ibid., p. 39.

110. Zohar Hadash on Lamentations (adapted). [See translation by Seth Brody in Rabbi Ezra ben Solomon of Gerona, *Commentary to the Song of Songs and Other Kabbalistic Commentaries* (Kalamazoo: Western Michigan University, 1999), pp. 153ff.]

111. [Zohar 2:8a.]

112. [Zohar 3:6a/b.]

113. [Zohar 3:98a.]

114. [Zohar 3:84a.]

115. [Zohar 3:164a.]

116. [Based on Zohar 8a/b.]

117. [*Tanya*, chap. 28.]

118. [This might be an overlooked error. I would expect him to be saying "evil" here.]

119. [*Reshit Hokhmah, Sha'ar ha-Ahavah*, chap. 4.]

INDEX